Strategic DNA

Strategic DNA

Lawrence Hobbs

AGATE

CHICAGO

Strategic DNA® is a registered trademark. All rights reserved.

Printed in the United States.

Library of Congress Cataloging-in-Publication Data

Hobbs, Lawrence.

Strategic DNA : bringing business strategy to life / Lawrence Hobbs.

p. cm.

Summary: "Demonstrates how to make and sustain connections between different management activities and focus strategy efforts for maximum effect"--
Provided by publisher.

ISBN-13: 978-1-932841-36-7 (hardcover)

ISBN-10: 1-932841-36-9 (hardcover)

1. Strategic planning. 2. Management. 3. Business planning. I. Title.

HD30.28.H595 2008

658.4'012--dc22

2008022318

10 9 8 7 6 5 4 3 2 1

B2 Books is an imprint of Agate Publishing, Inc. Agate books are available in bulk at discount prices. For more information, go to agatepublishing.com.

In memory of
Hans-Peter "H-P" von Sicard

Table of Contents

Acknowledgments

THIS BOOK IS A RESULT OF THE EXPERIENCE I GAINED DURING MY working career in North America and Europe. While any mistakes or contentious opinions are all my own, I have had the good fortune of continually learning from insightful employers, clients, and colleagues throughout my working life. Three people have had more influence on the thoughts represented in this book than everyone else combined, so to them I owe the greatest thanks. They are my wife, Angela, and my two mentors: Alain Dugas of Bombardier Aerospace and my late business partner, Hans-Peter von Sicard.

For more than 20 years, Angela has been a rock of support and a most constructive critic. She is an insightful reviewer who asks tough questions, holds me accountable, and provides a remarkable sounding board when ideas first see the light of day. Alain helped me understand the power of clarity and focus while demonstrating how quiet determination and teamwork can move mountains. Hans-Peter challenged me to integrate lessons I'd learned during different phases of my working life and provided the platform from which *Strategic DNA* emerged. Only his premature death prevented him from writing this book with me. He is sorely missed.

The many clients of Chinook Solutions each contributed in their own way. It would be impossible to mention everyone, but special recognition is owed to Dave Plett and Wayne Burns of Western Feedlots; Dave Snell of Ivrnet; Kellie Garrett and Daryl Nelson of Farm Credit; Dr. Susan Lea and Kelly Blackshaw of Foothills Health; Manuel Reta of GNP Insurance; and

Gary Wilkinson, Mike Marsh, and Ian Yeates of SaskPower. You'll never know how much you helped! Ian is worthy of special mention for the many helpful suggestions he made during the book's development.

Many of my colleagues and friends also supplied lessons that are reflected in *Strategic DNA*. In a two-minute rant he made 30 years ago, Martyn Wills unlocked my self-belief. At Canadair, John Holding challenged me to "step up a level," Norma Renaud helped me understand organizational and interpersonal dynamics long before "cultures" became so fashionable, and Louise Dontigny took the wind out of my sails just before they ripped. At Renaissance, Barbara Theurkauf and Allen Rupple coached me in managing consulting relationships, and our colleague, Dr. Lori Rocket, put everything into perspective so I could see the funny side of things.

Of course, you would not be reading this book if it weren't for the willingness of Doug Seibold and Eileen Johnson at Agate Publishing to seek value in a rookie author's work. While they must have seen something, it has taken Perrin Davis to make it readable. Thank you to all at Agate for making this possible.

You save the best for last, so here I must acknowledge my family. I thank my parents for unlocking my curiosity and indoctrinating me about the importance of fairness in all decisions. I thank my wife (again!) and our sons, Christopher and Richard, whose support has been more than I deserve.

Introduction

Decisions and Actions with a Family Resemblance

S TRATEGIC DNA IS A MODULAR APPROACH FOR DRIVING A COMPANY'S strategy through its decisions and actions, giving them a family resemblance. It integrates popular management methods with everyday business practices to ensure decisions are framed by a shared vision and actions work together in an overall master plan. *Strategic DNA's* clarity, alignment, and focus-building approach bring strategy to life for corporate "relatives" without compromising their individuality and resorting to centralized control.

Fix Broken Connections

Failing to connect decisions and actions to a bigger picture can cost businesses dearly in many ways, including failing to achieve goals, frustrating customers, accelerating costs, increasing inefficiency and unpredictability, driving staff to leave, and even causing management impotence. Eventually, most organizations experience some of the following broken connections:

- Value-eroding projects
- Understaffing strategically critical departments
- Duplicating efforts on isolated activities
- Making business-unit decisions that are inconsistent with corporate strategies
- Assigning deadwood staff to critical tasks
- Investing constrained capital in marginal opportunities
- Frittering resources away on truly unimportant tasks
- Undermining strategy with compensation systems

Leaders often try in vain to fix these broken connections using some of the methods endorsed by business literature—e.g., strategy maps[1], Balanced Scorecards[2], corporate cultures[3], professional project management[4], learning organizations[5], and so on—but unless these tools are properly integrated and implemented, they may turbocharge the problems. *Strategic DNA* makes strategy visible in everyday life by adapting and integrating these ideas in a way that clarifies purpose, increases alignment, and sharpens focus. In the end, the results, rather than the problems, get turbocharged.

A Recipe for Success

Proper connections are common in strategically successful organizations. Actions are consistent with vision because these organizations' leaders:

- Communicate their vision and strategy clearly
- Provide leadership from both above and alongside staff
- Get everyone "on the same page" and motivated
- Make people understand that the strategy is an important investment in the future
- Synchronize efforts so they are mutually supportive
- Concentrate resources on actions that produce meaningful results
- Stop or avoid nonstrategic distractions
- Pursue actions like a military operation
- Align everyday management practices to support the strategy
- Make sure they "walk the talk"
- Nurture contributors through necessary changes
- Measure progress and adjust for reality
- Learn from failed efforts
- Debug the process before automating it with software

These characteristics are so vital that their absence erodes results, and taking deliberate action to achieve them increases the level of success. *Strategic DNA* integrates everyday popular management practices into a pragmatic, modular learning cycle that tackles each characteristic, connects decisions and actions to the vision, builds broad support, and focuses efforts on producing desired results.

Strategic DNA's basic premise is that a company's ambition—its vision and strategy—is first clearly described in a "genome" that includes critical objcctives, their relationships, and the achievement targets that give them form. That genome is then *proactively* used to frame all significant discussions, virulently permeating its way into the details that achieve the vision.

The first elements of the premise—"objectives, relationships, and targets"—may be familiar to those who have adopted strategy maps and performance management systems like the Balanced Scorecard in the past. The proactive, determined extension of this genome to integrate decisions and actions is what makes it *Strategic DNA*. The steps described in this book explain how to design the vision and strategy to build alignment, prioritize projects and resources, mobilize workers, and effectively follow through on action plans. The *Strategic DNA* approach does more than simply combine visioning and balanced performance management: It integrates communication-centered practices—for effective organizational change management, portfolio management, competent project management, and strategy-driven budgeting—that drive vision into results.

In today's fast-paced business world, the actual strategy may be less important than the process used to develop and communicate it. If that process does not allow the organization to adapt its goals rapidly and without losing leadership alignment and work force mobilization, the strategy really doesn't matter!

Start with the End in Mind

Why is *Strategic DNA* necessary? Historically, managers managed and workers either did as they were told or did as they had always done before. In the modern workplace, people also need to know *why* they are doing what they are doing. In the modern knowledge economy, strategies consistently fail when people don't know why they matter, and eventually, valuable knowledge workers will simply move on. A clarity of purpose satisfies workers' quest for meaning and makes them want to get up in the morning. People need to understand the purpose of—and interactions between—goals, projects, plans, measurements, budgets, priorities, hiring decisions, and other significant decisions and actions if they are to feel engaged.

Communicating this complex model of a business's future to the people charged with building it is far simpler when they already know the intended result. They need not comprehend every detail of that eventual destination, as long as its general characteristics have been stated well enough to guide their direction. Therefore, starting with the end in mind is essential, even if the destination is expected to evolve over time.

It is amazing how many leaders put too much focus on turning strategy into action; both are merely steps along the way from vision to results. Leaders who focus on the strategies or actions themselves can do a great job and still utterly fail to produce the results that make it worthwhile, like a "successful" surgery after which the patient still dies! Clarity of purpose gives everyone something to focus on and makes it less likely that they will lose sight of the intended results.

Codifying the destination and principal waypoints into a *Strategic DNA* forces meaningful discussions about strategic ambition. It increases alignment, resolves issues, and identifies the desired outcomes that a results-focused organization should, and will, pursue.

Get Everyone on the Same Page

Leadership alignment and work force mobilization are at the heart of the *Strategic DNA* approach. Ideally, we'd all love to have complete consensus, but it is counterproductive if it means lowering the bar. Instead, what really matters to stakeholders is having input, feeling informed, and being empowered. If these prerequisites are met, employees can even accept and work to achieve a strategy they don't entirely agree with.

Strategic DNA tackles the diversity of leadership and stakeholder opinion right up front, in the techniques used to define the vision and strategy clearly. If not properly managed and harnessed, this essential diversity can rapidly become a showstopper liability instead of the powerful natural asset it should be. Once key stakeholders are aligned and on the same page, it is much easier to mobilize constituencies, get everyone pulling in the same direction, harmonize decisions made across silos, reduce energy consumed by nonstrategic activities, and drive results with focused implementation of the decisions.

Performance management, transparency, and visibility are often perceived as threatening, particularly in strongly unionized or large public sector organizations. Therefore, they should be introduced carefully by building understanding and buy-in and reassuring the team that the process is about excellence and accomplishment, not punishment for failure to perform.

Getting everyone to pull together in a desired direction is akin to a large-scale cattle drive. If the cattle are left to their own devices, they'll wander off, and if they're spooked, they'll run in random directions, burning energy and eroding their value. But if the cowboys—the managers—have their act together and work as a team toward the previously agreed-upon objective, they'll be able to get the herd to cover great distances very effectively. Workers are a lot brighter than Hereford steers, but as a group, work forces often exhibit many of their characteristics. Frankly, so do managers.

Do Only What Needs to Be Done

Failure to focus is the most common symptom of broken connections, and most managers would agree they are trying to do far too many things at once. It is natural to want to pursue every good idea, but success arises from evaluating those ideas rationally, performing only those that most contribute to achieving the vision, and determinedly refusing to work on any others. This ability to refuse to be distracted by nonstrategic ideas is the best way to judge whether an organization is sufficiently focused. Learning to do this in a flexible way, especially by not working on things that *used* to be important, is the secret to becoming adaptable without losing effectiveness. This is perhaps the most valuable skill any organization can develop, because no matter how well you do the wrong things, they're still the wrong things!

Strategic DNA decomposes a vision's desired outcomes to frame key decisions like project prioritization, resource assignment, progress evaluation, and performance assessment. This approach is intuitive to effective, results-focused organizations that treat their strategic agendas like military operations. They get what they want by keeping one eye firmly focused on their objectives and use the desired results as the framework for their significant decisions and actions. Focus is improved as clarity and alignment are pushed down through the organization, influencing what workers want to do, and to what managers want to assign their resources.

Do It Better Each Time

Strategic DNA sets the scene for ongoing strategic feedback and learning by framing objectives in clear, measurable terms, and making traceable connections back to them from the decisions and actions made during the strategy's lifecycle. Once the strategy's implementation is underway, the measurement of actual project and performance results provides feedback to confirm or challenge the assumptions and hypotheses that were used when the objectives were chosen. This traceability allows the strategy to be fine-tuned so objectives and projects can be refocused more realistically.

Strategic DNA Described

The twelve chapters of this book break down the why, what, and how of a strategy management lifecycle that can be scaled to suit businesses large and small. The lifecycle captures a clear and steadily deepening definition of the vision and strategy in many forms: a concise map, a text narrative, measurable achievement targets, a project portfolio, deliverables, schedules, accountabilities, resources, budgets, and other components. These integrated tools enhance management team effectiveness, increasing the organization's focus on strategic outcomes while pushing down empowerment and accountability. They provide a line of sight, letting individual contributors see how their actions are part of a bigger strategic picture and concentrating scarce resources where they do the most good.

In Figure 0.1, *Strategic DNA* is shown as a lifecycle of twelve chapters that start with building a vision and end with learning from achieved results. Each chapter describes activities and methods that produce decisions and actions framed by the genetic code of the *Strategic DNA*. The chapters are not strictly sequential, as efforts continue in several chapters simultaneously,

Figure 0.1 Strategic DNA Lifecycle

but the lifecycle represents the general sequence of events. Several of the steps can be iterative: For example, if a project has to be reevaluated because its detailed project plan reveals higher-than-expected costs, then Chapter 8's Step 5 would need to be followed by Chapter 5's Steps 7, 8, and 9.

The chapters suggest techniques for reconnecting disconnected activities and decisions in a way that builds understanding and alignment. Many of these techniques will be familiar, allowing you to build on the knowledge and practices you already have, but their integration and proactive orientation may not be.

Chapter		Questions Tackled
1	Vision Formulation	• What do we have to contend with? • Where do we want to go? • What do we want to become? • When do we want to get there?
2	Strategy Clarification and Mapping	• How will we get there? • How are things interrelated? • Are all our leaders on the same page?
3	Achievement Target Identification	• How will we know we're making progress? • How will we know when we get to where we want to go? • What value will the strategy produce?
4	Strategy Cascading	• How will we roll this out to divisions and departments? • What should be their strategies? • How will they execute the corporate strategy? • How will they contribute to the big picture?
5	Project Portfolio Selection	• What will we do to get there? • What will we stop doing to free up resources? • What should we do first?
6	Implementation Structure Organization	• How will we organize ourselves? • Who will be in overall control?
7	Resource and Accountability Assignment	• Who will be responsible and accountable for what? • What people, money, and other resources will we dedicate to it? • What is the business case?
8	Project Planning	• How will we manage the projects? • What is the plan and schedule for each project?
9	Work Team Mobilization	• How will we get everyone pulling in the same direction? • What must we communicate and to whom? • Are individual people's objectives aligned with the strategy?
10	Project Execution & Control	• How much progress has each project made? • What issues and problems are there? • What are we doing about the issues and problems?
11	Results Realization Measurement	• How will we measure and report results? • What are the actual results? • How do the actual results compare to the targets? • How much progress have we made overall?
12	Learning Analysis & Feedback	• Why aren't we getting the results we expected? • What is the impact of the results on the big picture? • What can be done to improve those results? • How will we modify the vision, strategy, plans, and resource assignments to accommodate reality? • What should we do differently in future?

Figure 0.2 Key Questions by Chapter

Figure 0.2 (see previous page) illustrates how each chapter answers key questions about the strategy and its progress to fruition.

Modularity

Fortunately, the *Strategic DNA* lifecycle is not a rigid process, so it doesn't have to be followed to the letter to produce great outcomes. The elements of this modular approach can be introduced where and when they can do some good. For example, a company may decide to introduce elements of the *Strategic DNA* process to help implement an existing vision at the corporate level only while using its established project execution approach. This company might start with Chapter 2, skip Chapters 4, 8, and 10, and move on to use certain elements of Chapters 6, 7, and 9. Even still, coordinating their decisions and actions would still produce great value. Of course, you'll get the most out of using *Strategic DNA* to frame decision-making and action-taking as broadly and proactively as possible.

Workshops

Many of the activities described in this book's how-to sections advocate a workshop approach to collective decision-making. Workshops have many advantages for implementing the *Strategic DNA* lifecycle, as they provoke discussion of issues that need to be addressed and resolved by the group that will drive the process.

A workshop setting will expose nonalignment, lack of clarity, lack of honesty, lack of focus, skewed priorities, and nonengagement. It provides a forum for peer discussions to resolve these issues, thereby minimizing distractions. Workshops are also particularly valuable when there are internal politics or face-saving considerations.

Large-scale wall charts can be very useful tools for workshops. (These can be easily and cheaply made from rolls of 4' or 6' wide brown Kraft paper.) Unlike projected PC images, wall charts get participants out of their seats to take ownership of their thinking. A digital camera is a handy way to record participants' work.

Software

A wide variety of software applications, such as business intelligence and project management tools, are often used to manage strategic activities. *Strategic DNA* does not assume that you will use these tools, and no particular products are recommended. As you read, you'll find that I've highlighted processes that are frequently automated, but I also provide manual alternatives in each case: There is little value in automating processes that aren't yet properly understood by their participants.

Chapter Structure

This book is organized into twelve chapters that address each part of the *Strategic DNA* lifecycle sequentially. Each chapter is organized into five sections:

Context	A discussion of the chapter's overall goals, the thinking behind the chapter, and its contribution to the overall cycle.
Why Do It?	An explanation of the value offered by the chapter's outcomes.
What to Do	Detailed descriptions of outcomes, tools, and deliverables.
How to Do It	A description of adaptable step-by-step processes and tricks of the trade that can be used to achieve desired outcomes. Useful templates, sample meeting agendas, and typical responsibility assignments are also provided.
Summary	A single paragraph that summarizes the role the chapter plays in the overall *Strategic DNA* lifecycle.

The same term can have different meanings for different people. I have tried to use terms in their most intuitive form, but I've also provided a glossary of principal terms to define their intended meaning in this book. The glossary also defines the types of teams and groups that I refer to in the book. Most organizations have their own language, and *Strategic DNA* terms should be adapted to suit that language during implementation.

Feedback, Please

This book is intended to share the insights I have gleaned from years of working with colleagues, clients, and seminar attendees to help them fix broken connections. I trust that you will find information that will be useful to you and will allow you to get more value from the work you presently do. I'd love to hear about your experiences with these ideas—share them with me at lawrence@strategicdna.org.

—Lawrence Hobbs
Calgary, 2008

1

Vision Formulation
Where Do We Want to Go?

THE *STRATEGIC DNA* LIFECYCLE BEGINS WITH DEFINING THE VISION an organization wishes to pursue. This vision provides the goal the *Strategic DNA* will be designed to achieve. Most organizations believe they have a vision, and many even have a vision statement. Unfortunately, most of these vision statements don't withstand scrutiny, and many are meaningless beyond the boardroom. A good vision definition is a description of a desired future state *that means pretty much the same thing to everyone.* It usually includes broad characteristics that the organization will have once it has achieved the desired changes.

Many strategic planning exercises do not include a visioning element because most organizations believe they already have a vision, think that a mandated mission would be too constraining, or are afraid that creating a vision would be tantamount to reopening Pandora's box. Think of a vision as a collective view of the overarching goals. The goals represent how different an organization expects itself to be in the future, and each of them should describe desired characteristics. You can expect a vision to evolve as internal, industry, market, and other factors change.

The vision formulation approach described in this chapter emphasizes the importance of collaboration among leaders in creating a single, focused view of the future. It doesn't really matter exactly what the vision says as long as it gives leaders, and, later, workers and other stakeholders, a shared sense of purpose. The approach described here can be scaled to suit your needs and used to produce either conventional visions that aim for incremental change or bold, innovative visions that will reinvent your business.

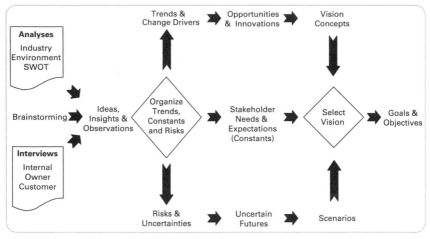

Figure 1.1 Vision Formulation Concept

Visions are developed to either preempt or respond to different factors that are capable of forcing a business to change. These change influences fall into three broad categories:

Trends or Certainties — Influences that are sure to happen; when they do, they will change the environment in which the business operates.

Risks or Uncertainties — Influences that might happen; if they do, they will significantly change the business environment.

Expectations or Constants — Values stakeholders continue to expect the business to provide, no matter what happens to the business environment.

Some visioning methods focus on uncertainties and can result in frustrating circular discussions as they try to plan for a future that is probably not going to materialize. These time-consuming discussions reinforce a mindset of avoiding failure and can produce risk-averse visions—thinking like a herbivore. In my opinion, the business jungle, like any other jungle, is ruled by carnivores. Some businesses know what they want and use sharp teeth to get it. This carnivore mindset is focused on being successful instead of avoiding failure. However, even trend-focused carnivores still need to recognize the risks—the bigger carnivores, for example—and the need to meet stakeholder expectations.

In this chapter, you'll learn how to balance trends, risks, and expectations when formulating your vision. Trends are used to calibrate the degree of change and explore ideas for satisfying stakeholder expectations. Risks are used to evaluate just how robust the ideas actually are. Figure 1.1 illustrates the concept that provides the basis for the process.[6]

If you are confident that your organization already has a clear, mobilizing vision, you may want to skip this chapter and begin with the strategy clarification processes of Chapter 2. If it in fact does lack clarity, you'll know it—the strategy clarification process will force you to revisit your vision anyway.

Why Do It?
To Say What We Wish to Become

A vision is a high-level statement of ambition. Identifying and describing that vision are natural first steps in the process that actually achieves it. The ideal outcome of the formulation process is a clearly articulated ambition with tangible goals that can serve as the basis for developing the *Strategic DNA*. By identifying what an organization wishes to become, the visioning process answers the question, "What do we want our *Strategic DNA* to make us look like?"

To React to Current and Predicted Business Pressures

Properly developing a vision means assessing the prevailing and anticipated conditions in the operating environment. This typically involves an analysis of trends and risks, an inwardly focused analysis of strengths, weaknesses, opportunities, and threats (SWOT), and a review of competitive, customer, social, and other environmental pressures. Often, this assessment is done in the context of cultural values and—particularly in the public sector—the mission.

Even organizations that are completely focused on their missions still have a vision, even though they may not think they do. Such organizations have a vision to continue to fulfill their mission even as their business environment evolves. Their strategy is focused on protecting their mission by accommodating environmental changes.

To Leverage the Insight of Informed Insiders

In the interest of good governance and transparency, detailed analyses are required if only to demonstrate the vision-makers' due diligence. Although these analyses set the context, they may also bring about "analysis paralysis." Updating earlier analyses and leveraging informed leadership insights can often be more effective. After all, the leaders usually participated in those analyses and, as such, they understand their implications best.

Vision formulation activities provide participants with an opportunity to volunteer ideas and ask questions. People are often afraid to ask questions that they believe are foolish, or mention ideas that they think might be too obvious. The low-risk visioning context of these activities can produce some real gems by drawing them out.

To Balance Outside-In and Inside-Out Views of the Future

Many formulation techniques emphasize analyzing external factors to identify and select visions and strategies. These "outside-in" approaches ask questions like "What do we need to be good at?" Although they can be very effective ways to identify what incremental changes are needed to maintain market share, satisfy customer needs, or respond to new competitors, they sometimes fail to exploit internal strengths and may leave internal weaknesses unaddressed. Too much outside-in means that an organization can only react to its environment and produce whatever outcomes are natural by-products of those reactions. These organizations are rarely able to shape their destinies.

Other methods use an internal focus to formulate visions and strategies, asking "What can we do with what we're good at?" These approaches use the firm's culture (values, mission, and ambition) and core competencies (knowledge, skills, experience, technologies, and financial capital) as the basis for identifying and selecting visions and strategies. These "inside-out" approaches can be effective ways to put internal strengths and capital to work, but they aren't as effective when insightful, innovative, visibility enhancing, or transformational visions and strategies are necessary.

There are clearly advantages and disadvantages to outside-in and inside-out approaches. To ensure that you get the best of both worlds, your visioning method should ideally balance the two.

What to Do
Build Alignment and a Sense of Ownership

How you clarify your vision is very important. In order for a leadership team to be aligned on a single common vision and able to mobilize its people and get everyone pulling in the same direction, it must share a collective sense of ownership. Buy-in like this is best achieved by having the entire leadership team develop the vision together and also involve other stakeholders in the process.

The Leadership Team

The list of people to involve in crafting a vision and strategy evolves over time and depends on the organization's structure, culture, and leadership personalities. In theory, only a business's owners *have* to be involved in visioning but, in practice, involving principal operational leaders reinforces success. In most cases, a vision should be developed by a leadership team that can collectively represent—in as high-profile a manner as possible—the interests of all who will be affected by the vision, and all who are required to make it happen. Typically, this would include the entire executive team, representatives of the owners, selected specialized thought-leaders, and others who can truly represent the opinions of customers and employees.

Carefully Focused Research and Analysis

Many vision development efforts spend far too much time conducting studies and analyses and far too little time facilitating dialogues among the leadership team. *Strategic DNA* emphasizes that although dialogues that build alignment and mobilization are crucial, proper research and analysis are still necessary as well—just not too much, and not to the exclusion of building that dialogue! Research and analysis should be carefully aimed at either supplying missing information in areas the leadership team is not yet comfortable or validating what the team already believes to be true. Several analyses can contribute to the vision formulation process.

Industry and Competitor Analyses

Industry and competitor analyses research the nature and conditions of an industry to reveal whether it offers attractive opportunities; weak, strong or emerging competitors; changing conditions; and increasing customer expectations.

Strengths, Weaknesses, Opportunities, and Threats

A SWOT analysis examines internal capabilities alongside emerging opportunities and threats. Although sometimes thought of as a strictly internal process, SWOT analysis can also be considered "outside in" because its inwardly focused element is usually an analysis of strengths and weaknesses compared against the rest of the industry.

Business Environment Scans

An environmental scan surveys the broader business environment for any factors that may have significant future impact, even if they may be slow to develop. This macroenvironment includes broad societal factors that can impact a business, such as demographics and environmental, health and safety, economic, political, and technological concerns.

Customer Needs Analysis

A customer needs analysis identifies what products and services existing and potential customers desire. Many different approaches are possible, including market research and customer surveys, but many businesses fall into the trap of assuming that they know what their customers want. Simply asking them for their feedback can be very enlightening. A customer needs analysis is a mandatory prerequisite to developing innovative value visions.

Understand Trends and Risks

The future always seems difficult to predict, because there are so many uncertainties that influence it. However, the real truth is that few uncertainties are truly capable of preventing well-founded visions from being achieved. Great visions and innovations almost always come from an understanding of the underlying trends (or certain change drivers) in the business environment.

When Bombardier Aerospace launched its Canadair Regional Jet in the late 1980s, conventional wisdom held that only turboprop aircraft were profitable on shorter routes, and the jet's higher speed gave no real advantage on short regional routes. The company has since delivered more than 1,500 regional jets and revolutionized the industry. Bombardier's apparent leap of faith was underpinned by several key trends and constants:

- People liked jets. They are quieter, smoother, faster, and more appealing than turboprops.
- Some people wanted to fly between secondary cities without having to change planes at a hub airport.
- A new generation of small, efficient engines was on the horizon that would make the regional jets more profitable to fly.
- Deregulated major airlines wanted to increase the feed to their hub-and-spoke systems by drawing passengers from smaller and more distant cities.

Uncertain risks, on the other hand, can be very useful for framing alternate scenarios for a hypothetical future but should not replace trends as the basis for the vision. Some organizations that place great faith in scenario-based approaches can become overly risk focused. A balanced approach that uses risk to assess the robustness of trend-based vision concepts typically works well. Think of trends as a foundation of bedrock and uncertainties as a foundation of shifting sand—which would you build your house on?

Recognize the Business Change Drivers That the Trends Imply

Trends are always forcing change, and many of them, such as e-mail, are irresistible. The challenge is to recognize and evaluate their potential effects early on, in a proactive way. If they are recognized early, they may present a business opportunity, thus making the mandatory change a positive experience. If they are recognized too late, an urgent scramble to catch up with everyone else may ensue.

Examples of business drivers that an analysis of multiple trends could identify include:

- Increasing sources and frequencies of risk events that threaten profitability.
- Operating costs of competitors falling due to consolidation, rationalization, and new delivery strategies.
- Customers expecting more consistent and predictable service experiences.
- Financial burdens of healthcare increasingly switching away from government and insurers and to consumers.
- Customers expecting a clearer understanding of their needs and more value placed on their business.
- New technologies rapidly transforming the products, channels, services, costs, and customers in the industry.
- Industry consolidation leading unions to become more militant.
- Increasing regulatory oversight restricting product flexibility and eroding margins.
- Entry by new competitors becoming easier because of technological advances.
- Finding friendly, knowledgeable, and empowered employees becoming increasingly difficult.

Get Inside Your Customer's Head If You Plan to Be Innovative

Earlier, I mentioned that analysis of customer needs is an integral element of basic research and analysis. Although that may be adequate for conventional visions, an added dimension comes into play when the vision needs to be truly innovative.

Most great innovations aren't the result of stunning leaps of insight pulled out of thin air. Great innovators look at the world from their customer's point of view, ask themselves what those customers truly value, and then figure out how to deliver it. In the business world, great innovators seek to identify, or even create, opportunities that go against industry conventions, because doing so can lead to market shifts, and ultimately market domination, instead of incremental market share. In most cases, this means understanding what potential customers—not existing ones—want to buy.

The airline industry is a great example of customer-focused innovation. Southwest, WestJet, Ryanair, and other "cheap-and-cheerful" airlines saw that traditional airlines were not providing many things their customers really cared about—low fares, simple pricing structures, and friendly employees—and instead provided many costly services that most customers didn't care much about at all—frequent flyer programs, business-class seats, meals, and free drinks. These discount airlines (see Figure 1.2) offered services that appealed to everyone, instead of just a few frequent business-class passengers. In doing so, they have reinvented their industry, sustained profitable growth, and put once-great airlines into bankruptcy.

Use Risk Scenarios to Test Trend-Based Vision Concepts
Although risks should not be the basis of a vision, they can be very

Service Characteristic	Traditional Airlines	Most Customers Value	Discount Concept
Fare Classes	Multiple Classes – First, Business, and Economy	Simple and Fair	Economy Only
Route System	Global Routes or Partnerships	Most Popular Routes	High–Volume Routes
Aircraft Types	Complete Range of Types	"Don't Care as Long as it's Safe and Cheap"	Single Type
Loyalty Program	Favored Treatment for Frequent Flyers	Resent Being Un-favored	Cheap and Fun Wins Loyalty
Free Food and Alcohol	Full Meal Services	"Doesn't Matter on Short or Cheap Flights"	"Pretzels or Cookies?"
Pricing	Complex and Confusing Fare Structures	Paying Same Low Price as Everyone Else	Simple, Consistent, Low Fares
Employees	Unionized Seniority, Mature, Often Cool	Friendly, Welcoming, and Attentive Experience	Young, High Energy, and Fun

Figure 1.2 Customer Value Analysis

helpful in evaluating whether a vision concept will withstand whatever the future throws at it. Risk scenarios can be an effective way to find out. In a risk scenario, significant risks are defined as center-crossing axes on a chart, thereby establishing a potential scenario in each quadrant. A vision concept can then be evaluated for each scenario to judge whether it would work in that hypothetical situation. The results may cause the leadership team to confirm, adjust, or discard the vision concept.

Figure 1.3 illustrates four possible scenarios confronting Bombardier's vision of creating a market for regional jets. The scenarios are predicated on two basic risks: First, will fuel prices be high or low, and second, will passenger expectations remain stable or dramatically change? The vision can be evaluated in the context of each of the four quadrants by determining the viability of the aircraft under a variety of circumstances surrounding fuel prices and passenger expectations.

- If fuel prices are low and expectations keep changing, airlines will value an aircraft capable of being used in many different ways (i.e., a broad mission profile).
- If fuel prices are high and expectations keep changing, airlines will need the scheduling and load flexibility smaller planes can offer.

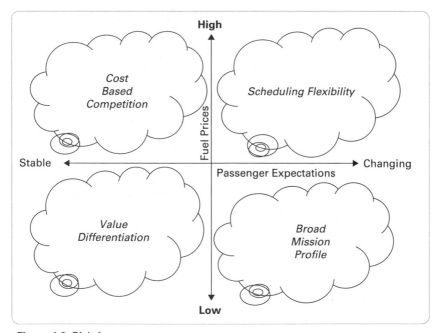

Figure 1.3 Risk Axes

- If fuel prices are low and expectations are stable, airlines will need aircraft that offer more value (newer, faster, quieter, and sexier) to the customer than other airlines' planes.
- If fuel prices are high and expectations are stable, airlines will need aircraft that cost less to fly than other airlines' planes.

How to Do It

Properly designing a vision is a complex and serious undertaking; unfortunately, it rarely gets the time and attention it deserves. In many ways, deciding what the organization wants to become in the future is more important than pretty much anything else, but somehow few businesses devote more than perhaps a two-day workshop to it. A short, intense workshop can work well if its participants are already well aligned and truly understand their business drivers, but a more extensive and in-depth visioning process is necessary when either of those conditions is not true—and that is usually the case.

The balance of this chapter describes the nine scalable steps of a vision formulation process. This process can be adapted to suit a single all-day workshop, but in its most extensive form, it could encompass three separate workshop meetings spread over several weeks. These three workshops (typically subdivided into groups: Steps 1–3, Steps 4–5, and Steps 6–7) usually take a full day each and tend to be more productive when they are off-site. Very large or complex organizations can expect this to take much longer. Figure 1.5 provides a sample agenda for workshop meeting(s).

The leadership team and the leader of the strategic planning team (who will serve as the facilitator) must participate in the workshops and discussions described below. Other members of the strategic planning team can also be included. Facilitating

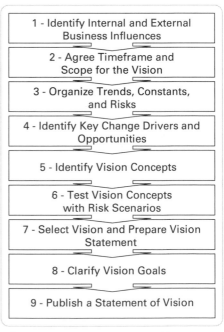

Figure 1.4 Vision Formulation Process

these early workshops helps establish the leader's credibility and authority in the minds of the leadership team. Research and analysis legwork, workshop preparation, and logistics should be delegated to a strategic planning team or external consultants.

On a practical note, members of the strategic planning team should be assigned to build lists of existing metrics and projects while the vision and strategy are being developed. The assigned team members can take note of metrics and

> Vision Formulation Workshop
>
> **Sample Agenda**
>
> Part 1 – Influences
> 1. Review Analysis Results
> 2. Set Time Frame and Scope
> 3. Brainstorm Business Influences
> 4. Organize Trends, Risks, and Constants
>
> Part 2 – Opportunities
> 5. Key Change Drivers
> 6. Challenges and Opportunities
> 7. What Customers Want
> 8. Vision Concepts
>
> Part 3 – Vision Selection
> 9. Concepts in Risk Scenarios
> 10. Vision Decision
> 11. Vision Statement

Figure 1.5 Sample Agenda for Vision Formulation Workshop(s)

projects when they are mentioned by participants during workshops and begin the sometimes lengthy research activities needed to build the lists. The list of metrics is needed in Chapter 3's Step 1 (see p. 60) and the list of projects is required in Chapter 5's Step 3 (see p. 109).

1. Identify Internal and External Business Influences
Who: Leadership Team Led by Strategic Planning Leader

The most valuable insight into critical factors like market evolution, business drivers, competitive pressures, trends, and risks usually comes from structured individual interviews and/or a brainstorming session. After all, leaders are subject-matter experts who are steeped in the business environment on a daily basis, but they may not realize just how much they already know. The combination of a confidential forum (private interviews) and a synergistic forum (brainstorming) allows a wide range of business influences to emerge, including many trends, uncertainties, hypotheses, guesses, and misconceptions. These insights can be supplemented with traditional research and analysis sources like environmental, industry, SWOT, customer, competitor, and other formal analyses.

Chapter 2 discusses the structured interview method in detail. The same method can be used here.

In the brainstorming session, move the meeting along quickly in order to avoid excessive discussion of any one business influence. These discourses often turn into a fruitless risk discussion. In this session, categorize influences into related subject areas. A useful list of categories might include:

- Demographics
- Economic
- Legislative
- Financial
- Cultural
- Environmental
- Customers
- Competitors
- Channels
- Technologies
- Skills

2. Agree on Time Frame and Scope for the Vision
Who: Leadership Team Led by Strategic Planning Leader

It can be very difficult for the leadership team to visualize the same future if they imagine different time frames for the vision. This is a basic issue, but it has a potentially dramatic impact. At one firm, an insurance company, operational leaders scaled their vision to be achieved in ten to fifteen years. Unfortunately, the firm's chief information officer (CIO) assumed the strategic plan had a three year time frame and thought they were crazy to think he could support that much change over three years. The leaders became a team again once the timing issue was clarified.

Although it may be lengthy, the time-frame discussion is essential. This discussion begins the alignment process in a neutral subject area and gets everyone looking outside the business as a whole instead of focusing on their own territories.

Some organizations, such as aircraft manufacturers, city planners, or electrical utilities, have extremely long vision lifecycles and must plan accordingly. To keep them in perspective, they may need to develop multi-term visions. A long-term context can help them maintain an overall sense of direction, and more intermediate stages allow them to see progress that would otherwise be invisible from the long-term viewpoint.

Defining the vision's scope makes a tremendous difference whether the vision is for the corporate level alone, for the whole organization, or for selected business units. Although it's not necessarily an intended outcome, this discussion can reveal important information about the business units' validity, compatibility, and synergy.

3. Organize Trends, Constants, and Risks
Who: Leadership Team Led by Strategic Planning Leader

This step provides two significant benefits. First, it avoids much fruitless discussion by extracting risks and agreeing to ignore them during the discussion. (Later, these risks will be used to test the robustness of the vision.) Second, discussing each business influence's likelihood and impact may reveal that some members of the team have divergent views. Making important decisions based on fundamentally different views of the situation can lead to costly errors.

Likelihood-Impact Matrix

The most straightforward method for organizing business influences is to plot them into a matrix like the one shown in Figure 1.6. One axis calibrates the potential impact of the influence on the organization, the second calibrates its likelihood of actually occurring, and a separate area captures constants.

		Minimal	Significant	Earth-shattering
Constant		No Choice—Stakeholders Expect		
	Certain	Worth Considering	Important Trend	Critical Trend
Will It Occur?	Probable	Worth Monitoring	Worth Considering	Important Trend
	Possible	Can Probably Ignore	Worth Monitoring	Important Uncertainty
		Impact If It Does Occur		

Figure 1.6 Matrix for Organizing Uncertainties

The matrix can be set up on a wall before the meeting. During the meeting, the facilitator can write business influences on small Post-it® notes.[7] The stakeholders should *collectively* decide where each note belongs on the matrix, and the facilitator should place them in the appropriate grids.

This process identifies which trends and risks *really matter* and ensures that the most important factors will be accommodated by the vision. By narrowing the number of business influences in this way, the leadership team reduces the distracting, unproductive wheel spinning of uncertainty discussions.

This is often a lengthy process, but team members must agree on the position of each business influence. This healthy discussion will build alignment and ownership and leaves participants feeling they have had a say in the foundation of the vision.

4. Identify Key Change Drivers and Opportunities
Who: Leadership Team Led by Strategic Planning Leader

Now that the risks and less important trends have been set aside, attention can be focused on clearly understanding the influences the vision must accommodate.

Key Change Drivers

Many change drivers will be common knowledge, but others may represent radical, out-of-the-box thinking. Both can contribute to suggesting new visions. While radical ideas may be risky and easy to dismiss, they could be the source of the next great innovation; therefore, they're worthy of proper consideration.

Facilitating this part of the process can be particularly difficult because of the sheer number of permutations and unique thought processes. One solution is to remove the probable and certain trend notes from Step 3's matrix (be sure you take a photograph of it or otherwise make a permanent record of it first) and place them on the boardroom wall or table. Encourage leaders to expand their thinking by organizing and reorganizing the notes into groups until their thoughts crystallize and the groups stabilize. Afterward, write a short, single sentence "headline" that summarizes the change that each group of notes implies.

Business Opportunities and Challenges

As the workshop progresses, some business opportunities and challenges will be better understood, and new ones will emerge. Systematic review of change drivers (in the context of stakeholder expectation constants) will ensure that a complete range of showstopper barriers and business opportunities are captured. Once that's done, the team can imagine the challenges and opportunities that are likely to emerge from them.

Facilitate the review of business change drivers by asking questions like:

- What effect will this business driver have on the industry's status quo?
- What opportunities will that create?
- How can we see this challenge as an opportunity?
- What could we do to seize that opportunity?
- What negative impact will that have on our existing business?
- What could we do to mitigate that impact?
- What would we do if we were new entrants in the market?

Innovative Customer Value Opportunities

Organizations with an appetite for particularly innovative visions can expand their opportunities by performing customer value analyses. The first step is understanding what future product and service offerings *potential* customers want. This means talking to them about what they value, and asking *existing* customers what they don't like about the organization's current products and services. Customers like to be asked these questions and often willingly participate in interviews, surveys, and focus groups. They love to tell you how you could make them happy!

Armed with the results of a customer value analysis, the team can review products and services to identify gaps between what is available, and what customers want. One way is to compare existing products against the customer's ideal. The Blue Ocean Strategy methodology described by Kim and Mauborgne[8] offers a more extensive approach for customer value innovation.

5. Identify Vision Concepts
Who: Leadership Team Led by Strategic Planning Leader

This step is about assessing how you can seize business opportunities and mitigate previously identified challenges. Alignment expands as vision concept insights emerge during the discussion about opportunities and challenges.

Each vision concept represents a configuration of opportunities the leadership team might choose to pursue and the assets and capabilities needed to pursue them. Different configurations of opportunities often reveal themselves naturally during discussions about business change drivers. Target the discussions by asking, "How do our capabilities and assets need to change in order to get us there?" This helps develop a high-level business case for each vision concept that will be a key consideration in the final decision.

Some vision concepts are likely to propose major transformational changes for the business and its product or service offerings. Other vision concepts may be more incremental in nature, advocating a stay-the-course approach. There is a certain amount of art and magic involved in this process, because collective creativity generates alternative vision concepts.

6. Test Vision Concepts with Risk Scenarios
Who: Leadership Team Led by Strategic Planning Leader

At this point, the potential impact of risks must be considered in the context of each vision concept. By removing the uncertainties from the discussions in Step 3, the visioning work has been allowed to focus on constants, trends, and opportunities, thus giving those spinning wheels some traction. Risks are reintroduced in this step to test vision concepts by evaluating how robust they might be if different uncertain futures come to pass. Traditional scenario planning methods can be used for this risk assessment.

Prepare risk axes diagrams for different pairings of the most significant high-impact risks revealed in Step 3. Evaluate each vision concept to see how it performs in each scenario or quadrant on the diagram. A favorite vision concept might not work smoothly in all scenarios, but this evaluation identifies what must be done *if* the concept is selected and the scenario comes to pass.

By the conclusion of this step, the leadership team should be reasonably well aligned about the challenges and ambitions the vision needs to address. Members should feel well informed about each vision concept and ready to decide which vision to adopt. Each vision concept now has a heritage soundly based on established trends, business drivers, and related opportunities. Each business case has been explored in principle, and risk mitigation strategies have been discussed for the main uncertainties.

7. Select Vision and Prepare Vision Statement
Who: Leadership Team Led by Strategic Planning Leader

Since the trends, risks, and constants have been defined and used to identify change drivers, business opportunities, and robust vision concepts, the team is poised to make an informed decision about which vision to pursue. The right one is usually fairly obvious at this point, but in some cases it may need further discussion, or sometimes, even the intervention of the CEO.

In relatively straightforward cases, when the list of proposed vision concepts is fairly short, the decision discussion can focus on the pressing need for and implementability of each concept. If leaders truly believe in a vision concept, they'll probably be confident that it can be successfully pursued.

In less straightforward cases, you can facilitate the vision selection discussion by providing a matrix that compares the business case magnitude and difficulty of each concept. In the business case matrix (see Figure 1.7) the axes are calibrated to reflect the leadership team's *perceptions of* a) the magnitude of benefits the vision concept could be expected to produce and b) how difficult its implementation will be.

While some organizations with complex, expensive, or risky visions prefer to judge concepts based on comprehensive business cases, others are content to rely on the leadership team's expert judgment. If the leadership team does not have the authority to make the final vision decision, the decision makers must be seen to, at least, consider the leadership team's input. If not, the alignment and motivational benefits expected from the vision formulation process could be completely undermined and may even backfire.

Magnitude of Potential Benefits	High	Wanna Bet the Farm?	Worth Considering	No-brainer
	Medium	Only When There's No Choice	Worth Considering	Worth Considering
	Low	Steer Clear	Why Bother?	Why Bother?
		High	Medium	Low

**Difficulty/Expense
To Implement Successfully**

Figure 1.7 Business Case Matrix for Comparing Vision Concepts

Preparing the Vision Statement

At this point, the team can begin articulating the newly selected vision in words. This is usually an extremely difficult task. Bad vision statements include phrases like "customer-delighting," "world-leading," "industry-dominating," "profit-producing," "employee-satisfying," and "society give-backing." They're usually worse than no statement at all.

A good vision statement describes what the organization is committing itself to become or deliver. It is a statement of intent that provides a compass heading—*not* an exact route—toward the desired future. It should be reasonable, realistic, and rational, but it should also represent a stretch from the organization's current state. Although many vision statements are very brief, there is no rule that it must be contained in a single sentence. The statement needs to use enough words to clearly, but still concisely, explain what the vision means. Aim for a vision statement that outlines where the organization plans to get to, what it will look like when it gets there, and a handful of major goals it expects to achieve *en route*.

For example, a leadership team could select a short, snappy vision like:

To be the best water utility in North America.

… only if it was sure that "best" would withstand scrutiny and mean the same thing to everyone. If not, the team might find it far more effective to aim for a vision like this:

To be the most effective municipal water utility in North America by…
- *Having a strong, stable, and adaptable work force.*
- *Delivering high-quality and effective services.*
- *Being broadly perceived as prudent and professional.*
- *Continually improving to meet changing customer needs.*
- *Leading the industry through innovative processes and behaviors.*
…sustainably protecting the city's ability to provide clean, safe water to its citizens.

Kickstart the discussion by organizing participants into subgroups and asking each group to develop a vision statement. Afterward, the whole group can review the submissions and collectively choose the best elements of each variation.

8. Clarify Vision Goals
Who: Strategic Planning Team

Once the vision statement is written, it may be tempting to throw out the workshop notes. Don't. The notes capture your hard-won foundational insights, and once they are consolidated, they will help you design your strategy, serve as a reference point, and tell the story of your vision.

Consolidate the vision story into a single document that captures the potential or expected outcomes of each goal, reveals the leadership team's thinking in more detail, and provides useful guidance for later, when you design the rest of your *Strategic DNA*. Whenever possible, identify and document potential objectives. Figure 1.8 shows the goals and potential objectives that made up the vision story of one conglomerate.

9. Publish a Statement of Vision
Who: Leadership Team and the Strategic Planning Team

At the conclusion of the vision formulation process, the leadership team may be tempted to keep the new or modified vision a secret, at least for a time. To justify this impulse, one participant in a vision formulation

Vision Goal	Potential Objectives
Streamline Divisional Activities	• Modern management techniques • Consistent value creation • Value-added products and services • Perceived as family of companies
Re-engineer Corporate Activities	• Promoting consistent corporate image • Balancing interdivisional planning • Enabling shared service offerings • Setting strategic orientation • Optimizing resource availability
Improve Governance	• Standardizing performance management methodologies • Enabling transparent decision making • Making accountabilities clearer • Protecting shareholder value • Enabling better control over divisions
Conduct Group-wide Programs	• Building a group-level project management office • Promoting cross-business teaming • Building value through customer sharing • Sharing best practices • Harvesting economies of scale
Invest and Diversify Asset Portfolio	• Divesting value-eroding assets • Reducing volatility in results • Avoiding value destroying decisions • Improving dealmaking

Figure 1.8 Vision Story Goals and Potential Objectives

remarked, "Since we haven't figured out how to do it yet, wouldn't it be better to avoid questions we can't answer by not announcing it until the strategic plan is finished?" Resist this urge. Doing so can be completely counterproductive, because the questions that may seem frightening are in fact desirable sources of insight and intelligence that will show you exactly how to achieve the vision.

Publicizing the vision statement has other advantages, too. It demonstrates your progress to other employees and emphasizes the leadership team's growing alignment. It begins the mobilization and realignment of the broader work force, particularly when they see that they'll have a role in developing the plan.

Deciding when the right time to publish is, of course, situation-specific and a function of the organization's values and culture. However, it can be argued that the only valid reasons *not* to publish are if the work force already has strategic exhaustion (has little enthusiasm because of unachieved, volatile, or massive recent strategic changes), or if the leadership team lacks credibility and thus must have real answers ready when the new vision is revealed.

At this point, the leadership team has developed a new vision and should be reasonably well aligned around it. It has developed goals and objectives—strategic priorities—for making the vision come to life. The team now knows what it wants the *Strategic DNA* to produce.

Summary

This chapter lays the foundation for the *Strategic DNA* by clearly defining the vision it will be designed to produce. At present, the vision's *Strategic DNA* has very little form. It's little more than a compass heading. Layers of detail will be added in each subsequent chapter.

2

Strategy Clarification and Mapping

How Do We Plan to Get There?

NOW THAT YOUR VISION IS CLEARLY DEFINED, STRATEGIC PLANNING can begin. Many organizations establish long-term visions and retain them through several strategic planning cycles, so subsequent planning iterations often start at this stage. These planning cycles begin either by formulating a new strategy for the existing vision or by clarifying an existing strategy. The approach described in this chapter is equally applicable to both.

Imagine if General Eisenhower had led the invasion of Normandy without using maps to explain his strategy. Although he had a massive army of enthusiastic people keenly mobilized around a shared vision of defeating the German armies, his forces would have struggled to win the battle. How would the Navy know where to land and sweep for mines? Where were the beaches, towns, hills, woods, and roads? Where were the obstacles and concentrations of resistance? Where were the German tanks, and where were the Allied tanks? How would soldiers know who to shoot and where to drop bombs? Without maps of the strategy, commanders would have found it difficult to communicate goals, thrusts, objectives, obstacles, and interdependencies. People cannot easily execute a plan they can't visualize and don't understand!

Executives who use strategy mapping to clarify, document, and communicate their strategies echo the same message: "If you do nothing else, do this." Whatever else occurs as they plan and implement their strategies, they believe that strategy mapping is important for the clarity, alignment, and mobilization it fosters.

It is hard to get everyone on the same page if that page does not yet exist. Surprisingly, many organizations create greatly detailed strategic plans and still don't have a single-page summary illustration their people can understand. The reason the strategy map is so powerful, and so popular, is that it is the "same page" that everyone needs to get on.

It can be a great challenge to ensure that key stakeholders are aligned around a clear and common interpretation of the strategic intent. Clarification exercises frequently become formulation efforts when a previously unrecognized or unacknowledged lack of alignment is revealed.

The map is the backbone for the strategic plan. The act of developing it is crucial to the effective alignment of the leadership team and the subsequent mobilization of their respective forces. When properly defined, it provides an overall roadmap that can be followed from the present situation to the desired future state—from the status quo all the way to the ambition. This is as true for today's businesses as it was for the Allied armies in 1944.

The dynamic and unique conditions faced by each organization means that there are almost as many different ways of developing strategies as there are CEOs. The fundamental requirement is that it must be a clear, concise, and changeable tool that is capable of sharing the big picture, keeping up with the fast pace of today's business environment, and remaining current in highly reactive sense-and-respond strategies.

Strategy mapping produces a graphical big picture in which objectives are visually organized and interrelated with each other with an illustration of cause-effect logic (e.g., "If we have *satisfied customers,* they will come back and buy more"). In *Strategic DNA,* this is where the strategic genome is mapped to define the strategy's overall anatomy. Like the DNA of the human genome, the information contained in the strategy map is outcome-focused and oriented toward what the organization will look like once the strategy has been achieved.

Why Do It?

An organization realizes several benefits when it chooses to use a strategy map. The map is a superb tool for communicating the strategy in a nutshell, clearly articulating the strategic intent and setting direction for the business. It is the core genetic code that guides the decisions people make and the actions they take. The process of building the map adds great value as leaders work through key questions, issues, and alternative viewpoints to reach a truly aligned single point of view.

To Communicate in a Concise, User-Friendly Format

A picture is worth a thousand documents. Many organizations produce extensively detailed and documented statements of their strategic intent, sometimes compiled into a strategic plan of telephone-directory proportions. Such bulky plans are intimidating and, at first sight, powerfully discourage people from actually reading them, even if they contain a brief executive summary. *A strategic plan serves no real purpose if nobody reads it.*

All the information included in telephone-book plans usually does have value, but most of it is better kept in the background as supporting documentation. A strategy map is the opposite of a telephone-book plan. It is a single-page overview that tells the story of the strategic intent. On the map, individual *strategic objectives* are positioned systematically to demonstrate the relationships between them and reveal the logic that underpins key strategic thrusts. Figure 2.1[9] illustrates a strategy map from Ivrnet Inc., an Internet communications company.

One of the most powerful characteristics of the map as a communication tool is that it reveals to individual employees where their activities contribute to achieving the overall big picture. Providing this line of sight begins the

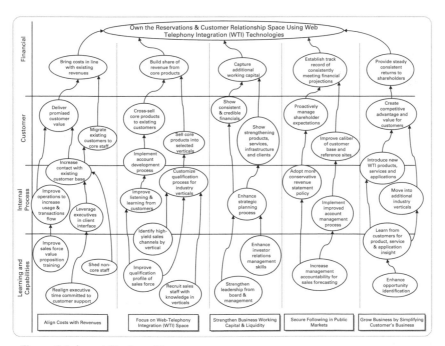

Figure 2.1 Ivrnet Strategy Map

process of making the strategy an everyday influence and helps mobilize the work force in pursuit of the vision.

The map enhances the strategy's implementation, facilitates collaboration and coordination, focuses creative energies, and provides a daily reference for everyday activities.

To Tell the Story of the Strategy and State the Strategic Intent

Strategic Objectives

In a human body, DNA provides information to control physical characteristics (e.g., making hair blond or making the person short). In *Strategic DNA*, this genetic code is programmed into the strategic objectives (e.g., "find more customers" or "reduce carbon footprint") and reflected in everything from the achievement targets to the resource allocations and management reports that are derived from them.

In describing the road to the vision, the strategy map identifies characteristics the organization will exhibit once the vision is successfully achieved and the milestones along the way. To exhibit those characteristics, the organization needs to change. When taken together, the changes define the strategy it intends to accomplish. Each characteristic change represents a strategic objective, and their illustration on the map (usually as an oval or bubble) is thus a statement of strategic intent. An objective's inclusion on the map provides unequivocal direction to the work force and other stakeholders.

Cause-Effect Logic Relationships

Although the strategic objectives are the fundamental molecules of *Strategic DNA*, the way they are arranged together, as with human DNA, ultimately drives the anatomy of the final business configuration.

Individual strategic objectives are related to each other on the strategy map using a cause-effect logic linkage that reflects the natural value chain and culture (see Figure 2.4 on page 30). These logic links illustrate how the achievement of one objective enables the achievement of another and captures the underlying hypotheses for the strategy. This interconnection of the objectives, in effect, allows the map to tell the story of the strategy.

Understanding and illustrating relationships between strategic objectives answers unasked questions about an objective's importance, its achievement through preceding objectives, the interdependencies of related metrics, and variances between actual and expected results (discussed further in Chapters 3 and 12).

The Vision Stairway—Thrusts Building Toward the Ambition

Strategic thrusts lend a second dimension to the map's high-level structure. Each thrust documents chains of cause-effect logic that lead to a particular major outcome. The term "thrust" has naturally proactive, action-oriented implications and is clear and simple enough for use with the broader work force.

Strategic thrusts lend themselves to illustrating how an intended strategy builds toward achieving the vision. Building strategic ambition is illustrated by a vision stairway in Figure 2.2; there, thrusts build on each other to move two companies toward their visions: One example features a vision of industry-transforming technologies and the other reveals a vision of corporate growth through creative products.

Thrusts are not strictly sequential—one thrust need not be complete before another can begin—but more results can be expected earlier from more foundational thrusts (shown on the left of the map). Results from more visionary thrusts (those placed on the right) arrive later, as they build on improved foundations laid by earlier thrusts. This adds implicit cause-effect logic to the explicit relationships illustrated as lines on the map.

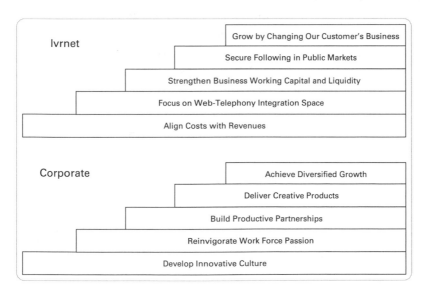

Figure 2.2 Stairways to Heaven—Thrusts That Build the Ambition

The logic of strategic ambition provides the highest-level overview of the strategy—ideal for discussion by the CEO in the firm's annual report.

The vision stairway is most useful for communicating the strategy to the work force and other stakeholders. Exposing people to the complete map for the first time can cause confusion and resistance, but presenting the stairway sets the stage for subsequent explanation of the complete map.

To Clarify the Meaning and Align the Leaders Around It

It is not just the finished map that provides advantages. A more precisely defined and broadly understood strategic intent emerges from the *process* of building the map. The degree of precision can then be further developed using the achievement targets listed in Chapter 3. Such broadly held and precise understanding of strategic intent is rare without some form of strategy map. The map-building process surfaces and addresses significant issues, resolves areas of contention or divergent intents, and aligns the stakeholder group around a single view of the strategy.

Alignment and Sharper Focus

By clarifying the strategy through an approach that builds alignment, the mapping process reduces and consolidates multiple objectives into a critical few that require focus. This sharpening of the collective focus tackles areas of known divergence and helps identify previously unrecognized differences in expectations, interpretations, or opinions.

The discussion and identification of logical relationships among objectives and their arrangement into thrusts helps develop stakeholder alignment and focus. The relationships codify common knowledge, hypotheses, and assumptions; link desired outcomes to areas of investment; and reveal high leverage areas of opportunity. The relationships illustrate how organizational capabilities must evolve and lay groundwork for business cases that justify investment.

Clarity

When it is performed as a team sport, the very act of constructing the logic clarifies the meaning of each individual objective. As a result, the team is aligned on a shared understanding. Specific words emerge during this process that might be interpreted in different ways by different people. Identifying and clarifying the meaning of these key words greatly enhances the strategy's precision, but it cannot be considered to be truly precise until it is quantified by specific achievement targets (see Chapter 3).

For example, imagine the discussion surrounding a vision to "be the best service provider in North America." "Best" could be interpreted in terms of competencies, quantity, size, quality, price, speed, share, frequency, and probably a hundred other ways. Although the clarification discussion begins during strategy mapping, the objective does not become clear until it is described by a specific achievement target (e.g., "rank first in the J.D. Power annual survey by 2009").

To Help Mobilize the Work Force

The pursuit of the strategy and achievement of the vision invariably depends on the ability of leadership to mobilize the people whose efforts will produce the desired results. Harnessing and motivating the work force in the chosen direction requires several elements.

- A clear message
- Leaders aligned on a single interpretation of that message
- Effective communication tools and techniques
- An expectation of rewards for success, and consequences for failure

The strategy map can provide, at least in part, the first three elements listed above, but the fourth is largely supplied through the tools and techniques described in Chapter 9. The map will provide the basic framework around which those rewards and consequences are built.

What to Do
Capture Insight, Input, and Involvement

Effective strategy mapping uses insight gathered from key stakeholders and their constituencies. It begins the process of aligning everyone around the strategy map their insight inspires. Key stakeholder involvement is essential; their input is invaluable, and it's even more important to convey to them that their contributions are valued. The fruit of their involvement is used to develop a "straw-man" strategy map they can validate and finalize. Stakeholder input, recognition, participation, and validation cements the earlier alignment and ensures that conceptual and emotional ownership of the map is in the proper hands—theirs.

There are really two basic approaches for building a strategy map: "full" or "lite." The lite method—using earlier documentation or a focus group meeting—usually takes less time. It is effective when the vision is clear and the stakeholder alignment is strong. The full method, which uses a combination of research, interviews, straw men, and workshops, can take more time. It is effective when the vision is unclear, the alignment is unstable, the group prefers to use a straw-man map, or the culture requires deep involvement and commitment before it buys in.

The full method—research plus interview plus draft plus validate—is described in this chapter. It relies on private interviews because they usually reveal deeper insights. Hidden agendas, challenges to the conventional wisdom, and emotional considerations are far more likely to emerge in private discussions. Failing to discover such aspects usually makes the validation process far more difficult. The considerable time investment to conduct and synthesize interviews and prepare a straw-man map results in fewer iterations of difficult discussions and a more rapid and robust alignment. This is especially valuable for joint ventures, large corporations, and the public sector, where getting competing stakeholders to collaborate can be very challenging.

Stakeholder Group

The stakeholder group is usually very similar to the leadership team that developed the vision. Some senior executives and owners may no longer be involved (they may have stepped aside to empower operational executives to design and implement the strategy), and representatives from other groups that will be involved in implementing the strategy may be added.

Identify Strategic Objectives

The interviews identify the personal objectives of the stakeholders. Although their many points of view can initially cloud the landscape, stakeholder interviews can provide raw material for building the draft strategy map. Objectives that conflict with each other help identify areas of disagreement and nonalignment while revealing opportunities to address issues and improve alignment. Most truly strategic objectives emerge as goals; their achievement represents significant progress toward the *actual* realization of the vision. This includes objectives that are prerequisites for subsequent objectives.

Strategic objectives are briefly defined on the draft map and are further clarified by supporting information. Ideally, the initial short-form wording of objectives should be meaningful in tangible, everyday terms. Although their precise meaning will not be clarified until achievement targets are defined in

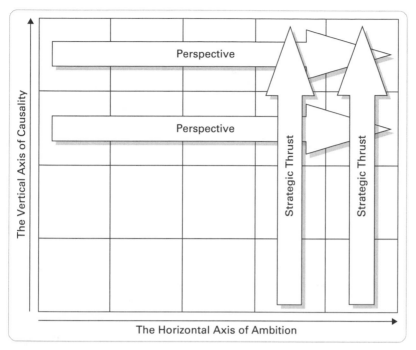

Figure 2.3 Strategy Map Axes

Chapter 3, the short-form wording usually provides enough clarity for draft validation discussions.

Organize the Axes of the Map

The two principal dimensions of the map are the axes representing the cause-effect logic and the building ambition (see Figure 2.3).

The Vertical Axis of Causality

The axis of causality is conventionally shown running top to bottom, with *desired outcomes* at the top and *foundational investments* at the bottom. This provides a framework for demonstrating dependencies between strategic objectives by illustrating their cause-effect relationships. The cause-effect model usually takes the form of a Balanced Scorecard[10] structure (or a derivative of it) and organizes objectives into perspectives, or different points of view. The perspectives, which include financial, customer, internal process, and learning and growth viewpoints, are organized in a sequence that aligns with the organization's culture and reflects its internal points of view and values. The Balanced Scorecard architecture is not obligatory, but

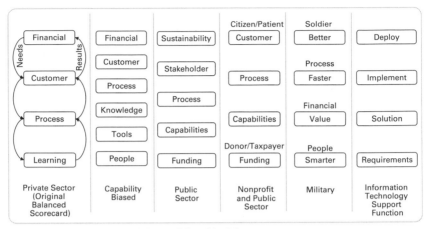

Figure 2.4 A Selection of Cause-Effect Models

corporate and business unit strategies usually benefit from such an approach. Strategies for support functions, such as Human Resources or Information Technologies, are less likely to need a Balanced Scorecard structure.

Figure 2.4 provides six examples of cause-effect models. Most are loosely based on the Balanced Scorecard, but their perspectives are reorganized or redefined to suit the organization's values, culture, and philosophy.

Perspective names can cause considerable debate. In one workshop, a public-sector board kept returning to an endless debate about whether to refer to a perspective as "client" or "customer" because of the political implications. The right name is the one that communicates its intent most intuitively. Figure 2.5 provides some common names.

The Horizontal Axis of Ambition

The axis of ambition is conventionally shown horizontally, with

Standard Perspective	Alternates or Elements
Finance (Financial Outcomes)	Sustainability, Profitability, Shareholder
Customer	Stakeholder, Client, Shareholder, Employee, Bettor, War-Fighter, Patient, Audience, Parents, Artistic Impact
Internal Process	Processes, Services, Programs, Practices, Internal, Do, Activities, Workflow, System, Faster
Capabilities/Innovation	Learning and Growth, Innovation, Infrastructure, People, Technology, Knowledge, Smarter, Resources
Funding (Financial Inputs)	Financial, Capital, Investments, Resources, Donors

Figure 2.5 Perspective Name Examples

immediate priority foundational thrusts on the left and less tangible and more visionary thrusts on the right. This axis provides a general time sequence, but it is not necessarily consecutive. Thrusts on the left side of the map tend to be more clearly defined, produce more immediate results, and/ or establish foundations on which later, and initially less tangible, thrusts will build.

Ivrnet used a conventional Balanced Scorecard for its cause-effect model; see Figure 2.6.

Define Relationships Among Individual Objectives

Using the example shown in Figure 2.7 (see next page), the logical relationship between the objectives helps explain the story as follows: "If we want to grow profits, we must offer customers targeted and competitive products." The relationship between each pair of objectives can be explained similarly until the complete logic chain demonstrates how the company can grow profits: "We must first teach our people to understand customer value and identify profitable customers, channels, and products." A critical question—"How are we going to grow profits by serving our customers?"—

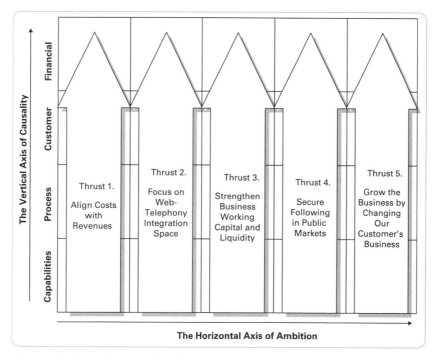

Figure 2.6 Ivrnet Strategy Map Structure

is answered by the relationships that illustrate how helping employees understand customer value and profitable customers will improve customer segmentation. In turn, customers can be offered targeted products that ultimately make profit. Similarly, the question "How can we improve our segmentation?" is answered at least in part by the relationship that points to training employees to identify profitable customers.

The strategy map explicitly shows the cause-effect relationships *within a thrust* as lines connecting two objectives. It should only *imply* relationships among different thrusts. This keeps thrusts disentangled, simplifies the map, facilitates individual accountabilities for results, and reduces the incidence of turf wars.

How to Do It
1. Collect and Review Background Information
Who: Strategic Planning Team

Collect and review all relevant information to build a solid understanding of existing visions, strategic plans, and their supporting data. In addition to the vision documentation prepared in Chapter 1, this may include all the traditional components of strategic planning activities, such as value and mission statements, environmental scans, SWOT analyses, competitor

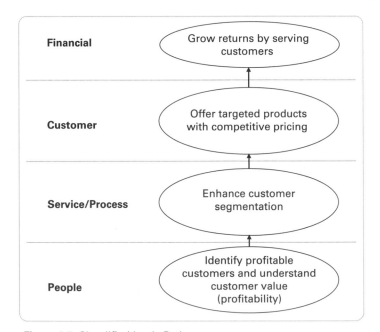

Figure 2.7 Simplified Logic Path

analyses, industry benchmarks, literature reviews, and expert advice.

Often, in-house strategic planners are tempted to gloss over this step, as they have long been exposed to, or even were part of developing, the background material. When external consultants are engaged, they take this step very seriously in an effort to better understand the client's needs. Consequently, consultants can sometimes be more up-to-date than the insiders. In-house strategic planners should review the background information carefully before beginning a strategy formulation or clarification exercise.

2. Establish Cause-Effect Logic Framework

Who: Strategic Planning Team

The cause-and-effect logic framework defines the perspectives

Figure 2.8 Strategy Clarification and Mapping Process

that calibrate the vertical axis of the strategy map. Establish and agree on a framework in this step, as it will be necessary for the next step, organizing the interview guide. The framework, as shown in Figure 2.4, is often self-evident to the strategic planning team as it reflects the organization's values and philosophy. When in doubt, refer the question to the strategy owner or the full stakeholder group.

3. Prepare Interview or Focus Group Guide

Who: Strategic Planning Team

The interview guide is a multirole document that provides structure to a series of stakeholder interviews or focus-group discussions. It is designed to guide the interview process, achieve the goals of the interviews, and reveal insight about the strategy and the environment in which it must be pursued.

The most effective interview guides are organized in sections that reflect the agreed-upon logic framework from the previous step. If the interview guide is structured in this manner, many of the relationships among objectives will reveal themselves naturally during the interviews. The guide should test preexisting thrusts, objectives, achievement targets, and initiatives, as well as probe implementation obstacles. The sections of a typical interview guide might be as follows:

1. Vision exploration
2. Current plans
3. Financial
4. Customer
5. Process
6. Capabilities
7. Barriers
8. Initiatives

On a practical note, review Chapters 3, 4, and 5 before developing the interview guide and design your questions to gather some of the information you will need later, when you are adding metrics, projects, and organizational accountabilities to the *Strategic DNA*.

Open questions encourage an interviewee to provide free-ranging, broad opinions, including unconventional or innovative ideas. Closed questions sharpen the subject's points and opinions and reveal areas of focus and degrees of alignment across the interviewees. Use both open and closed questions for each section. This iterative questioning approach carefully distills detailed points of view from broader opinions without stifling creativity.

For example, questions in the customer section might include:

- Who are the company's customers? (Open)
- What do those customers most value? (Open)
- How would you segment the customers, and how much of the business does each segment represent? (Open)
- How would you prioritize this broad list of values? (Closed—refers to a table)
- What is needed from each customer segment if we are to achieve the sustainability goals discussed earlier? (Open)
- Which of the following outcomes would the customer need if we are to achieve the sustainability goals discussed earlier? (Closed—refers to a table)

4. Conduct Structured Interviews and Harvest Insight
Who: Individual Stakeholders and External Interviewer

Conduct private structured interviews with each stakeholder to:

- Gain an understanding of the business issues
- Capture insight from subject matter experts
- Build collaboration by acknowledging and validating stakeholder opinions
- Identify existing and intended thrusts, objectives, achievement targets, and initiatives
- Identify relationships between objectives
- Discover the degree of clarity and alignment around the preexisting vision and strategy
- Reassure stakeholders that they are part of the planning process and encourage buy-in
- Identify others who should be contacted for additional insight

The interviews typically last around one to two hours and are conducted by a respected outside consultant in an environment that is comfortable and convenient for the interviewee. This private, one-on-one format provides political safety, allowing the subject to talk, reveal his or her insights, and sometimes vent about perceived issues. Such safe interviews provide interviewees with a rare opportunity to explain why something is an issue; doing so is daunting in the everyday environment. Diamonds of insight are frequently hidden in the rough of venting.

Interview the following stakeholders:

- The stakeholder group that will participate in the strategic planning workshops (including the entire executive team)
- Senior leaders of departments/divisions that must implement the strategy
- Recognized thought leaders
- A high-level representative of individuals directly impacted by the strategy, which could be a board member, shareholder, customer, employee, strategic venture partner, or similar constituent

Compile interview notes and background review notes and synthesize them to produce a body of knowledge that will be very useful as you progress through later steps. Focus the synthesis on capturing and documenting the complete diversity of stakeholder opinion, including how they perceive the thrusts, objectives, relationships, related measures, initiatives, and implementation obstacles.

5. List and Distill Draft Objectives
Who: Strategic Planning Team Supported by External Interviewer

Use the synthesized notes to create a draft of strategic objectives, and then distill it to eliminate duplication and combine related subobjectives. Some draft objectives will be echoed by several interviewees; these can be considered broadly supported. Others will be more personal, either because they greatly affect the interviewee's own business unit or are a prerequisite that allows the interviewee to pursue a subsequent objective.

Numerous draft objectives are also implied during the interviews but not explicitly stated. Exploring relationships with a systematic analysis of responses based on the defined logic framework can shake these out. For example, standard Balanced Scorecard framework questions might include:

- "If we are to achieve that financial objective, what would customers need to see?"
- "Which processes must be changed to achieve that?"
- "What capabilities need to be improved to support that?"

Additional draft objectives may be suggested by the research conducted during Step 1. Also, review of the practices of other organizations that are striving to achieve similar strategies can sometimes reveal adaptable draft objectives.

The Power of Perspective

The arrangement of the interview guide ensures that draft objectives will be discussed in the context of the perspectives defined by the logic framework. Draft objectives emerge as interview responses are analyzed, one perspective at a time, so they can be easily categorized. Subdividing perspectives into layers or bands can also help draft objectives to emerge. For example, customer perspective objectives might be considered for internal, external, and customers' customers, and capabilities perspective objectives might be considered for knowledge, technology, and people.

Objective Documentation

Document each draft objective with sufficient data so its meaning will remain clear over time. The following guidelines should help you document draft objectives:

- Be brief. Chapter 3's achievement targets will precisely clarify the meaning, so the wording doesn't have to.
- Write objectives in a consistent format—"enhance service," "expand market share."
- Use action-oriented verbs like *increase, reduce, develop, grow, build,*

improve, maximize, provide, satisfy, reward, and so on.

- Encourage stakeholders to change the wording during Step 9's validation workshop, as it will help them assume ownership of the map's content.

It is not always possible or desirable to base strategic objectives on hard facts and figures; they can often only be derived from intuition and insight. Therefore, strategic objectives can be framed either relative to the current configuration of the business (e.g., *more, enhance, grow*) or described in absolute terms (e.g., *provide, implement, establish)*.

Distill Objectives

An overabundance of objectives is not unusual. Analysis of them often reveals opportunities for consolidation. Generally, each subject area will generate a number of objectives, all of which belong to a single perspective. For example, if several objectives relate to different aspects of improving customer experience in the company's call center, they can be consolidated into a single objective as long as doing so doesn't lose their intent.

6. Identify Strategic Thrusts
Who: Strategic Planning Team

Thrusts tend to have one of three pervasive characteristics.
1. They are already well defined and universally understood.
2. They are already defined but poorly understood or inappropriate.
3. They are not defined.

Appropriate thrusts are frequently self-evident or emerge naturally from interviews. There are usually no more than four or five of them. When thrusts are not readily obvious, establish them by analyzing the draft objectives with one or more of the following techniques:
- Start with the vision goals and explore first "what do we want to become?" and then "what must be done to get there?"
- Brainstorm high-level goals that summarize the strategy.
- Group objectives that naturally belong together and then translate the groups into an action-oriented statement of intended change.
- Capitalize on the personal insight of the interviewer (now the most broadly informed person after the CEO).

Design thrusts to be measurable, since they are, in effect, major objectives. Use a single format to name thrusts, either verb-object style ("increase operational effectiveness") or in a simpler outcome format ("operational effectiveness"). Summarize each thrust with one or two objectives in the map's top perspective, each representing a significant strategic outcome. Achievement of these top objectives represents the thrust's overall achievement and also sets the scene for accountability (see Chapters 7 and 11).

Sequencing the Thrusts

Thrusts are not usually sequenced until after they have all been defined, but sometimes, thinking about the sequence helps crystallize their definition. The principal consideration when sequencing thrusts is that they must reflect the organization's building strategic ambition. Thus, the sequence should position thrusts that lay foundations on the left and graduate to more visionary thrusts on the right.

As a rule of thumb, thrusts on the left tend to be more clearly defined than the right side's less tangible ones. They tend to produce more results sooner, and although ideally there should be activity in all thrusts at all times, work tends to concentrate on left-side thrusts earlier in the implementation. This means that more initiatives (see Chapter 5) are related to the left side of the map early on, and emphasis shifts to the right as time goes by.

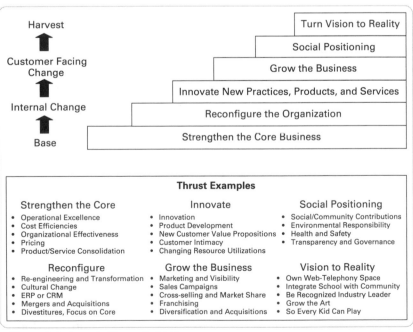

Figure 2.9 Generic Thrust Guidelines

The Vision Stairway Formula—A Generic Thrust Model

In the same way that horizontal perspectives usually reflect variations on the Balanced Scorecard theme, a high proportion of strategy maps follow the same basic stairway formula (see Figure 2.9). This formula is useful when designing thrusts. It is based on the common-sense logic of a) fixing problems with the existing situation (i.e., strengthen the core business), b) effecting significant change to the business, and c) realizing or harvesting the dream.

7. Map the Strategic Genome (Sequence the Objectives)

Who: Strategic Planning Team

Organize the draft objectives into a strategy map by sequencing them in the context of the defined vertical thrusts and horizontal perspectives.

Locate Objectives in Strategy Map Grids

Position the objectives that emerged from the interviews in the perspectives to which they would naturally belong (e.g., an objective that produces a customer outcome would be located in the customer perspective, and an objective that produces an improved business process would be located in the internal process perspective). This straightforward approach reflects the sequence of the interview guide, so objectives emerge naturally in their related perspective. Figure 2.10 illustrates the placement of objectives (denoted by gray bubbles) on the strategy map grid.

Alternatively, as long as the thrusts are well understood, the objectives should be placed under them. The choice of whether to start with the perspectives or the thrust is simply personal preference. The perspective-

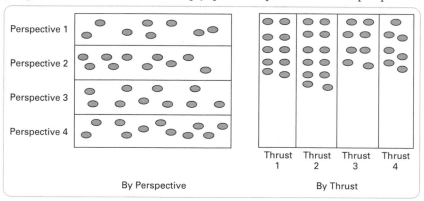

Figure 2.10 Organizing Perspective First or Thrust First

first approach is more intuitive for experienced Balanced Scorecarders, and the thrust-first approach is usually preferred by action-oriented thinkers.

Either way, the next step is to analyze the objectives once more and adjust them on the second axis. Once the analysis is complete, each objective will be located in its appropriate perspective/thrust box, as seen in Figure 2.11. With experience, you'll be able to finish this in a single step.

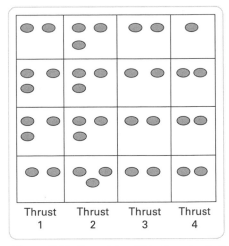

Figure 2.11 Organizing Objectives by Both Thrust and Perspective

Homeless Objectives

Invariably, some "homeless" objectives emerge that do not seem to belong in any of the boxes. Perhaps the objective has little to contribute to any thrust's success, or perhaps it simply isn't strategic. Sometimes this occurs when an objective is inherited from an earlier strategy, but it is often a reflection of diverging interviewee opinions.

It is best to park homeless objectives, since they only serve as a distraction. They can be dealt with during later validation discussions, when they may reveal errors that require adjusting the thrust definitions.

Develop Logic Paths for Each Thrust

By examining the location of the objectives in each box, it should be possible to develop cause-effect logic relationships for the objectives of each thrust. Many relationships are self-evident based on either interviewee insight or a visual review of objectives among preceding and succeeding perspectives. Review the objectives from the top of the thrust down, as this reflects a top-down, start-with-the-end-in-mind viewpoint.

Ask three interrelated questions about each objective to help identify its logic relationships, either among the thrust's boxes or within a single box.

1.   Do any of the thrust's objectives in the same perspective need to be completed before this one can be achieved?
2.   Do any of the thrust's objectives in the preceding (lower) perspective need to be completed before this one can be achieved?

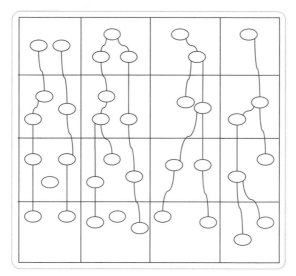

Figure 2.12 Preliminary Draft of Map

3. Are any prerequisite objectives missing from the thrust?

The result is a preliminary draft of the strategy map shown in Figure 2.12.

Avoid relationship links between objectives in two different thrusts, because they lead to significant measurement and accountability confusion when the strategy is implemented. The logical relationship between such objectives is implied by the very nature of the vision stairway, rather than by an explicit link on the strategy map.

Normalize Logic Relationships

Once the preliminary draft has been prepared, the resulting logic can be reviewed for completeness. Incomplete logic may appear as:

- An objective with no relationships
- A relationship that jumps through a perspective (e.g., a direct connection between a financial objective and a process objective without an intermediate customer objective)
- An objective that has no relationship with objectives in preceding perspectives (except for those in the bottom perspective)
- A path of relationships that fails the sanity test—it simply does not make sense
- A thrust with very few objectives

Incomplete logic can be readily apparent to a newly expert

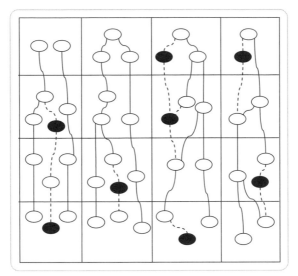

Figure 2.13 Adding Objectives to Resolve Incomplete Logic

interviewer, but it is most often discovered through a disciplined review of the chains of objectives and relationships within each thrust. Resolve incomplete logic paths by defining additional objectives, as shown in Figure 2.13.

Flesh Out Undefined Thrusts

Occasionally, a thrust will have few objectives. This is common when innovative new visions and strategies are being formulated. In this case, define new objectives from scratch by decomposing the thrust from the top perspective down. To do so, reuse the questions used to distill the objectives in Step 5.

The logic of decomposed objectives can also be validated by reviewing the logic path from the bottom up in a similar manner. Pose questions like:

- Will the achievement of this learning/capabilities objective enable the achievement of this/these internal process objective(s)?
- Will the achievement of this internal process objective enable the achievement of this/these customer objective(s)?
- Will the achievement of this customer objective enable the achievement of this/these financial objective(s)?

The result of this step is a *draft* strategy map. It should only be considered a draft until the stakeholders validate it as a group.

Too Many Objectives?

Although the overabundance of objectives was consolidated in Step 5, you still may have too many. While it may be possible to consolidate more of them, undistilled objectives actually serve a purpose. Stakeholders who are using the map for the first time may be uncomfortable with its function or impact on their world. Keeping undistilled objectives aids alignment by letting everyone see their piece of the big picture reflected in it.

By the time the map reaches its second iteration, stakeholders are conscious of its impact on priorities and resource allocations and lobby for their agendas. Those already overabundant objectives start breeding! By the third iteration, stakeholders have learned—the hard way—that their map should be more sharply concentrated on key objectives. Organizations that go through all three iterations may be slower to internalize the need for a tighter ambition, but ultimately, they will achieve a very keen focus.

8. Prepare Draft Strategy Map and Narrative
Who: Strategic Planning Team

In Step 9, the draft map will be validated and adjusted by the stakeholder group during a workshop meeting. In this step, produce the tools to facilitate that meeting, including:

- A PowerPoint-based graphic that illustrates the vision stairway
- A PowerPoint-based version of the strategy map
- A wall-chart version of the strategy map
- A strategy narrative

Vision Stairway and Strategy Map PowerPoints

The PowerPoint strategy map provides the single-page view of the strategy that serves as the "same page" everyone needs to be on. The first time people see the full strategy map, it can appear somewhat confusing and overwhelming. Avoid that confusion by first showing the stairway before introducing the full map. Color-code the stairway's steps with the same colors used for the thrust's objectives on the map.

The custom animation feature of PowerPoint allows a meeting facilitator to introduce the strategy map one objective at a time, so the thrusts will appear to decompose into the objectives and their relationships. This allows the stakeholders to digest the map in small pieces. Identify the thrusts along the bottom of the slide so the connection to the stairway is intuitive. Use highlighter pen colors to color-code thrusts in PowerPoint, as this will simplify additions, changes, and cross-references to paper-based documents during workshop meetings (you'll simply use highlighter pens to do so).

Strategy Map Wall Chart

A strategy map wall chart is an invaluable visual aid for workshop meetings. The chart should be about 6' by 20 to 25', so all participants will be able to see it clearly. Each strategic objective should be identified with a movable color-coded bubble. The colors, which coincide with the colors of the thrusts, should be consistent with the colors used in the PowerPoint.

The wall chart is used to adjust and fine-tune the objectives. The objectives may be reworded, removed, relocated, or replaced, so don't attach them permanently to the background, and don't include relationship lines.

Strategy Narrative

The strategy narrative is a written version of the strategy map. Many people understand a picture more readily than written words, but some prefer to read text. Most stakeholder groups include both types of people, so it pays to present the content in both formats (both will be needed later anyway). Once completed, the strategy narrative becomes the written story of the strategy and supplements the visual map. It provides a script that can be used to explain the map to people and captures additional details about individual relationships among objectives. This narrative may be printed on the back of hard copies of the map to provide a handy explanation. A simplified example is shown in Figure 2.14.

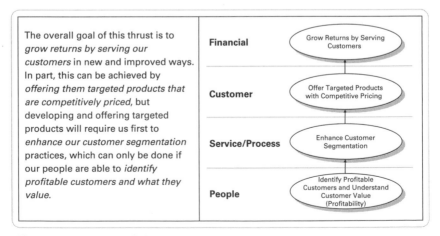

Figure 2.14 Example of Narrative

9. Validate and Adjust Strategy Map

Who: Stakeholder Group and Strategic Planning Team Led by Strategic Planning Leader

Armed with the results of the interviews, the draft strategy map, and its corresponding narrative, you can bring the complete stakeholder group together in a workshop (see Figure 2.15 for a basic agenda).

The principal goal of the workshop is to validate and finalize the strategy map that establishes the structure of the *Strategic DNA*. Going forward, this structure will frame decisions and actions. Secondary goals include aligning the group with the map's content, resolving differences of opinion, and transferring ownership. The ultimate outcomes of the meeting are an aligned group of stakeholders and an approved map that clearly defines the strategic intent.

This is the point where stakeholders get on the same page. When this has been done well, the stakeholder group will be aligned around a single-page illustration of a broadly supported strategy and mobilized to take it forward. Do not allow the strategic planning lifecycle to move forward until this step has been successfully completed. Imagine a soccer team where each player thought the goal was in a different place. No matter how good their intentions are, they'll always find it difficult to score goals.

The length of the workshop should be determined by how aligned the stakeholders are and how much time they're willing to invest in improving the situation and resolving issues. Working through the issues—particularly those that have not previously surfaced—can take considerable time.

First, brief the stakeholders on the synthesized findings of the interviews. Carefully introduce the thrusts and the map by first unveiling the stairway and then, using the PowerPoint of the strategy map, explain the story of the draft strategy. Unveil the strategy map wall chart and use it to facilitate the discussion of the draft; as you go along, carefully validate the objectives and their relationships, and revise the large objective bubbles on the wall chart to record the stakeholders' conclusions. Encourage the stakeholders to

---

Strategy Validation Workshop

Sample Agenda

1. Review Interview Synthesis
2. Review Stairway and Draft Map
3. Validate Thrusts
4. Revise Each Thrust and Its Objectives
5. Approve Final Map

Figure 2.15 Sample Agenda for Strategy Validation Workshop

revise the bubbles themselves, because by correcting, improving, rewording, removing, destroying, creating, or relocating the bubbles, the stakeholders assume intellectual and emotional ownership of the strategy.

10. Finalize Strategy Map and Narrative
Who: Strategic Planning Team

Now that the workshop is complete, fine-tune the strategy map documentation and distribute it to stakeholders. Complete outstanding action items and confirm the agreed-upon resolutions to any contentious or complex issues outside the workshop setting. It is also usually advisable to follow up with each stakeholder to ensure that he or she truly concurs with the results of the meeting.

11. Making It Public
Who: Stakeholder Group and Strategic Planning Team

Once all have agreed on the strategy map, it can be released to the broader group of stakeholders. However, this is sometimes not done until later, during either the strategy-cascading, portfolio-selection, or work-team mobilization stages. Distributing the map to a broader community can greatly enhance transparency by making the strategic planning more visible. While this is usually a desirable outcome, throwing the map out to the world without explanation or context can be construed as threatening and may cause confusion.

Unveiling the map as part of a coordinated communications program is the most powerful way to deploy it, particularly if the program is part of an executive or work force mobilization event.

Summary

The activities performed in this chapter give overall structure to the *Strategic DNA* by virtue of a strategy map that defines thrusts, objectives, and the relationships among them. The structure is defined in a way that addresses issues and builds alignment of the leadership team and other stakeholders.

3

Achievement Target Identification

How Will We Know We Are There?

THE STRATEGY MAP PROVIDES AN OVERVIEW OF THE OBJECTIVES AND tells the story of the strategic intent, but all the organization's goals cannot be described in detail on a single page. Setting achievement targets for each objective describes that intent at a much more granular level, providing a framework for performance measurement techniques used to evaluate progress towards each objective. In this chapter, we'll look at the performance metrics and achievement targets behind each objective (see Figure 3.1).

The Detailed Meaning of Key Words

A particularly good example of the need for a more detailed description of an objective came to light at a food processing company. At first glance, the senior managers and board members appeared to be closely aligned about their strategic intent. Unfortunately, the strategy clarification process revealed that they were actually quite far apart. In this case, the critical word in their vision statement was "largest," as in "… become the largest

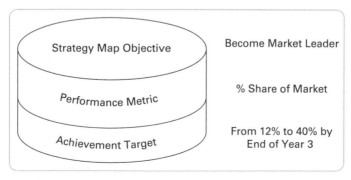

Figure 3.1 Metrics and Targets Make Objectives Tangible

food processing business." Individual interpretations of "large" varied dramatically. To some, it meant most profitable, and to others, it meant garnering the greatest revenues. Some thought it meant processing more food each year than any other firm, and others believed it meant having more physical locations than anyone else. The CEO thought it meant being the industry leader.

Their animated conversations about their strategic achievement targets revealed that "large" really meant behaving as a major player in the industry (e.g., by joining government trade missions, supporting university education programs, influencing industry standards, and pushing industry technologies to new levels of sophistication). Although these key words had first emerged during the vision formulation and strategy clarification processes, their true meaning only crystallized once related achievement targets were defined.

A Balanced Scorecard

In their Balanced Scorecard program[11], Kaplan and Norton explain that modern businesses are letting themselves down by focusing almost exclusively on measuring financial outcomes. They suggest a framework that looks at business objectives from four different perspectives—financial, customer, internal business processes, and learning and growth capabilities. The undeniable logic of this balance, and the astounding results some have achieved using it, has made the Balanced Scorecard process very popular with all types of businesses.

Much of this popularity stems from how the perspectives aid the understanding of the cause-effect logic by readily identifying relationships among business objectives. When carried over from objectives to performance metrics, this structured logic reveals measurable indications of future performance outcomes.

In Chapter 2, an adaptation of the Balanced Scorecard was used as the strategy map's vertical axis of causality. This lays the groundwork for selecting intuitive and meaningful achievement targets that provide a crystal-clear statement of strategic intent.

Why Do It?
To Make Objectives Explicit and Tangible

The main reason for establishing achievement targets is to clarify and communicate goals in a way that everyone can understand. Associating a *performance metric* (something to be counted) and *achievement target* (the number of these somethings desired) with a strategic objective makes it more tangible. For example, "to become a market leader" is an objective that most can agree with. But until the performance metric is identified and the achievement target is set, the objective often means different things to different people. Each stakeholder might interpret "market leader" in different terms—markets, revenues, shareholder capital, number of employees, number of customers, number of stores, and so on. They may also have different interpretations of what it will take to become the leader: Do they need to be 51 percent, or just 1 percent ahead of the number two company? Does this domination need to be worldwide or just domestic? Associating a specific achievement target with an objective clarifies its intent. If the objective reads, "to become a market leader before the year 2012 by capturing 51 percent of all North American sales of networked widgets," everyone will understand it clearly.

Quantifying strategic objectives provides precision and clarity about the objective's intent and transforms potentially vague ideas into everyday terms that people can understand. During the period when the objective is only generally described, stakeholders can interpret it as they please and continue to pursue their own agendas. As achievement targets introduce more granular clarity, alignment can become increasingly challenging. This "no pain, no gain" effort encourages the group to pull in the same direction, but it can be extremely difficult to accomplish.

To Quantify the Expected Value of the Strategy

If you are armed with a defined achievement target for each of the objectives at the top of each thrust, it is possible to establish a view of the overall value the strategy is expected to create. For private-sector companies with a financial perspective at the top of each thrust, the value would be stated in financial terms. For public-sector and nonprofit organizations, which often list customer perspectives at the top of each thrust, the value may be stated in customer-outcome terms. It can describe the anticipated benefits in the strategy's business case, and in many ways, it is what makes the rest of the strategic implementation possible.

To Motivate Desired Behaviors

Establishing targets motivates people to perform in a certain way. From our earliest days in grade school, people are measured to establish and evaluate performance expectations. We are motivated to work harder primarily because of the consequences a low grade would bring—embarrassment with our peers, shame in the presence of our parents, or failure to achieve goals like getting into a particular school.

The use of performance measurement to motivate behaviors in the modern business world has its roots in the groundbreaking research conducted by Elton Mayo at Western Electric's Hawthorne Plant in Cicero, Illinois. In describing the "Hawthorne Effect"[12], Mayo explained that an individual's behaviors may change simply because they know they are being studied. This principle has long been reflected in the use of performance metrics and targets in the workplace. Using metrics to motivate individual behavior has its limitations. People can react negatively if they perceive the targets to be unfair or irrational, and they may become demotivated if they feel others' actions are inconsistent with the targets.

There can be an osmosis-like effect where measurement naturally influences performance, but relying on it to achieve desired outcomes has a downside. In the business world, this sort of osmosis is compromised by competing influences, like rapidly changing competitive forces, collective agreements, interdepartmental rivalries, interpersonal relationships, and so on. Supplementing the osmosis effect with more assertive target-driven decisions, such as variable compensation and appropriate resourcing, adds a more reliable source of motivation and directly affects actual results.

To Set Timing for Performance-Improvement Expectations

Periodic interim targets encourage an organization to stretch its performance at a preferred pace. Progress toward an objective is easier to see when it's measured against expectations documented in interim and final targets. Without interim targets, there may be little sense of progress, and motivation may be lost long before the final target is approached. By balancing short- and long-term outcomes, interim targets set timing expectations for performance improvements, allowing quick wins to be celebrated and motivation to be refreshed.

Performance-improvement expectations may also be shared among the divisions, departments, and individual workers involved in making the strategy happen. Expectations set at the corporate level can be shared among business units using the strategy cascading approach described in Chapter 4. Performance expectations for individuals can then be developed as part of the work-team mobilization process described in Chapter 9.

To Calibrate Strategic Evaluation and Learning

Setting achievement targets enables progress toward the objectives to be quantified and used as feedback for strategic evaluation and learning. In time, this may become the most valuable reason for setting the targets, because it allows the strategy to be continually adjusted until the objectives have been met.

The detailed definition of the strategic objectives, their cause-effect interrelationships, and their associated measurable achievement targets provide a hypothetical model of the business that can be used to evaluate actual results. Comparing actual measurements to what was originally anticipated validates or challenges underlying assumptions and hypotheses. It allows the model to be recalibrated (or fine-tuned) based on lessons learned during the implementation of the strategy and supports continual improvement of strategic efforts. In some mathematically sophisticated organizations, finely calibrated models have been used to produce dynamic computer models of the system in support of enhanced (and usually financial) decision-making. Chapter 12 provides practical processes for learning analysis and feedback for nonmathematicians.

What to Do
Choose the Right Achievement Targets

A well-chosen achievement target translates an objective into a desired, measurable improvement that reflects stakeholder wishes and needs. It drives change by influencing behaviors, so people try to do the right thing the right way. Targets for objectives lower down the strategy map drive change by influencing the achievement of subsequent objectives.

The best performance metrics are relatively easy to capture, calculate, and maintain. The information or its source data should ideally be available already, with clearly identified responsibilities for collection, calculation, and dissemination. This avoids expensive and time-consuming information systems development activities; sometimes, however, for just the right metric that expense may be unavoidable.

Ultimately, the most important characteristics of a well-chosen achievement target are:

- The ease with which it can be understood and communicated.
- The clarity with which it establishes expectations.
- The encouragement it gives to stretch performance.

Conversely, poorly chosen achievement targets can spread confusion,

Method	Question
Translation of Meaning	What exactly do we mean by that objective?
Financial Business Cases	What additional economic value does the objective represent?
Stakeholder Expectations	What do the stakeholders expect this objective to achieve?
Internal and External Comparisons	What is the performance of northern region or John Doe & Co.?
Existing Metrics Inventory	What do we measure today? How much do we need to improve that?
Current Baseline Performance	How well we perform today? How much better could that be?
Behavioral Improvement	How will we know if people are doing what we want them to?
Hypothesis Validation	How will we know what we believe is actually true?

Figure 3.2 Methods for Exploring Metrics and Targets

Metrics in This Perspective...	...Should Motivate Specific Outcomes or Behaviors
Finance (Financial Outcomes)	Improved Economic Results
Customer	Customer Needs and Desires, Satisfaction of Expectations
Internal Process	Improved Ways of Working
Capabilities	Improved Knowledge, Skills, Tools, Infrastructure, and Cultures
Funding (Financial Inputs)	Better Focus to Application of Resources or More Available

Figure 3.3 Types of Outcomes and Behaviors by Perspective

undermine strategy, cause people to pursue the wrong goals, unnecessarily consume resources, and seriously demotivate workers. This last point comes into play when establishing the desired level of performance: It is all too easy for managers to set discouraging targets that negatively affect the achievement of objectives and the strategy as a whole.

Identify Appropriate Metrics and Targets

Several points of view can be taken when exploring the most appropriate way of measuring progress toward an objective. Each of them has value, but the best method for each objective must be evaluated on a case-by-case basis. These different points of view can be explored using the questions in Figure 3.2.

The strategy map's structure can be valuable for identifying metrics for each objective. Each of the perspectives has a naturally corresponding type of metric (see Figure 3.3).

Understand Predictive Indicators and Outcome Metrics

The identification of predictive indicators and outcome metrics is simplified by basing metrics on the strategy map's cause-effect arrangement. Predictive, or lead, indicators can provide an early indication of future performance. They are particularly valuable when the value of the outcome, or lag, metric cannot be expected to move until much later. Predictive indicators allow the organization to react to a failing strategy long before the failure might otherwise have been discovered.

Outcome metrics are the most intuitive, as they measure actual performance in terms of the outcomes produced. The outcome metric of one objective may be a predictive indicator for a subsequent objective, with the strategy map identifying the logical relationship. For example, an expenditure on information technology training for teachers is an outcome metric for an objective to increase teachers' technology competencies, but it is also a predictive indicator for a subsequent objective to improve students' computer skills.

Review the Existing Portfolio of Metrics

Every organization has a number of performance metrics already in use. Usually, most of these metrics are used in daily operations, but a few are periodically compiled or calculated to satisfy reporting requirements or provide strategic insight. Most have far too many such metrics and expend substantial resources to routinely gather, collate, and calculate measurements that have little meaning. Reducing the number of things being measured can yield substantial savings.

The proliferation of measurement data has caused many organizations to turn to *ad hoc* data mining and business intelligence software to generate meaningful indicators of progress. These tools are essential when you are manipulating huge amounts of data, but they rarely compensate for a failure to focus on measuring just the right things—the metrics that matter. Whenever possible, adopt existing metrics to minimize the time, cost, and effort spent implementing the strategy, and reassure employees that they have been measuring the right things, at least in some cases.

Stop Measuring Valueless Metrics

Existing metrics that do not matter strategically and operationally have little value in general. They are distractions that consume resources unnecessarily, and they should be eliminated.

In this automated computerized age, it can be surprising to learn just how much it costs to measure something. Some performance measurement projects have even been justified by the savings achieved by reducing other measurement efforts. Measurement costs are often intangible, but they can include costs related to:

- Time filling in extra fields on forms
- Time asking customers additional questions
- Dedicated industry or customer surveys
- Annual benchmark research updates
- Computer processing and storage
- System interfaces
- Software customization
- Results analysis
- Report generation
- Paper printing and distribution
- Management review and discussion
- Target setting
- Unnecessary nonstrategic corrective actions

Reducing the number of metrics increases the focus on the metrics that really matter. The sharpened focus lends itself to a dashboard approach that raises visibility and awareness of the current values of key performance metrics. When coupled with modern database management tools, dashboards allow a manager to drill down to explore and address the root cause of undesirable trends.

Listen to the Voices of the Customer, Market, Shareholders, and Other Stakeholders

Stakeholder expectations are a wonderful source of measurement inspiration; in fact, many would argue that they are of overriding importance. If your real bottom line is what the stakeholders expect, your strategy is best described in those terms. However, it can be a challenge to identify all the stakeholders and prioritize their relative desires. Using stakeholder expectations to frame achievement targets can greatly simplify otherwise complicated measurement decisions.

Consider Noneconomic (Social, Environmental, and Health and Safety) Metrics

Performance metrics were predominantly financial in nature before the 1990s. The Balanced Scorecard changed all that by shifting some of the emphasis to customers, business processes, and learning and growth capabilities. The scope of performance measurement priorities has since broadened again, in part due to stakeholder demands for transparency and good governance. This rebroadening also occurred in part because of an increased awareness of the impact business activities have on society and the environment. Some approaches specialize in tackling environmental and social metrics, but a balanced approach can actually accommodate them without losing the benefits of the balance.

Objectives in the social arena still fall onto the strategy map by virtue of the need to achieve targets from the perspective of society (a customer), sustainability (financial) outcomes, society-friendly business behaviors (business processes), and societal development (capabilities). Similarly, environmental or health and safety objectives fit readily into the perspectives. Noneconomic thrusts, objectives, and metrics can all be built into the strategy map and achievement targets.

A professional theater company provided a most interesting example: The top perspective on its strategy map, and its overall vision, was framed in terms of artistic impact. The board, management, and employees of the company all agreed that artistic impact was the ultimate goal, so strategic outcomes needed to be expressed in those terms. In effect, however, this is essentially a customer perspective in disguise. The company's objectives and metrics were all designed to satisfy the expectations of a broadly defined group of customers—not just the audience, but also the artists themselves, sponsors and donors, and so on.

Be Careful with Expensive Benchmarking

Benchmarking is a popular tool for comparing performance relative to other business entities. Part of its popularity is rooted in the reassurance it offers about how internal performance compares to that of outsiders. Unfortunately, benchmarking can also result in either analysis paralysis or very complex metrics. It is often an expensive proposition, particularly when the information must be purchased, researched, or developed from a blank page.

Benchmark data can provide false reassurances—the fool's gold of performance comparisons—by disguising performance as the best of a bad bunch and keeping the eye on the wrong ball. My earlier example of major nondiscount airlines showed that they clearly fell into this trap by comparing performance amongst each other and disregarding the superior performance of rapidly emerging discounters in areas that mattered most to their customers. This fool's gold trap can be offset by benchmarking efforts that examine other industries for analogous performance examples, as well as direct comparisons against competitors.

One aspect of benchmarking that is well worth considering is that of internal comparisons. Many organizations are looking for best practices elsewhere in the industry when one of their own business units might provide far more relevant, and easier to acquire, information. Organizations that are being outperformed by their competitors may find that one of their internal divisions is actually performing better than any of their competitors, thus presenting a real opportunity to transfer knowledge and techniques among divisions.

Benchmarking should really only be used when it is absolutely necessary and appropriate for the situation. It is probably needed if:

- Other efforts are stagnating.
- Competitors appear to understand customers better.
- Other organizations are using revolutionary technologies that could be useful in yours.
- External stakeholder expectations make it politically necessary.

Consider Special Types of Measurements

Sometimes, there just isn't a single output metric that properly represents the intent of the strategy, or it is simply impossible to use the right metric. Special types of metrics are available for these situations, the most useful of which are the composite index and the proxy.

Composite Indices

Simple, absolute metrics can be difficult to identify, as the complexity of the objective and sometimes the political concerns of multiple stakeholders combine to ensure that no single metric will be acceptable to all. Although it is preferable to battle through the issues and concerns until all agree on a simple, absolute metric, it is often impractical or politically impossible to do so. In these cases, a composite index may be an effective metric that all interested parties can agree to.

A composite index combines several metrics that are individually more absolute together in a mathematical function. The Dow Jones stock index is perhaps the most famous example. Another fine example was developed by a public school board with a vision to "satisfy individual education needs" of each student, which meant that a true reflection of systemwide performance had to reflect the school board's six "common essential learnings" (CELs):

1. Communication
2. Numeracy
3. Technological literacy
4. Critical and creative thinking
5. Values and skills
6. Independent learning

An index was proposed that combined the established measurement for each of the six CELs and tracked overall long-term progress in them. Actions that increased one CEL at the expense of another did not significantly increase the total index. The contribution of each CEL to the overall index set its weighting, and the index made historically subjective performance monitoring much more objective.

Proxies

A proxy may be used to provide a close approximate indication of actual performance. It may not be conceptually ideal, but it can intuitively represent performance until a better metric is available. A proxy is normally adopted when the ideal metric requires unavailable or prohibitively expensive data, or when technically better metrics are not intuitive to the stakeholders. Proxies are not usually used as long-term substitutes for ideal metrics; for example, if you were attempting to measure changes in the proportion of a city's population that is physically active, you could measure the trend in citywide sales of running shoes as a proxy until sufficient data is collected.

Establish Performance Baselines

All strategic objectives represent a change from the current situation. The magnitude of the desired change is calibrated by the achievement target as an increase or decrease from the current baseline level of performance. For metrics to be meaningful, the baseline must be quantified and clearly stated.

When conceiving of a new achievement target for an objective during strategy formulation work, a stakeholder group frequently does not know what the present level of performance is, as it has never before been measured. In such cases, the most convenient practice is to select the metric, set targets as a percentage improvement against the (unknown) present value, and declare that its present value, once it has been measured, will become a baseline against which performance can be tracked.

Set Achievement Targets

Once metrics have been selected, the degree of improvement desired is identified and quantified as targets to be achieved. Figure 3.4 illustrates how the value produced by the vision is made up of the value created by each thrust, which is in turn made up of the value produced by each objective in the thrust's chain of logic. Simply put, the intended value of the vision is calibrated by setting the achievement targets. The most practical method for doing this is to first set targets for each thrust and then decompose them to the level of each objective.

Discussing each thrust's value in outcome terms focuses attention on the strategy's business case. The discussion highlights the explicit link between the objectives and the business case; in many cases, it can be a rude awakening. Until stakeholders become comfortable with the value each thrust must produce, there is little point in proceeding any further. One private-sector manufacturer became increasingly uncomfortable as 30 percent of its $20 million strategy was allocated to the very first thrust, an operational efficiencies undertaking. The dawning realization that operations

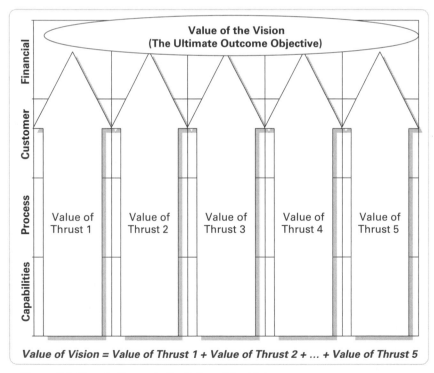

Figure 3.4 Thrusts Generate the Value of the Vision

would thus have to find $6 million in cost efficiencies led the company to question its strategic assumptions more realistically.

The achievement targets chosen should require the organization to stretch its performance to an explicit degree and in a stated timescale. The stretch quantifies the gap between the current performance and the level at which the vision will be considered achieved. This makes the intent of the strategic objectives much clearer. For example, the intent of an objective of "increase share of major contracts" becomes much clearer when it is understood as "increase dollar share of $1 million plus contracts from 18 percent to 33 percent by 2012."

Achievements against targets

Figure 3.5 Achievement Target Identification Process

are often used to trigger performance rewards or consequences. For multiyear strategies, interim targets are set annually, quarterly, or per reward period to maintain motivation and momentum. Targets should still be set even if decision makers are unsure about what they should be. Such targets can be communicated to employees as preliminary or subject to change, along with a commitment to revisit them at a preplanned interval. At least this correctly communicates the overall intent.

Decompose Through the Organization

Achievement targets are often readily decomposed and shared across the organization. One example is a sales force with individual, departmental, and product quotas that are adjusted relative to corporate goals. Less intuitive are targets that have a different anatomy in each business unit, such as customer satisfaction at an electrical utility. At an electrical utility, a corporate-level customer satisfaction target of "99 percent satisfied or very satisfied by 2012" may work for its customer care division, but this might have to be translated to "99.99 percent power availability" for the transmission and distribution divisions and "97 percent average generator duty cycle" for the electricity generation division. Other targets might need to be specifically developed to address objectives specific to those business units. (This is discussed further in Chapter 4.)

The relevance of achievement targets—and how they sound as they decompose through the organization—frequently does not get enough attention and can result in meaningless targets. For example when an executive team was setting goals in terms of "economic value added," first-line managers found it impossible to explain the metric to their employees, partly because they didn't understand it themselves. When the targets were restated as "return on utilized assets," employees were able to understand explanations of why they wouldn't be getting new computers.

How to Do It
1. Collect Existing Metrics Portfolio
Who: Strategic Planning Team

Many organizations measure too many things, and most of those metrics do not have established targets. Ideally, this needs to be turned around so that there are only a few key metrics, each with established targets. The first step in this process is to prepare an inventory of the existing metrics as a spreadsheet.

Many existing metrics will be well known and easy to document from readily accessed data sources, including operational and financial reporting systems. Others will have emerged during the interviews and workshops in previous chapters.

In this step, collect existing measurement data from all available sources and compile it into a metrics inventory. A consistent spreadsheet form works well and simplifies the mail-merge production of workbooks in the later steps.

2. Establish Benchmarks
Who: Strategic Planning Team

External performance benchmarks frequently add little value unless the success of the strategy will be judged against them. Whether they're established here, after Step 5, or not at all varies from one organization to another.

The goal of the first benchmarking activity is to understand the objective's intent. Once the intent of the objective is understood in more detail, design a data search that contains the scope of the work by only seeking to calibrate specific achievement outcomes. The design work generally falls into two streams of discussion. In the first stream, the objectives to be benchmarked are reviewed to better understand their desired outcomes. This may have been captured in Chapter 2, but what you have may lack detail. The second stream resolves this issue by exploring stakeholders' perceptions with more discussions of what outcomes they need the objective to actually produce.

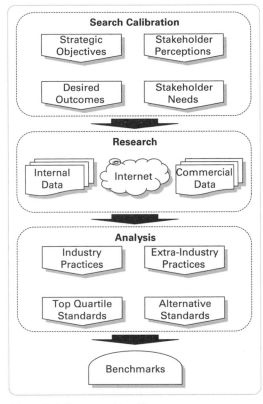

Figure 3.6 Benchmarking Flow

Conduct research following the data search design to identify relevant reference points. Consider data from three sources: the organization, the public domain (including the Internet), and commercial sources, such as pollsters or Dun & Bradstreet.

The next activity is to analyze what others measure as their benchmarks and what their level of performance is. Arrange this information into performance quartiles for conventional industry metrics and offer alternative approaches drawn from external analogies. Update the metrics inventory spreadsheet to include industry standard and alternative references.

Figure 3.6 illustrates the steps needed to identify performance benchmarks.

3. Relate Existing Metrics to Strategy Map Objectives
Who: Stakeholder Group and Strategic Planning Team

Relating the metrics in the inventory against the objectives on the strategy map takes place in a workshop setting with or without a straw man. The preferred method is without a straw man, because it fosters alignment and the buy-in needed to dispose of unnecessary metrics. The straw-man method is more popular when inventory is very large or the executive team prefers to delegate the legwork. In this method, the strategic planning team prepares a straw-man metric scheme for validation and adjustment by stakeholders in the workshop. The method adopted depends on the availability of stakeholders, the preference of the executive team, the degree of buy-in desired, the number of existing metrics, and so on. Figure 3.7 shows a sample agenda.

Workshop Method

This method engages the entire stakeholder group in analysis and decision-making during the workshop. Reuse the strategy map wall chart to guide decisions about which inventoried metrics relate to which strategic objectives. Write each metric on a Post-it® note and, after suitable discussion, stick it in its proper place on the map, as illustrated in Figure 3.8. The stakeholder who cares most about an individual metric is the ideal person to stick the note on the map, as he or she will buy in to its placement. This is especially important for those metrics that do not seem to fit. The stakeholder begins letting go of the metric by placing it in a holding area for disposition later in Step 10. The notes—represented as small gray squares in the figure—will be distributed throughout the map, and many will end up in the "don't seem to fit" holding area at the bottom. Some objectives will have no notes attached to them, and others will have many; these gaps and concentrations are addressed in subsequent steps.

Straw-Man Method

The straw-man method is popular especially when the stakeholders have full confidence in the strategic planning team. The method recognizes stakeholders' specialized knowledge while leveraging strategic planners'

Achievement Targets Workshop

Sample Agenda

Part 1 — Metrics
1. Relate Existing Metrics to Map
2. Vision and Thrust Metrics
3. Objectives Metrics
4. Finalize Scheme
5. Assign Owners

Part 2 — Targets
6. Thrust Targets
7. Decompose Stretch
8. Vision Value
9. Disposition Unused Metrics

Figure 3.7 Sample Agenda for Achievement Targets Workshop(s)

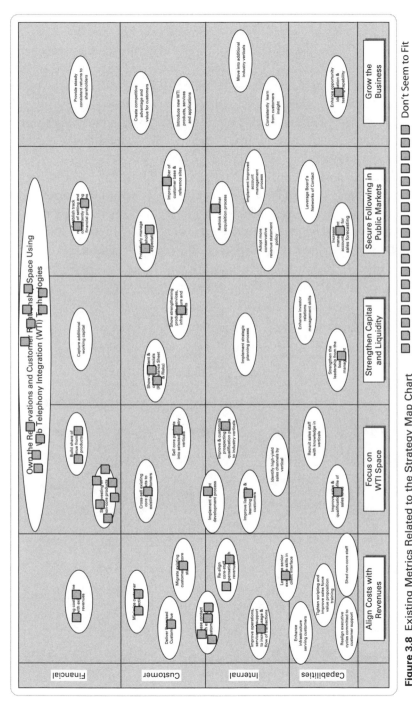

Figure 3.8 Existing Metrics Related to the Strategy Map Chart

expertise in the whys and wherefores of performance measurement.

Prepare for the workshop by reviewing the metrics inventory and relating them to strategy map objectives. Use your earlier exposure to stakeholder thinking covered in Chapters 1 and 2 and your prior knowledge of the performance management discipline to frame this analysis. Record the analysis in an additional column on the inventory spreadsheet. (The objectives should be numbered, if they haven't been already.) Using numbers like 1.06, where "1" represents the thrust and "06" identifies the objective, can be very helpful.

Once each metric has been related, manipulate the spreadsheet to reorganize them by objective and extract the "don't seem to fit" metrics. Use the spreadsheet and the template shown in Figure 3.9 to identify multiple candidate metrics for each objective on a single sheet. Using a spreadsheet to collect the data, and Microsoft Word's invaluable mail-merge capability, configure the template to produce a workbook for use in the workshop.

In the workshop, the stakeholder group now only has to review and

Strategic DNA Metrics Worksheet

Thrust #	Objective #	Objective		

Candidate # 1

Definition				Data Source

Availability	Current Performance		Definition Responsibility	

End Year 1	End Year 2	End Year 3	End Year 4	End Year 5

Candidate # 2

Definition				Data Source

Availability	Current Performance		Definition Responsibility	

End Year 1	End Year 2	End Year 3	End Year 4	End Year 5

Candidate # 3

Definition				Data Source

Availability	Current Performance		Definition Responsibility	

End Year 1	End Year 2	End Year 3	End Year 4	End Year 5

Figure 3.9 Candidate Metric Template

approve or adjust the straw man before moving on to the next step. This review still takes a lot of time if stakeholders are really engaged in the effort, but this investment is necessary if they are to take ownership of the work back from the strategic planning team. Consider it a warning sign if it is dispensed with quickly.

4. Establish High-Level Metrics
Who: Stakeholder Group Led by the Strategic Planning Leader

The inventory has now been related to the strategy map objectives, but are they the right metrics? This question is best answered by starting with the metrics for the vision as a whole and for each thrust. Key metrics are usually self-evident, but for strategies that explore new directions, new metrics may have to be designed.

This step is usually conducted in the same workshop used for the previous step. The stakeholders participate in the discussion about the thrust metrics, but sometimes, a CEO or parent corporation dictates vision and thrust metrics.

Vision Metrics

The vision metric represents the desired result of the vision in its entirety. If it is difficult to decide on a single overall metric, the vision may not be clearly articulated or broadly supported. In such cases, adopt an index made from the *thrust metrics* or some other proxy. Discuss the challenges this will create when mobilizing workers or customers around the strategy. It is essential to establish this metric, but if the stakeholder group cannot resolve the question, the metrics for each thrust must be established first, before returning to the vision metric discussion.

Thrust Metrics

Thrust metrics are the same as the metrics for the uppermost objective in each thrust and represent the desired outcome of the thrust in a nutshell. During the discussion, occasionally remind the group that the thrust metrics will ultimately represent the value of the vision and strategy. When characterizing whether a proposed metric is appropriate, consider these questions:
- How do we want the business to look in x years from now?
- Is it easy for people to understand? Is it intuitive? Does it add clarity?
- Will it tell us whether the objective is being achieved?

- Will it encourage people to do what we want them to?
- Will it cost a fortune to measure?

In the example in Figure 3.8, two of the five thrusts have no existing metrics related to them, so new metrics will certainly have to be defined. The other three thrusts have many metrics, but none of them may be the right one—they may not clarify what the stakeholder group truly means.

5. Establish Objective Metrics
Who: Stakeholder Group Led by the Strategic Planning Leader

Decompose established vision and thrust metrics to design metrics for each objective. Review the existing metrics that were related to each objective to see if one of them can be adopted. Design new metrics where gaps exist or when no existing metric is appropriate.

The following questions, and the questions from Step 4, help identify the appropriateness of existing metrics.

- Will the metric ensure that prerequisites are in place for subsequent (higher up the map) objectives?
- Will it recognize important progress toward the vision?
- Does it really matter?

This review usually results in more existing metrics being relegated to the "doesn't seem to fit" area, and more gaps emerging as each metric's unsuitability becomes recognized.

Design new metrics by focusing on identifying a metric that adds detail to the intended meaning of each objective. The questions are again a great help when leading the group through this discussion, but many metrics are self-evident from the discussion of surrounding objectives and metrics.

Useful approaches for facilitating the identification of new metrics include:

- Considering what successful achievement of the objective should look like.
- Reviewing succeeding (higher up) objectives for required inputs (see Figure 3.10)
- Considering the types of outcomes or behavioral changes normally related to the perspective (see Figure 3.3).

Each objective should only have a single intuitive metric, but in practice, some may have more. If key stakeholders cannot agree on two or less metrics for an objective, they are not yet really on the same page about the strategy (the usual case), or the objective warrants an index metric (the rare case).

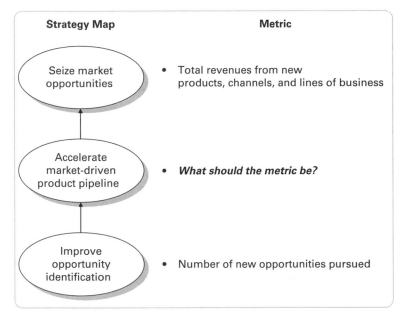

Figure 3.10 Insight from Preceding and Succeeding Objectives & Metrics

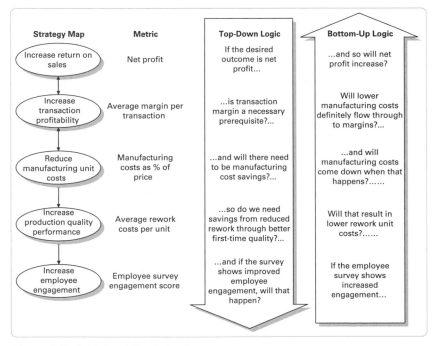

Figure 3.11 A Chain of Metric Logic

6. Validate Completed Logic Scheme
Who: Stakeholder Group Led by the Strategic Planning Leader

Now that metrics have been established and rationalized for each objective, you may validate their logical relationships using the strategy map as the frame of reference. Although some existing metrics will be adopted for use in the model, thus speeding implementation and reducing organizational resistance, they may detract from the original intent of the related strategic objectives. Reviewing the metrics and their relationships as a complete, integrated scheme provides a final test that the chosen metrics are logical and appropriate. Be sure you validate the integrated scheme during the workshop.

First, validate the logic from the top down. Starting from the top objective of a thrust, state its metric and describe how the metrics for each of the preceding (lower) objectives contribute to the succeeding (higher) objective. Then ask the group, "Did that make sense to you?" If they agree that it does, repeat the process for each of the preceding objectives until you reach the bottom of the thrust. Discuss any of the statements that do not pass this sanity test, and revise the metrics if necessary.

By the time you reach the bottom of the thrust, adjustments have been incorporated, and stakeholders are usually comfortable with the logic. If not, repeat the process from the bottom up to revalidate the logic from another point of view. (Figure 3.11 on page 67 provides a simplified example of one chain of logic.) Once you are finished, the top-down description can also be used to add granularity to the strategy narrative you prepared in Chapter 2.

7. Assign Preliminary Owners and Define Metrics in Detail
Who: Stakeholder Group Led by the Strategic Planning Leader

Assign preliminary owners for each metric. They should become the single points of authority for their respective metrics and be responsible for finalizing the formula for its calculation, documenting any necessary assumptions, compiling supporting information, and developing plans for locating and assembling the information. The preliminary owner may not be the person who ultimately has operational responsibility or accountability for the metric, but he or she should allow initial progress to be made and achievement targets to be set.

Owners are often appointed by the CEO or business-unit leaders, but the legwork is frequently delegated to the strategic planning team. This is typically the last activity of the first part of the workshop. If you schedule a separate session to set the targets, you'll have time to document related information and assemble it into a new workbook. Figure 3.12 provides a template that will help you define metrics in detail—but some of its fields may remain blank until later in the *Strategic DNA* implementation.

8. Establish Stretch Achievement Targets
Who: Stakeholder Group Led by the Strategic Planning Leader

Since you now have a complete, validated, and broadly supported measurement scheme, you can tackle the difficult target-setting activity.

Objective							
Strategic Thrust							
Objective							
Related Portion of Strategy Narrative							

Metric							
Metric Name							
Availability Status	Currently measured and reported	Metric will be available by	Customization planned	Customization needed		Manually compiled	Not available or planned
Implementation Plan							
Measurement Definition & Intent							
Assumptions & Constraints							
Calculation Algorithm							
Data Sources							
Accountabilities	Metric owner	Target setting	Review and assessment		Reporting		Data capture
Data Capture Process							
Report Generation Process							
Frequency of Reporting							
Reporting Forum or Distribution List							
Audit Process							

Achievement Targets						
Interim & Final Targets						
Current Level	2008	2009	2010	2011	2012	

Figure 3.12 Metric Definition Template

It's difficult because stakeholders have begun to see how much more performance is expected from their respective business units. Managers may energetically attempt to minimize their department's degree of change; and only those with the confidence or courage to stick their necks out are more accepting of the challenge to stretch their departmental performance.

Achievement targets should be a stretch, but not completely out of reach! If targets are too easy, they'll have little impact on performance. If they're too hard, they'll discourage the very behaviors they're supposed to motivate.

When establishing targets, it is helpful to know the current baseline performance level. Unfortunately, this can be hard to discern at the time the decisions are being made, so most achievement targets are first expressed as a percentage change against a yet-to-be-defined baseline. An absence of quantified baselines, however, is no excuse for not setting targets. Many strategy implementations begin to fail when performance targets are not set. The discussion about achievement targets should be held in a workshop setting with the same stakeholder group. In rare cases, it may be done at the same meeting as previous steps in this process; ideally, it is a reconvened meeting. As the facilitator, you should be armed with a new workbook that includes a completed template for each adopted metric and—whenever possible—actual current performance data. Having the same stakeholders in the room permits peer pressure to keep the metric owners honest.

The activity starts at the top of the map, establishing clear, unequivocal targets for each of the strategic thrusts and the vision as a whole. These numbers must make sense. If the achievement target at the top of a cost efficiency thrust does not represent significant cost savings, people will question the strategy's value. Employees and mid-level managers seeing high-level achievement targets for the first time have made some of the following comments:

- "Oh, it's OK. They're not really serious about cutting costs that much … look!"
- "They've got to be kidding. Where do they think we can find another 15 percent from operations? They must be smoking something!"
- "Wow, I guess they're serious about this!"

Design the targets to prompt this third reaction—it's tough, but not impossible, and well worth pursuing.

Logic Decomposition of Targets

Once achievement targets have been set for the vision and thrust metrics, it is possible to decompose the performance change into its component parts using the strategy map's chain of logic. Using the example shown in Figure 3.11, the discussion could be steered by answering questions like:

- How much net profit are we aiming for?
- Will the change be linear, front-loaded, or back-loaded? What are the interim targets?
- If we are going to meet those profit targets, how must the transaction margins change, and how fast must they change?
- What level of cost reductions is needed in manufacturing? How soon is it needed?
- What does that imply for rework costs? How quickly must that change?
- How much more employee engagement must we strive for? How soon should we expect this engagement?

Shares of Stretch

Where multiple predecessors contribute to achieving a target, an additional discussion must establish how much of the improvement will be driven by each predecessor. Figure 3.13 illustrates this "stretch–share allocation." The share can be used to calibrate calculations for each predecessor's targets.

Interim Targets

Interim targets set expectations for the rate of change in the metric

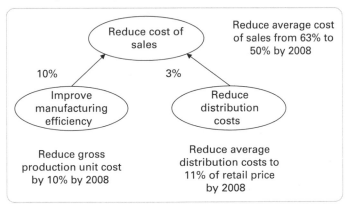

Figure 3.13 Allocating Shares of Stretch Between Contributors

and recognize progress toward the final target by indicating the level of achievement expected at specific interim periods (e.g., at the end of each year in a five-year strategy). Interim targets often cannot be set until after an objective owner has been assigned (see Chapter 7).

9. Quantify the Vision
Who: Stakeholder Group Led by the Strategic Planning Leader

Now that thrust metrics are identified and their achievement targets quantified, it's time to calculate a total value of the vision. As illustrated in Figure 3.4, the value of the vision is the sum of the value created by each thrust. State thrust value in outcome terms framed by the achievement targets related to the top objective(s) for each thrust. The value for a thrust is the total amount of change from baseline to target achievement levels for each top objective's metric(s).

For commercially minded businesses whose strategy maps have a financial perspective at the top, outcomes are usually framed in some combination of economic terms—EVA, profit, revenue, capitalization, share price, and so on. Organizations that have a customer perspective at the top (including stakeholder, donor, citizen, taxpayer, patient, and so on) may find it more difficult, as they must combine nonfinancial values like customer satisfaction, achievement test scores, program output volumes, discharge timeliness, patient readmission rates, average time in program, and so on.

Whenever possible, compile the value of the vision during the workshop and state it to the stakeholder group. If you do, you can confirm they are confident about the benefits the vision is supposed to produce. If they have any discomfort with the scale of change it represents, they'll let you know.

10. Disposition of Unused Metrics
Who: Stakeholder Group Led by the Strategic Planning Leader

What remains is to determine the disposition of metrics that didn't seem to fit. If they don't fit the strategy, they probably aren't strategic metrics. The best thing to do is simply stop measuring them (unless they are needed for operational purposes).

However, managers can perceive a loss of personal credibility when their metrics are discontinued. In such cases, carefully manage the change so those managers continue to support the overall strategy. Your argument is clear, nonetheless: "Unless a valid strategic or operational reason can be shown for continuing to expend resources on their measurement, let's stop measuring them!"

Lead the group through this discussion for each previously parked metric and assertively press for a disposition of each.

Summary

This chapter adds precision, depth, and measurability to the description of the *Strategic DNA* by defining performance metrics and achievement targets for each thrust and objective. Achievement targets make the *Strategic DNA* more exact and tangible by enabling specific tests that evaluate whether each characteristic of the vision has been produced.

4

Strategy Cascading
What Will That Look Like for Each Business?

EVERY JUNE, RESIDENTS OF THE CANADIAN CITY OF CALGARY, ALBERTA are treated to the excitement of chuck-wagon racing at the Calgary Stampede. Teams of four magnificently powerful horses tow heavy covered wagons around a track at incredible speeds. Imagine what would happen if those horses were harnessed individually to their wagons, without a center pole or any other connection between them. When the driver signaled them to go, they'd all pull in different directions. As for the wagon, it would either go in the direction the strongest horse wanted to go or fall apart. This is exactly what happens in a business when its departments, divisions, and strategic business units aren't pulling in the same direction. Strategy cascading harnesses the actions of the entire team together.

At heart, strategy cascading decomposes a high-level strategy throughout all business units. For example, a conglomerate's strategy establishes the framework within which each subsidiary company should design its strategy. Each subsidiary's strategy in turn sets the scene for its divisions, regions, profit centers, and so on, all the way down to the level of each department, and even each individual. With *Strategic DNA*, the strategy cascading process ensures there is a *family resemblance* among efforts of different organizational entities; it is an effect akin to the unique DNA of a child being similar to that of his or her parents and siblings.

This is a natural extension of the strategy mapping discussion from Chapter 2. The needs for, and benefits of, clarity and alignment apply to any group of stakeholders, whether they are individuals or whole divisions. Chapter 2 addressed the development of a strategy map to align stakeholders on a single strategic agenda, and this chapter tackles the challenge of coordinating the strategies of independent or quasi-independent entities, whether they are internal or external. Strategy cascading represents the first stage of decomposition and can even be used to take the strategy down to the level of individual managers. In Chapter 9, Work Team Mobilization, you'll explore decomposing strategy down to the level of the individual employee.

Owners Becoming Activists and Demanding Performance

Business owners have recently become far more assertive about ensuring their expectations are satisfied. Private-sector shareholders, and the boards of directors that represent them, demand that managers consider their input, keep their commitments, and are accountable for the business's performance. In the public sector, boards of directors, trustees, and governors are taking their responsibilities more seriously than ever before and are moving beyond purely political and electoral considerations to real transparency and accountability. Notorious scandals like Enron, WorldCom, and Hollinger provide almost daily reminders that leaders don't just get fired or thrown out of office—sometimes, they go to jail.

Such high-profile incidents have encouraged shareholders to force their boards to hold managers more accountable for their actions while legislation like the Sarbanes-Oxley Act provides teeth for enforcement efforts. As a result, managers have become more focused on outcomes, and businesses have had to seek better, more transparent governance processes.

Yet despite rhetoric to the contrary, many large organizations—particularly those in the public sector—still suffer from weak accountabilities. Their managers' actions sometimes cloud the waters, compromising transparency and allowing stakeholders to compete rather than collaborate. Such organizations probably have the most to gain from a system that visibly connects front-line performance metrics with corporate vision goals.

Scale *Strategic DNA* for Companies Large and Small

Private, public, and nonprofit organizations come in many shapes and sizes, ranging from individual entrepreneurs to Wal-Mart, the American Cancer Society, and the government. Yet with the possible exception of small firms, all need to clearly state their strategic intent and communicate it to their different levels. Complexities and communication mechanisms vary with the nature of the businesses.

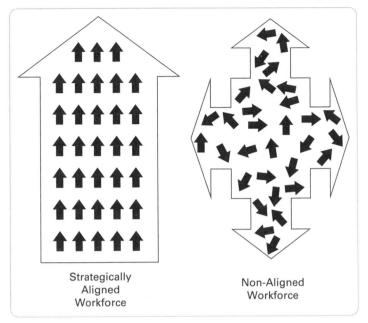

Figure 4.1 Effects of Non-Alignment

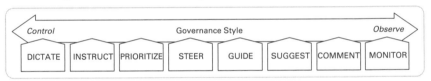

Figure 4.2 The Governance Style Spectrum

Small and mid-sized enterprises may find that the preceding three chapters provide enough depth for their strategy, but larger organizations—where CEOs cannot personally coach each employee—may need to develop vision goals, strategic objectives, and achievement targets for each business unit as well. Independent divisions and operating companies within larger organizations will each need their own versions of strategy maps and achievement targets, but smaller units may only need to be accountable for a subset of objectives and targets from the parent's strategy map.

Why Do It?
To Enable Good Governance

The strategy cascading mechanism enables good governance by allowing corporate owners and leaders to influence, or control, group and individual priorities using whatever motivational styles they prefer. Figure

4.2 illustrates the wide variety of governance styles available to a leadership team, ranging from strong autocratic control at one end of the spectrum to uninvolved observation at the other. The degree of influence represented by the governance style can be adjusted as appropriate to the culture and needs of the current situation, and can even vary from one part of the organization to another.

Each style has its strengths and weaknesses. At one extreme, a dictatorial style is tightly controlled, hierarchical, top-down, and vision driven; it can stifle innovation. At the other extreme, a monitoring style is loose, decentralized, bottom-up, budget driven, and creative; if unchecked, it can lead to anarchy.

Establish Governance Styles

Strategic DNA permits a leadership team to implement the governance style that suits the culture and situation. Its integrated practices can be applied with varying degrees of rigor to set expectations, control decisions and actions, and frame reporting requirements. For example, *Strategic DNA* might be used to provide the general guidelines managers are expected to respect when making their decisions, or it might be used as a rigid filter for approving funding requests.

Reinforce Direction from Parent Organization

When used as a funding filter at the corporate level, *Strategic DNA* speeds approval of clearly strategic funding requests and denies, or at least delays to death, any requests not aligned with strategy. This reinforces direction from the parent and greatly encourages business units to be better aligned with the parent's priorities. Corporate-level objectives and achievement targets are reinforced when the cascaded structure is used to guide the assignment of resources and authorization of other commitments. (This is further addressed in Chapter 7.)

Structure Parental Progress Reviews and Divisional Reporting

Cascaded objectives and achievement targets allow a corporate parent to review business-unit progress in big-picture terms, giving divisional reports a family resemblance and allowing performance results to be rolled up. However, if the parent fails to review progress formally against the shared *Strategic DNA*, or allows units to opt out of the reporting structure, the cascade is undermined. (This is further addressed by the reporting scheme in Chapter 11.)

Properly Focus Variable Compensation

The chosen governance style tends to calibrate the level for performance rewards and consequences. More autocratic styles require a greater spread between rewards and consequences than more motivational styles. However, the difference is usually most noticeable in the proportion of reward attached to group versus individual performance. More autocratic styles mean more personal accountability.

Whatever the style, cascaded *Strategic DNA* makes it possible to link individual performance expectations to corporate achievement targets, so people are motivated to work in ways that support the strategy. As a result, employees are less likely to do the wrong things for the right reasons.

To Balance Top-Down and Bottom-Up Inputs to the Strategy

The more levels an organization has, the less effective bottom-up and top-down strategies will be on their own. In a purely top-down strategy, lower levels are not required to provide feedback, so impractical strategies are neither challenged nor corrected. Bottom-up strategies rarely fare better as they churn in the anarchy of empowered individuals pursuing uncoordinated and hidden agendas. In this situation, leaders will find it impossible to control the corporate supertanker's course. To be effective, large organizations must combine the structure and direction of top-down strategy with the pragmatism and insight of bottom-up strategy (see Figure 4.3).

To reduce resistance to change and gain proactive participation, managers and workers have to buy in to the strategy. However, you *can* have too much of a good thing. A surplus of positive feedback can result in the irrational and volatile groupthink the stock market is famous for. Therefore, the strategy cascading process must also encourage the controlling and stabilizing influence of negative feedback. Negative feedback validates the *Strategic DNA* by subjecting it to constructive criticism. As a result, the *Strategic DNA* is debugged and any ivory-tower naïveté is removed. It becomes practical all the way down to the individual's level.

Although subsequent planning iterations are necessary to fine-tune the strategy, stakeholders will see that they have been listened to as their best ideas are implemented across the business units.

To Make the Strategy Meaningful at All Levels

Decomposing corporate objectives into achievement targets for divisions, departments, sections, or even individuals makes them more meaningful to each stakeholder. Historically, many organizations have had success in doing this at certain levels (e.g., translating a corporate goal to increase market share into quotas for each salesperson) but have been far less successful introducing the approach for other types of objectives, such as work-force retention or innovation goals.

Motivate by Scaling to Front-Line Realities

In concept, strategic objectives should be decomposed so each front-line employee is focused on the correct targets and accountable for achieving a portion of them. This is usually very difficult to implement, leaving many

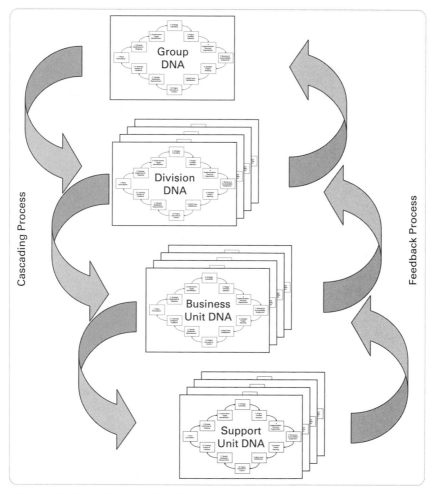

Figure 4.3 Cascading with Feedback

organizations settling for a less than perfect approach. Strategy cascading, if decomposed to departmental levels, can provide a workable framework for identifying personal objectives and targets (Chapter 9).

Share Out the Stretch and Divide Up Responsibilities and Accountabilities

The achievement targets for some objectives can be shared between business units. This visibly lessens the burden of the change and enhances a sense of working together for a greater collective achievement.

To Coordinate Independent Efforts

Whatever an organization's configuration may be, achieving its vision requires alignment and coordination of its business units' respective strategic agendas to produce team synergies—even if units are independent or quasi-independent profit centers. The cascading mechanism should allow units to continue operating independently while supporting coordinated interdependencies and permitting different degrees of independence.

For example, each time Microsoft introduces a new version of its Microsoft Project application, users expect it to continue to function with subsequent updates of Microsoft's operating system, Windows, and its general business application, Microsoft Office. Therefore, users expect Microsoft to coordinate and synchronize the development strategies of its Office, Windows, and Project divisions, no matter how independent they may be. Overall product portfolio performance, and ultimately marketplace success, will suffer otherwise.

Highlight Common Thrusts and Objectives Between Internal Businesses Units

The top-down goal of coordinating efforts across multiple business units is usually the principal motivation for strategy cascading. In *Strategic DNA*, this plays out as a consistent strategy map structure and a group of common objectives with achievement targets shared out among participants. Ideally, these strategy maps have identical perspectives, consistent (if not identical) thrusts, and many objectives in common with the parent's map.

Parent organizations ultimately want to promulgate their strategy, achieve synergies and economies of scale, and get all business units pulling in the same direction without suffocating each's specialization, individuality, and innovation. The challenge is in influencing each unit's strategic direction while allowing each to tackle its own priorities.

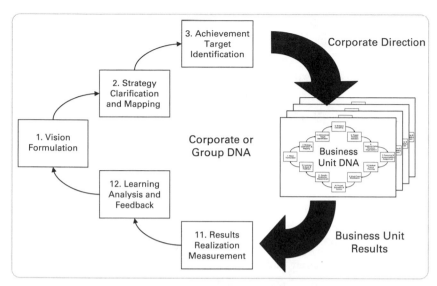

Figure 4.4 Integrating Cascaded Strategies to Govern the Big Picture

The conceptual approach is illustrated in Figure 4.4. The corporate level establishes its *Strategic DNA*, which is then used as an input to each unit's internal *Strategic DNA* lifecycle. Results from the multiple units' efforts are then rolled up to inform the corporate level's realization measurement and learning analysis processes.

Reduce Silo-Driven Inefficiencies

Synergies and economies of scale are realized when coordinated efforts are based on improved intersilo understanding. Shared thrusts, objectives, and targets reduce the effects of operational silos by making collaboration more desirable to each silo and introducing subtle peer pressure: "We've done our bit. Have you done yours?" The cascaded *Strategic DNA* improves the environment for assembling interdepartmental work teams (discussed further in Chapter 9) and encourages individuals to make decisions and take actions that suit more than just their own department's best interests.

Joint Ventures, Public-Private Partnerships, Trade Agreements, and Other Collaborations

Coordination of cascaded strategies is essential for interorganizational visions like corporate joint ventures, public-private partnerships, or international trade agreements. Imagine what would have happened if Boeing, GE, Rolls Royce, Goodrich, Honeywell, and all the other companies involved had not adjusted their strategies to reflect their mutual collaboration in the development of the new 787 Dreamliner aircraft. Similarly, public-private partnerships and shared societal change programs (such as the Kyoto Accord, the North American Free Trade Agreement, or the introduction of the euro) would be impossible if multiple independent organizations were unable to coordinate their strategies for the good of a common agenda. Cascaded *Strategic DNA* provides a mechanism for the integration, alignment, coordination, and reporting of independent and shared objectives.

Post-Acquisition Integrations

Combined ventures resulting from a merger, acquisition, or consolidation can benefit greatly from cascaded *Strategic DNA*. Many of the common problems that ultimately cause mergers to fail could be avoided with the clarity, alignment, and focus on outcomes that cascaded *Strategic DNA* enables. By establishing and communicating cascaded achievement targets for the merged entity, the burdens of performance expectations are shared transparently, and the focus shifts from sibling rivalry to family harmony.

What to Do
Repeat and Synchronize Chapters 1–3 for Each Business Unit

Strategy cascading is essentially an appropriately scaled repetition of the strategy formulation processes. The corporate-level vision, strategy map and achievement targets provide context and guidelines for the development of the vision, strategy, and targets for each business unit.

Larger organizations might then repeat the cascading process for each subsidiary's subunits. Here, context and guidelines would be provided by both corporate and divisional *Strategic DNA*s. Modern information technologies make it possible to connect multilevel strategic plans to provide timely dashboards, drill-down capabilities, and performance management functionalities.

Choose an Implementation Style

The pursuit of a vision may become routine once a *Strategic DNA* management process has been introduced, but using it the first time can represent a considerable, and often transformational, change in how an organization does business. There are many different ways of introducing

Fiaure 4.5 Horizontal Rollout or Vertical Slice Pilot

Pros	Cons
Cautious, careful	Can be very slow
Strategic business units set the pace	Requires strong intersilo collaboration
Encourages customized approach within corporate strategy framework	Opportunity for change resistance
Sends concurrent message to entire organization	Thinly spreads change agents and other experts
Fair impact on all organizations	Not concentrated where most value can be returned

Figure 4.6 Pros and Cons of the Horizontal Rollout

a new strategy management process; while each is unique, they tend to fall into three broad styles. Each implementation style has different strengths and weaknesses and is suitable for certain situations.

Horizontal Rollout

A horizontal rollout begins with the implementation of the new strategic management process at the corporate level. This learning opportunity exposes the leadership team and key change agents to the process. This is followed by implementing the process for all divisions at the same time; later, the next level of subdivisions will undergo implementation. Level by level, each organizational level will receive the strategy. The approach is illustrated on the left side of Figure 4.5.

While horizontal rollout is the usual way strategies are pushed through an existing management system, it can be problematic when used for the first time; at that point, there are few experienced change agents within the organization. If the whole organization tries to roll it out for the first time at the same time, the lack of experienced change agents make the situation considerably more difficult. However, horizontal rollout is often

Pros	Cons
Usually quicker	Transitional period where SBUs work differently
Strategy quickly cascades two or three levels	Can amplify change resistance
Concentration in high value or change friendly business units	Can produce "us and them" cliques
Early lessons speed later efforts	Less clear message
Useful for prototyping strategic hypotheses	Sends mixed messages and can imply leaders lack confidence in their convictions
Defers resistant organizations until knowledgeable resource pool is stronger	Resistance festers and has time to get organized

Figure 4.7 Pros and Cons of the Vertical Slice Pilot

seen as a more democratic approach; as such, it is sometimes favored by large unionized and public-sector organizations.

Vertical-Slice Pilot

Like horizontal rollout, a vertical-slice pilot begins with implementation of the new strategic management process at the corporate level. Once the leadership team is aligned on the corporate strategy, the process and strategy are implemented in selected divisions that are either enthusiastic early adopters or those that offer the most immediate strategic potential. Using this approach means that some areas of the organization will not be impacted by the change until considerably later. The business units selected for the change act as pilots, permitting already knowledgeable resources to be concentrated where they can do most good. Those who are involved in the pilot implementations will be available to train a broader group of change agents for later implementations throughout the organization. The system may then be implemented across the other divisions as a demonstrated, debugged success. The vertical-slice pilot is illustrated on the right side of Figure 4.5.

While this approach is less representative of how the system will subsequently be used, it can demonstrate quick wins. The resulting pool of knowledgeable change agents can greatly simplify later rollouts to other business units. This approach is popular with private-sector organizations.

Single-Thrust Focus

Like the previous methods, the single-thrust focus begins with implementation of the new strategic management process at the corporate level. A single thrust is then selected and pushed out into the entire

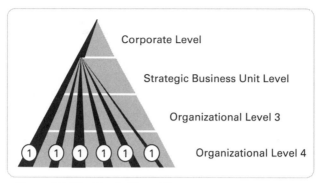

Figure 4.8 The Single-Thrust Focus

organization to tackle an urgent challenge. As a result, the big-picture strategy receives little attention.

Single-thrust focus is not usually recommended, but there are times when it is appropriate. For situations where organizations need to react quickly, like emergency cost cutting, unexpected trade barriers, food/water safety issues, or hostile takeovers, the single-thrust focus can be particularly useful, particularly if the organization is unsure how to proceed and is poorly aligned. However, repeatedly using this approach can cause urgency fatigue, and a broader implementation should be considered once the fire has been extinguished. Figure 4.8 illustrates the single-thrust focus.

Diagnose Change Readiness

Few newcomers understand the process of introducing a cascaded strategy well enough to make an informed decision about which implementation style to adopt: True understanding often doesn't emerge until the implementation is well underway, and lessons are learned the hard way. Using a change-readiness diagnostic to evaluate the current situation

Pros	Cons
Rapidly develops strategy when direction is unknown and need is urgent	Strategic DNA really only at corporate level
Single thrust cascades completely across whole organization	Risk of urgency fatigue
Fights a single fire	Organization unaware of anything except the fire
Rapid results	Organization doesn't see bigger picture
Sense of achievement and momentum for broader implementation	Limited skill development for broader implementation

Figure 4.9 Pros and Cons of the Single-Thrust Focus

	Mandatory Objectives	Mandatory Targets	Component Objectives	Component Targets	Unique Objectives	Unique Targets
Corporate	Reduce costs	$50M	Diversify business offerings	30% increase in product portfolio	Modify governance structure	New structure implemented
Business Unit 1	Reduce costs	$19M	Acquire boat manufacturer	12 new products	Expand sales force training	50% increase in training hours
Business Unit 2	Reduce costs	$29M	Develop new aircraft	1 new product	Reengineer accounting processes	100% of processes completed
Support Function	Reduce costs	$2M	Support expanding sales channels	20% more sales channels	Upgrade People soft system	Upgrade completed

Figure 4.10 Examples of Cascaded Objectives and Targets

and culture can help a leadership team identify the most appropriate implementation style before the change becomes painful.

Change-readiness diagnostics reveal which business units will readily adopt the new approach, which will work productively with the implementers, and which will energetically resist and undermine the implementation. A good diagnostic can reveal specific challenges that must be addressed to smooth the implementation.

Change-readiness diagnostics examine criteria through either a survey or interview method. A typical diagnostic looks at:

- Leadership profiles
- Commonly perceived needs
- Clearly comprehended vision
- Mobilized stakeholders
- Support-system infrastructure
- Progress management
- Short-, medium-, and long-term perspectives

Mandatory, Component, and Unique Objectives

Corporate-level strategic objectives may guide the development of business unit strategies in several different ways, as shown in Figure 4.10. Like the objectives, the strategic thrusts may also be mandatory, component, or unique.[13]

Mandatory Objectives

Mandatory objectives must be directly reflected in each business unit's strategy map. The performance metric must be the same in each case, so a corporate achievement target can be readily subdivided among the units.

For example, if a corporate target is reducing costs by $50 million, each unit in the organization must make cost cuts that total (organization-wide) $50 million.

Component Objectives

Component objectives are framed in the context of a corporate objective, but they are restated and quantified to be meaningful to each business unit. For example, a corporate objective of diversifying business offerings can be achieved through divisional objectives of acquiring a boat manufacturer, developing new aircraft, and accommodating new sales channels. Subsequently, appropriate achievement targets can be designed for each component.

Unique Objectives

Unique objectives may not bear any direct relationship to a corporate objective; instead, they pertain specifically to the business unit. They may be indirectly related to corporate priorities, but in any case, they must be consistent with corporate values and the unit's mission.

How to Do It

Unless a parent organization wishes to be seen as dictating to its divisions, business units must participate in the process at the corporate level. Their level of involvement often reflects the organization's degree of decentralization. Divisional leaders should participate in discussions that share measurable objectives among their units.

At this point, you may discover just how close your family is. Widely different departments of a conglomerate may only share a handful of financial objectives, but different regions of a bank or government agency, for example,

Figure 4.11 Strategy Cascading Process

may share more than 90 percent of their objectives.

The cascading process uses the parent's vision, strategy map, and achievement targets as a basis for developing objectives and targets in each business unit. When the cascade is between corporate and divisional levels, the divisions' strategy maps reflect the context of the parent's map but maintain individuality in each division. A cascade between a department and its personnel uses other objective communication tools, such as an employee performance evaluation form. Read more about employee objectives in Chapter 9.

1. Identify Implementation Approach
Who: Leadership Team Led by Strategic Planning Leader

This step establishes how the new cascaded approach will be implemented. This discussion may evolve into a complex debate about the merits of the horizontal rollout versus the vertical-slice pilot, but if the single-thrust approach is appropriate, the conversation may be very brief. The strategic planning team can recommend an approach, but the decision should be made in a leadership team meeting that involves representatives from the corporate level and some or all of the business units.

Consider the following when selecting an implementation approach:
- Motive for introducing the new approach
- Desired governance style
- Sense of urgency
- Individual leaders
- Each division's likelihood of success
- Each division's change readiness

If yours is a large or change-weary organization, perform a change-readiness diagnostic to discover where the implementation may encounter resistance. Additional information about change-readiness diagnostics is provided in Chapter 9 and Figure 9.5.

2. Identify Business-Unit Phasing
Who: Leadership Team

This natural extension of the first step is usually achieved during the same meeting. Phasing differs depending on which implementation style is chosen, but the heart of the issue is figuring out which units should adopt the new approach during which planning cycle. The phasing for a vertical-slice implementation is illustrated in Figure 4.12 on page 90.

The balance of this chapter applies to each division that is selected to participate in the planning cycle.

3. Identify Mandatory Objectives and Metrics
Who: Leadership Team and Corporate Strategic Planning Team

The previous steps identified the business units for the first implementation. Next, you will analyze corporate-level objectives, performance metrics, and achievement targets to determine which of them will guide business-unit *Strategic DNA* development. At this point, each subsidiary strategy inherits a family resemblance from the corporate strategy. The strategic planning team may be delegated to prepare a draft, but the corporate leadership team should ultimately make all decisions.

The analysis is often quite straightforward, as mandatory objectives and performance metrics must be meaningful to everyone in their original form. The portion of the achievement target allocated to each unit is sometimes identified during this step, but they can only be finalized in Step 7.

In this step, consider whether to make the corporate map's thrusts mandatory. Mandatory thrusts effectively dictate the structure for the subsidiary maps and ensure cascaded strategies have a *strong* family resemblance. If your environment usually resists corporate will, ensure that your mandatory thrusts are meaningful to those who will be forced to accommodate them in their *Strategic DNA*.

4. Identify Component Objectives and Metrics
Who: Corporate and Business Units' Leadership and Strategic Planning Teams

Although it is similar to the analysis that reveals mandatory objectives (and often conducted at the same time), identifying component objectives and metrics requires more input from the affected business units. This step is primarily focused on translating corporate objectives and performance metrics into terms that are more meaningful to divisional managers and employees. Component objectives and metrics also propagate family characteristics, but they do so less forcefully than mandatory objectives.

This analytical process explores how a business unit might be expected to contribute to the broader corporate objective. In the example shown in Figure 4.10, the corporate objective of diversifying product offerings is translated into objectives that include acquiring a boat manufacturer and developing new aircraft. These objectives contribute to the broader corporate objective and thus, they become components of it.

Planning Cycle	Business Units
Year 1	Corporate only
Year 2	Northern and southern regions
Year 3	All other regions plus human resources and information technologies
Year 4	International, legal, finance, and purchasing

Figure 4.12 Example Implementation Phasing

At this point, compile all business units' analysis results into a single scheme for review, adjustment, and approval with the corporate leadership team. Although achievement targets are discussed here, they aren't established until subsidiary strategies are developed in Step 5.

5. Perform Strategy Clarification and Mapping in Each Business Unit
Who: Business Units' Leadership and Strategic Planning Teams

This step might best be summarized as "Repeat Chapters 1 and 2 for each selected business unit," with Chapter 1 being optional. This is the heart of the strategy cascading process. Each selected unit formulates a vision, clarifies its strategy, and prepares a map, with its own needs, the corporate strategy, and mandatory and component objectives as its guide. The vision formulation process is optional, because although many organizations share a common single vision, some diverse, decentralized conglomerates, governments, and municipalities may have divisions with very individualized visions (that, of course, still retain the family's shared values). Large units may even have their own stakeholder groups, executive teams, and strategic planning teams.

The outcome is a strategy map that describes the business unit's strategy and provides a clear line of sight to the corporate bigger picture via the mandatory and component objectives. The map then integrates unique objectives with mandatory and component objectives.

6. Perform Achievement Target Identification in Each Business Unit
Who: Business Units' Leadership and Strategic Planning Teams

This step can be summarized as "Repeat Chapter 3 for each selected business unit." Each team identifies performance metrics and targets for its thrusts and objectives from its own unique perspective. This accommodates achievement targets for mandatory and component objectives and also develops performance metrics and achievement targets for any unique objectives.

7. Apportion Shares of Mandatory and Common Achievement Targets
Who: Strategic Planning Team

Each business unit now has its own *Strategic DNA* separate from, but aligned with, the corporate *Strategic DNA*. In earlier steps, the corporate leadership team may have developed expectations for how much of the targeted achievement should be expected of each unit. In Step 6, leadership teams identified the degree of achievement that can be reasonably expected. Compile these two sets of expectations to reveal the achievement share gap—the difference between corporate expectations and the sum of the units' ambitions.

In this step, calculate, present, and discuss share gaps with all levels of the organization in a joint working session to find adjustments that will eliminate the gaps. Possible adjustments may include lowering corporate expectations, increasing business-unit ambitions, or making some form of compromise.

8. Establish Reporting Process Framework
Who: Strategic Planning Team

The cascaded *Strategic DNA* serves as a framework for the reporting infrastructure. Its mandatory and component metric interrelationships allow corporate-wide performance to be calculated in Chapter 11.

Leadership teams establish reporting expectations to guide the development of progress, measurement, and reporting processes (for projects in Chapter 10 and metrics in Chapter 11). Establish expectations for the formats, media, frequency, and content of the information and determine how the information will be rolled up between levels. Document the expected frequency of progress review meetings and who will be expected to participate.

9. Coordinate Business Unit Strategic Planning Processes
Who: Strategic Planning /Program Teams

In this step, coordinate each business unit's efforts to perform the processes in Chapters 5 through 12. This work is performed by the strategic planning teams until much later in the process, when the program teams will take over. Cascaded *Strategic DNA* acts as a framework for coordinating the balance of the strategic planning work, and the corporate *Strategic DNA* management process sets the timing for the work.

Summary

This chapter spreads the *Strategic DNA* along the branches of the organizational family tree to ensure each unit has its own *Strategic DNA* aligned with the corporate vision. Connections are made between business-unit thrusts, objectives, metrics, targets, projects, resources, and the corporate *Strategic DNA* to ensure they all share a family resemblance—no matter how distantly related, or seemingly independent, they may be.

5

Project Portfolio Selection
What Will We Do to Get There and What Will We Stop Doing?

THE FIRST FOUR CHAPTERS DESCRIBED A VISION, QUANTIFIED ITS measurable strategic objectives, and then decomposed them. In this chapter, your organization will decide what it will do to make those dreams become a reality. The strategy map is the backbone for the strategic plan, and the portfolio of projects is its legs.

Business, Not Busyness

Businesses like to be busy. Bosses like to see employees working up a sweat. Unfortunately, no matter how efficiently an employee does the wrong thing, it's still wrong. It's even worse if they're being paid overtime to do it. This chapter is about figuring out what those employees should be working on and, equally importantly, what they *shouldn't* be working on.

Project Prioritization—The Glass Ceiling of Strategic Planning

Strategic planning efforts frequently grind to a halt at this "choosing what to do" stage. In fact, it is probably the most likely place for a planning effort to stall. Even if stakeholders can agree about what projects to do, they soon lose alignment when discussing what to do about unstrategic projects. It is one thing for a stakeholder to agree that a project from another department is important, and quite another to get him or her to agree to delay or stop one that truly matters to his division. The consequences of what will happen to projects that don't get chosen make prioritization difficult, but those consequences—reduced costs, increased focus, more available resources—are precisely why the decision must be made:

- *Strong*. It must make sense and be meaningful to those that will perform the chosen projects.

- *Supported.* Stakeholders' actions must visibly, verbally, and emotionally reinforce the decision instead of undermining, resisting, or distracting attention, energy, and resources from the chosen projects.
- *Stick.* The course of action must be followed until it has been successfully completed.

Getting people to understand, agree to, and respect *Strategic DNA*-based project prioritization is perhaps the greatest challenge your leadership team will face in the pursuit of its vision. Chapters 1 through 4 emphasized the need for involving a respected and representative cross-section of stakeholders when developing the vision, strategy and achievement targets. That involvement set the scene for tough prioritization discussions. Hopefully, that effort developed a single, broadly supported vision. If not, any misalignment will be found out in this chapter!

Terminology
Initiatives, Actions, or Projects?

The *projects* that move a strategy forward are often known interchangeably as initiatives, actions, priorities, or *programs*. For our purposes, projects are temporary undertakings intended to produce specific results, and program refers to a coordinated set of related projects. Strategic projects can be treated differently than operational projects, but any relaxation in their governance can prove to be a false economy. By definition, strategic projects are the most important efforts any organization undertakes. They must be properly managed and executed, and carefully governed without being suffocated by unnecessary bureaucracy.

Portfolios and the Strategic Program

When designing your strategic program, select strategic projects from a complete list of current, planned, and "new idea" projects. This selection of strategic projects is the portfolio. The portfolio can then be prioritized and sequenced to define the strategic program.

Why Do It?
To Identify What Needs to Get Done

Project prioritization recognizes that it is neither desirable nor possible to do absolutely everything. Even if a project seems like a good idea, there may be better, and more strategic, ones out there as well. The capacity to pursue projects is always limited, so organizations should choose to do only those that matter most, and choose *not* to do those that matter least. This reflects the traditional 80/20 rule: If 20 percent of the projects produce 80 percent of the benefit, concentrate available resources on the 20 percent first to get at least 80 percent of the way there.

To Avoid Project Chaos

Every business, from a local entrepreneur to a multinational corporation like Nestlé, tries to do too many things at once. Leaders readily agree their businesses are trying to juggle too many projects, but their efforts to halt this project chaos are usually frustrated. Figure 5.1 illustrates project chaos as arrows pushing the organization in random contradictory directions. This directly relates to the lack of alignment illustrated earlier in Figure 4.1, and it ultimately results in a self-perpetuating cycle—nonalignment encourages project chaos, which reinforces nonalignment, thereby increasing project chaos, and so on. The extreme difficulty of breaking this cycle explains why so many strategic planning efforts grind to a halt at this stage. Project chaos is very common, especially in decentralized organizations or bottom-up strategies. The result is often volatility, stifled ambitions, and nonstrategic priorities.

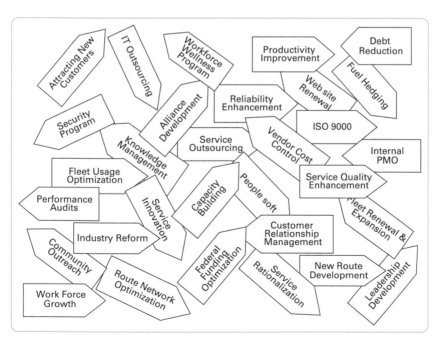

Figure 5.1 Project Chaos

To make matters worse, so-called "great new ideas" keep randomly emerging in meetings, water-cooler conversations, magazine articles, on the drive to work, and so on. These new project ideas tend to be justified by local managers on their own merits, in isolation from the big picture. It can be many weeks before senior managers become aware that resources are being expended on them.

To Set Project Priorities with Strategy, Not Comfort, Instinct, and Emotion

Intellectually, of course, most managers know they can't do everything at once and are frustrated by this inability to focus and achieve. Unfortunately, they often have their hands tied behind their backs, as priorities keep changing. These priorities may be driven by perceptions, politics, big shots, budget constraints, or all these factors combined! Even when they are well intentioned, such as when a leader tries to solve chaos by dictating priorities, typical methods of prioritizing projects all seem to be bad reasons for doing something:

- *Rank*—"Because she wants it … It's her pet project."
- *Force of personality*—"Keep him quiet."
- *Amount already invested*—"We're just pouring good money after bad."
- *Share of the budget*—"If we do this, we can avoid layoffs."
- *Inertia or precedent*—"We've always done it that way."
- *Trendiness*—"It's the flavor of the month."
- *Power games and politics*—"They got theirs last year."
- *Management by magazine*—"Well, *HBR*, *Fortune*, or *Gartner* said so."

To fix this problem, use the *Strategic DNA* as a filter for prioritizing projects and new project ideas in a way that is broadly communicated, understood, and supported. Simply put, the most worthwhile projects contribute to making the vision happen. If a project will significantly move the measured value of a performance metric toward its achievement target—thereby helping to achieve a strategic objective—it is definitively worthwhile. Similarly, if a project produces prerequisites for another strategic project, it's strategic too. Projects that do neither are irrelevant, distracting, and a waste of resources.

Some nonstrategic projects may seem to have value on their own merits, which can make it very difficult to persuade others that they do not belong on the strategic agenda. Finding the project an appropriate place in the operational agenda—where the project can justify itself in direct cost-benefit terms—often resolves concerns. People will continue to raise the issue until they understand the project's proper place.

To Stop Wasting Resources on Less Important Actions
It always seems that stopping projects is a much tougher challenge than choosing the right things to do, but it is worth doing. If only 20 percent of the projects produce 80 percent of the achievement, completely stopping the other 80 percent would have little negative impact and would save a lot of effort and money. It would also free up resources needed to do a better job with the 20 percent that is truly important. In one example, an insurance company reduced its portfolio from seventy-four projects to seven, avoided $5 million in unnecessary costs, and finally started to make strategic progress.

Reduce Volatility
Unfortunately, resource attrition is costly in more than just financial terms. By spreading key people so thinly, few projects can have the critical mass of competencies and capabilities that are necessary to be efficiently successful. Crucial projects get neglected or starved of key capabilities until their issues become urgent enough to force reactive problem solving. The resultant volatility reveals itself as:
- Continually changing priorities
- Lack of integrated picture
- Confused timing
- Uncoordinated inefficient efforts
- Duplication of efforts
- Confused work force
- Inconsistent approaches
- Unreliable execution
- Attrition of resources on nonstrategic projects
- Insufficient support for strategic projects
- Strategic exhaustion
- Weak governance and poor accountability
- Poor results
- Departure of good people

These problems are cemented in place when internal politics and face-saving considerations prevent significant adjustments. *Strategic DNA's* emphasis on alignment gets the faces on board with the priorities. When those priorities are clearly communicated to, and understood by, the broader organization, volatility problems are reduced or avoided, decisions to halt projects are better supported, and faces are saved all around.

To Send a Message About the Strategy's Importance

Communicating which projects to do and *not* to do can send several messages. Choosing the right things focuses attention on projects that reinforce the strategic agenda. Choosing the wrong things undermines the strategy, implies that the leadership team is not serious, and distracts attention from the pursuit of the vision. For example, if the strategy is to reinforce domestic operations, but the projects are all aimed at expanding foreign markets, people will draw their own conclusions about how serious or competent the leadership team is.

Telling people what not to do can either reinforce or undermine the strategy. If people do not understand why a seemingly essential project is being put on the back burner, they will be confused, unmotivated, or defy orders and continue the project anyway. Similarly, if people are allowed to continue working on clearly nonstrategic projects, onlookers will conclude that management isn't serious about the strategy. If, on the other hand, nonstrategic projects are canceled, recognized superstars are redeployed to strategic projects, and top executives are seen to be actively engaged in their progress, the broader work force will get the message. The work force usually judges the value of strategic projects by the company they keep.

Therefore, concentrating key resources and killing other projects sends a clear message to middle management and the work force—they are serious. However, the killing of projects will still be resisted. This resistance tends to be greater in large bureaucracies or whenever the leadership team does not truly share a single agenda. Alignment and clear communication can only go so far in such organizations; nonstrategic distractions often have to be killed more than once.

Clearly Distinguish Between Operational Maintenance and Strategic-Change Projects

Many actions are compulsory. They maintain daily operations and occupy most of the work force's time. In budget-driven, bottom-up organizations, discretionary projects are usually embedded in operational

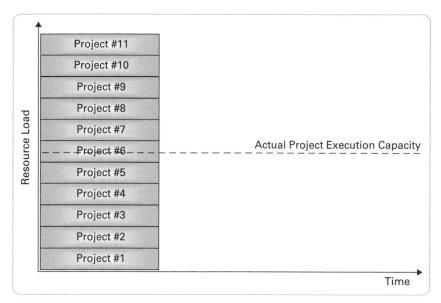

Figure 5.2 Ambition Exceeds Capacity

budgets. Killing embedded projects causes confusion and resistance, as middle management and the work force see their operational budgets being cut. Distinguishing embedded change project resource allocations from operational and maintenance budget provisions, even if they are comingled on budget line items, removes this confusion and thus reduces resistance.

To Increase Success of the Most Important Projects
Concentrate Attention of People

Eliminating low-value distractions forces people to concentrate on the projects that remain and greatly improves their likelihood of success. Canceling nonstrategic projects, redeploying recognized superstars, and focusing executive attention lets the work force know that the success of the strategic projects matters. Sometimes simply making the decision and sticking to it is enough. As one CEO once remarked, "We're really good at executing once we set our minds to it. It's a shame we can't seem to make up our minds."

Avoid Stifled Ambition

Figures 5.2 and 5.3 illustrate what happens when an organization tries to do too many projects at once. Figure 5.2 shows how the ambition to do projects is often greater than the ability to execute them, and Figure 5.3

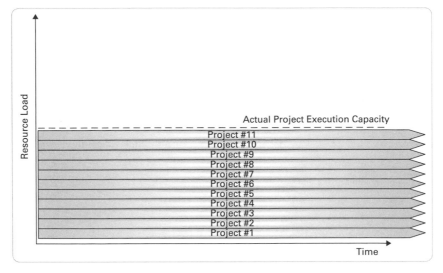

Figure 5.3 Capacity Stifles Ambition

shows the typical results: few projects get finished, they are rarely done well, and they often continue forever, just like the Energizer bunny.

What to Do
Agree About Which Projects Matter

If selecting the projects that matter most is to be strong, supported, and "sticky," the leadership team and other stakeholders must be aligned around the choice of projects. The decision process needs to include all involved constituencies and should reach a consensus about what projects are chosen.

The decision-making process should begin with discussions in areas in which the stakeholders are more likely to agree. This includes discussions that frame the decision to be made.

Frame the Decision for Capacity and Capability

The effects of capacity/capability constraints were illustrated earlier in Figure 5.3. Understanding and articulating these constraints provides an outer boundary for the decision framework. Figure 5.4 identifies several aspects that can be considered when establishing constraints.

Frame the Decision for the Profile of a Strategic Project

One effective way to get a group of stakeholders to frame the project prioritization decision is to ask them first what an ideal outcome might

Consideration	Question
Cash Flow	• How much can we afford to invest in strategic projects and when? • How big is the discretionary budget for strategy? How many projects does that represent?
People	• How many people (or FTEs) can we allocate to these projects?
Simultaneous	• How many projects can we manage effectively? • How many good project managers do we have?
Governance	• How much time can leadership make available for reviewing and reacting to strategic project progress reports?
Rate of Change	• How much organizational change can we cope with at any one time (or at this time)? • How fast do we need to achieve the vision?
Risk	• How much risk are we willing to accept?

Figure 5.4 Considerations for Capacity and Capability Constraints

realistically look like. There is no standard formula for this, as an ideal strategic project can be very situation-specific. Figure 5.6 summarizes the most essential characteristics.

Typical Profile

Because the *Strategic DNA* defines the leadership team's intentions, any project that explicitly contributes to its objectives and achievement targets is clearly strategic. If its contribution is merely implicit or tenuous, the project may not be very strategic—even if it is large or expensive. This linkage should be an overriding consideration when deciding whether to pursue a project.

The use of *Strategic DNA* for filtering projects is illustrated in Figure 5.5 (see next page). If your leadership team still wants to pursue a nonoperational project that is not linked, your *Strategic DNA* does not truly reflect their intentions and should probably be revised.

Strategic projects that involve even modest amounts of work result in significant outcomes, particularly when they are considered alongside the objectives they enable. As an integral component of a broader strategic program, these projects rarely stand alone and are of enduring interest to the leadership team. They are supported by the dedicated efforts of some employees, managed and reported on formally at the highest levels of the

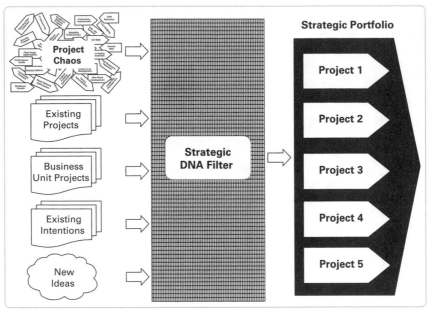

Figure 5.5 Filtering Projects with Strategic DNA

organization, and protected by executives looking to remove obstacles to the project's success. If a project does not fit this profile, it is probably not very strategic.

It may still be too early in the planning process to quantify a project's

Characteristic	Question
Strategic DNA Contribution	• Does the project directly contribute to achieving Strategic DNA objectives and achievement targets? • Does the project directly enable another project that will itself contribute?
Magnitude	• How much time will the project take to accomplish? • How costly is the project likely to be? • How much of our key resource capacity will the project consume?
Risks and Rewards	• Why do we want to do this project? • What results can we expect? • What is the impact if it is not successful? • What is the likelihood that it will be truly successful?
Organizational Impacts	• Which business units or infrastructure capabilities would be affected? • Is this an appropriate time to make those changes?
Timing of Returns	• How long will it be before we will see acceptable outcomes?

Figure 5.6 Characterizing the Profile of a Strategy Project

real business case, but the high-level business case should be understood in preliminary, unquantified terms. If the conceptual business case for the proposed project cannot be described in general terms, it should not be considered a strategic project.

Design the Strategic Program

A strategic program is designed by selecting and sequencing projects that will pursue the strategy and ultimately achieve the vision. The program contains a portfolio of projects that complement one another and are properly coordinated to achieve success. The portfolio accommodates four basic principles:

- Portfolio waves
- Portfolio balancing
- Minimized compromises
- Symbolic of the new world order

Portfolio Waves

The challenge of choosing the right things to do is a little more sophisticated than simply deciding which projects to choose or kill. A group of projects can only be successful and timely if the capabilities they collectively consume (resources, use of infrastructure, management attention, and funding) are within the organization's capacity. When

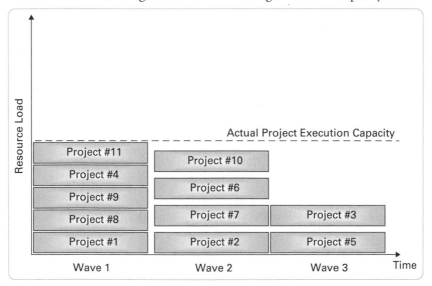

Figure 5.7 Portfolio Waves—Ambition Achieved Within Capacity

a strategic program demands more than the delivery capacity, either the capacity has to be increased (e.g., by hiring more project managers) or project schedules must be staggered.

It is rarely possible to increase capacity rapidly, so instead of doing too many projects at once, organize the portfolio into groups of projects that can be performed in achievable batches. These "portfolio waves" identify what to do first, second, third, and so on as resources become available. In practice, only the first few waves will be accomplished before the next planning cycle, so the inclusion of a project in a later wave is effectively a postponement. This planning technique is very useful when stakeholders cannot agree to cancel a project that should be killed.

Figure 5.7 illustrates the concept of portfolio waves. Projects in the second wave are not begun until resources become available as earlier projects are completed. In practice, of course, the projects in one wave do not all begin and end at the same time.

Portfolio Balancing

Balancing the project portfolio achieves overall goals while managing risk. In investment portfolios, stocks are balanced by government bonds, cash, real estate, and so on to achieve growth while softening volatility. Failing to balance the project portfolio can create several problems:

- Focusing projects on only one strategic thrust at a time can delay broader success.
- Simultaneously pursuing too many expensive projects with a slow return can mean financial constraints, or even bankruptcy, before returns are received.
- Too many projects that affect a single department at the same time can be counterproductive.
- One person cannot be everywhere at once, no matter how good he or she is.
- Too many projects that change a business process or computer system at the same time can be very disruptive.
- Quick wins reassure stakeholders that the strategy is sound, but longer horizons may be necessary for substantial value creation. Too much of either is not recommended.

Minimized Compromises

How much of the decision is based on firm absolute facts is related to the culture and the decision-making group's personalities and history. Ideally, they will choose to do the right projects based on their contribution to the *Strategic DNA*, business cases, and capacity. Strongly supported selection decisions need a good degree of consensus, but this forces compromises to ensure everyone's acceptance and support.

Compromise is excellence's enemy; it often undermines a strategy's success. A good method for minimizing the degree of compromise starts with getting individual issues out in the open, where they can be tackled. Confronting these issues before making decisions is sometimes difficult and always time consuming, but it usually results in tighter alignment and less compromise. It is always worth remembering that for an executive to shift support away from a project he or she has previously advocated, a tremendous leap of "face" may be required.

Symbolic of the New World Order

Sometimes the relative priority of a project is higher simply because it sends a message to people about a new way of thinking. These projects set precedents that influence subsequent actions. They are particularly essential when a strategy involves considerable cultural change.

Keep Killing the Undead Projects—"Buffy the Project Slayer"

Frequently, nonstrategic projects that are stopped don't stay stopped. Even killed, they may have a nasty little habit of starting up again—sometimes under another name, and sometimes in a different business area. This resurrection usually occurs for four principal reasons:

- *Miscommunication*—It isn't fully understood that the project has been killed.
- *Lack of clarity*—The strategic priorities aren't understood by all.
- *Lack of alignment*—The project is still important to someone who doesn't care why they weren't chosen.
- *Momentum*—Managers still have financial and labor resources available to support them.

Preventing these undead projects from coming back to life can be an ongoing challenge for a leadership team. A tongue-in-cheek name for this approach is "Buffy the Project Slayer," a reference to a TV character's battles with a seemingly endless supply of undead vampires. It begins during the project portfolio selection process, as project and project ideas are killed off in multiple battles until only a few strong projects survive in prioritized implementation waves. The undead projects will try to return even after being killed unless the leadership team remains alert and keeps "rekilling" them throughout the subsequent stages of the *Strategic DNA* lifecycle.

Assign Interim Project Sponsors and Managers

Strategic project portfolios are usually selected long before projects have been defined by charters and business cases. Once the scope and business case for a project has been worked out, the portfolio selection can be confirmed. Interim project sponsors and project managers should be appointed to prepare project charters and preliminary business cases. These people may not be the final ones to occupy the role, but they should be knowledgeable and capable enough to take responsibility for business case development.

Project Sponsors

Project sponsors are senior managers who act as project owners and customers. They provide conceptual leadership, frame projects within the strategic intent, appoint the project manager, ensure coordination between multiple projects, acquire necessary resources, and remove obstacles to progress. Project sponsors are usually drawn from the stakeholder group that participates in the project portfolio selection.

Project Managers

Project managers work for the sponsors and perform or direct the activities needed to complete the project. Their first assignment from the sponsor is usually to produce the project charter and business case. To achieve this, they collect input and advice from specialists in the business. Sponsors should be discouraged from trying to perform both roles themselves.

How to Do It

The first two steps in the portfolio selection process frame the selection decision and are best conducted in a single meeting. The meeting includes those who will participate in the rest of the process—usually the same group of stakeholders who participated in Chapters 2 and 3. Getting stakeholders to fully support the eventual portfolio selection is far easier when they have each participated in developing the framework.

The framing discussions may be included as an agenda item at the end of the achievement targets workshop in Chapter 3, but stakeholder groups rarely have more mental energy to invest at that point.

1. Identify Capability Constraints and Delivery Capacity

Who: Stakeholder Group Led by the Strategic Planning Team

Develop a draft statement of capability constraints and delivery capacity that can be presented as a straw man. Develop the straw man carefully, as stakeholder groups often insist on accepting them virtually unaltered. Avoid circulating the straw man before the meeting, as it will be misunderstood and taken out of context, leading some stakeholders to react defensively.

The intent of the meeting discussion is to reach agreement about the number of strategic projects that can be supported at any one time. This may be

Project Portfolio Selection Process
1 - Identify Capability Constraints and Delivery Capacity
2 - Clarify Profile of the Ideal Project
3 - Collect Existing Portfolio of Projects
4 - Filter Existing Projects to Remove Non-Strategic and Low Value Projects
5 - Relate Remaining Projects to Strategy Map Objectives
6 - Identify New Strategic Project Ideas
7 - Select Balanced Portfolio Waves & Develop Initial Master Schedule
8 - Assign Interim Sponsors/Managers
9 - Disposition Unselected Projects – Choosing What *Not* to Do
10 - Formally Charter Selected Projects

Figure 5.8 Project Portfolio Selection Process

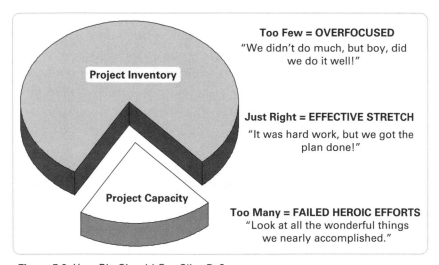

Too Few = OVERFOCUSED
"We didn't do much, but boy, did we do it well!"

Just Right = EFFECTIVE STRETCH
"It was hard work, but we got the plan done!"

Too Many = FAILED HEROIC EFFORTS
"Look at all the wonderful things we nearly accomplished."

Project Inventory

Project Capacity

Figure 5.9 How Big Should Our Slice Be?

Capacity/Profile Decision Meeting

Agenda

1. Review Strategy Map
2. Present Straw Man Capacity
3. Discuss Capacity/Capability
4. Establish Agreed Project Capacity
5. Present Straw-Man Profile
6. Discuss Profile of Ideal Project
7. Establish Agreed Profile of Ideal Project
8. Preview Portfolio Selection Workshop

Figure 5.10 Sample Agenda for Capacity and Profile Meeting

conditional based on the size of projects and the business units they relate to. The point the discussion should try to reach is illustrated in Figure 5.9. How many strategic projects represent an effective stretch? Too few will make the organization over-focused, and too many will result in failed heroic efforts. Figure 5.4 outlines key questions that can facilitate the discussion.

2. Clarify Profile of the Ideal Project
Who: Stakeholder Group Led by the Strategic Planning Leader

Now that capacity constraints have been identified and described, attention turns to clarifying the ideal project's profile. Facilitate the discussion with another straw man using individual characteristics of the profile illustrated by familiar examples. For example, a change-weary organization may decide that one characteristic of its ideal project is that it should not require significant organizational change. Other desirable characteristics may include inexpensiveness, certainty, high benefit-to-cost ratio, engagement of the work force, promotion of innovation or sustainability, and so on. The questions listed in Figure 5.6 can help facilitate this discussion.

The outcome of the discussion is an agreed-upon profile defined in terms of the desirable characteristics that can be used to evaluate projects. This step is crucial for developing buy-in for eventual project selection, because the profile will be used during Step 4 to filter out nonstrategic projects and concepts. It is far more difficult for stakeholders to resist the results of the filtering if they helped design the filter.

3. Collect Existing Portfolio of Projects
Who: Strategic Planning Team

For some organizations, this may be the first deliberate effort to build a single list of all ongoing and planned projects. It often provides unexpected insight, as some leadership teams had no idea that so many projects were going on. (Some may already have a current or updatable inventory of projects.)

Most large organizations and even some smaller businesses suffer from embedded or hidden projects that have funding buried in operational budgets. These projects can make it more difficult to build the list, but it is important to plumb the depths of the organization to find them.

Several methods for identifying ongoing or planned projects are listed below. These methods can be used cumulatively, as each method tends to reveal projects the other methods may have missed.

> **Project Portfolio Selection Workshop**
>
> **Sample Agenda**
>
> 1. Review Strategy Maps and Targets
> 2. Review Profile
> 3. Review Capacity
> 4. Filter List for Nonstrategic and Low Value
> 5. Relate Remaining Projects to Map
> 6. Analyze Gaps and Identify New Projects
> 7. Group Related Projects
> 8. Identify Natural Project Sequences
> 9. Select Balanced Waves
> 10. Assign Interim Responsibilities
> 11. Disposition Nonselected Projects

Figure 5.11 Sample Agenda for Project Portfolio Selection Workshop Meeting

- Assign a strategic planning team member to build this list when work begins at the start of Chapter 1 or 2. The designated team member may note projects as they are mentioned conversationally in workshop meetings.
- Incorporate a question in the structured interview guide (Chapter 2). If the question is worded well, it will tease out what projects matter to the interviewees.
- Consult the finance department to identify recognized projects that are receiving funds or for which funds are budgeted or forecast.
- Review existing budget and planning documentation to identify actions that are clearly not everyday operational activities or maintenance.
- Interview business-unit managers to discuss what their staff are working on, or what they plan to work on. (Asking a broader question can identify some projects that they don't even think are projects.)
- Interview project managers and other office personnel to identify what they are working on or planning to work on.
- Interview members of the information technology staff to identify what system changes they are performing or have been asked to perform.
- Repeat this process for each business unit and attempt to group related projects together.

This inventory effort captures any information available about projects' business cases and magnitude (in time, person-days and/or dollars), their leaders, the stakeholders for whom the work is being done, and their stage of progress. Some of this information may only be available in very general terms, such as a categorization of small, medium, or large by the information source.

When completed, the inventory provides a list of current and planned projects. This list serves as a basis for the selection of the strategic project portfolio, so each project on the list may be considered a decision candidate.

4. Filter Existing Projects to Remove Nonstrategic and Low-Value Projects
Who: Stakeholder Group Led by the Strategic Planning Leader

Complete the next six steps in a single project portfolio selection workshop. This process rarely takes less than a day, but I recommend that you break it up—perhaps an afternoon and then the following morning.

In this workshop, the stakeholder group decides collectively which projects are strategic priorities and which are not. Several steps are taken, with the first being to eliminate nonstrategic or low-value projects. These steps can be the most difficult, but they are the most critical ones as well. The discussion may be very emotional. It is sometimes necessary to try several approaches until one is found that suits the group's culture and current situation. Several useful facilitation tools are available; their effectiveness depends on the culture and personalities involved in the stakeholder group.

Already Existing Tools
- Corporate strategy map and achievement targets
- Cascaded business unit strategy maps and achievement targets (if applicable)
- Agreed-upon profile of an ideal project
- Agreed-upon capacity to perform strategic projects
- Inventory list of existing and planned projects

Specialized Tools

Begin the workshop with a framework refresher by reviewing the strategy map, the agreed-upon capacity, and the agreed-upon profile. Run through the inventory list to identify any low-hanging fruit that can be eliminated. (If everyone agrees that a project is nonstrategic, the decision about that project has been made.) If one or more people think a project is strategic, it should survive until the next round. The result of this first filter should be a shorter inventory list.

The following list of tools can be used. Read on to learn more about them. Use one or more of the tools in turn to reduce the number of projects remaining on the inventory.

- Straw-man categorization
- Decision scoring model
- Decision facilitation software
- Post-it® notes
- "Parking lot" wall chart or flip-chart sheet
- "Red dot/green dot" wall chart
- "Vitally important" wall chart
- "Impact/difficulty" wall chart
- Portfolio wave wall chart or flip-chart sheets

Straw-Man Categorization

If the inventory reveals a surprisingly large number of existing and planned projects, it can be helpful to perform a straw-man filtering process prior to the workshop. Document why projects have been recommended for the nonstrategic category, and make sure the stakeholder group takes ownership of the nonstrategic categorization during the workshop.

Post-it® Notes

Prepare a numbered note for each project. Once a project has been categorized as nonstrategic, its note can be placed in a parking lot for disposition in Step 9. Whenever possible, encourage the project's greatest supporter to place the note in the parking lot, as this begins his or her ownership, or tacit agreement, with its eventual disposition. It is far less powerful when the facilitator places the notes.

Scoring Models and Facilitation Software

The scoring model uses a weighted assessment for each desired characteristic in the profile. The model can be arranged either as a Microsoft Excel spreadsheet or within specialized decision-facilitation software. An Excel model is useful for assessing a large number of projects or preparing a straw man, but facilitation software is usually better when evaluating fewer projects in a group workshop setting. This is because the software helps overcome negative emotions and draw out real opinions.

As an example, one software tool, Aha![14] presents each desired characteristic as a multiple-choice question that the stakeholder group must answer collectively. The group's responses generate red, yellow, or green colored tiles for each characteristic until the profile of the project has emerged. The result is an intuitive visualization of how closely each project fits the ideal profile, as well as a scored ranking of the short list. As questions are answered, issues emerge and different points of view are discussed. By the end of the process, most issues have been uncovered and tabled, and the group is better aligned about the relative merits of each project. This alignment usually makes the nonstrategic categorization and the selection of the implementation waves much more straightforward. Be prepared for this scoring discussion to be time consuming.

Red-Dot/Green-Dot Selection

The red-dot/green-dot wall chart can quickly reduce a long project list. Occasionally, it is so successful that no further iteration is needed. En masse, each stakeholder sticks a red (nonstrategic), a green (strategic), or no dot at all next to each of the projects listed on a wall chart. Projects with many red dots and no green dots are clearly nonstrategic; projects with many green dots are probably strategic; and those with no dots are not strongly supported. Nonstrategic project owners are then encouraged to place the corresponding self-adhesive note in the parking lot.

The chart is popular with stakeholders because it feels very democratic, allowing all participants to have their say.

Impact/Difficulty Wall Chart

The impact/difficulty grid illustrated in Figure 5.12 is a favorite tool for quickly seeing which projects fall into the 20 percent group that produces 80 percent of the benefit. The vertical axis of the grid illustrates the level of strategic impact the project is expected to have (with high/immediate at the top). The horizontal axis illustrates the project's potential difficulty (with easy on the right). Encourage each project's owner to place his or her project on the grid personally, as peer pressure will lead to honesty.

Projects in the top right corner are low-hanging fruit: they are simple, cheap, or fast, and they should have a big impact. They are clearly strategic and readily yield results. Projects across the top of the grid represent the top 20 percent, as they will have the most impact. Consider risky projects in the

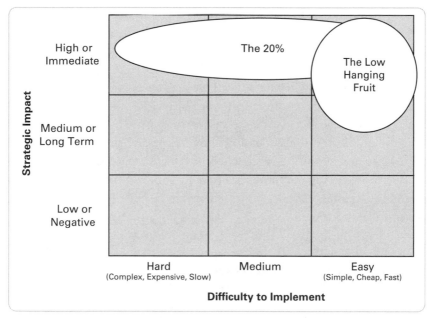

Figure 5.12 Impact and Difficulty Wall Chart

top left corner with caution. Medium-impact projects that are easy to do are often preferable to high impact, hard-to-do projects.

Vitally Important Wall Chart

Somewhat surprisingly, this grid (see Figure 5.13) has been effective with groups for whom the impact/difficulty grid failed. The grid works because it separates *vitally* important projects from those that are *merely* important, or desirable. It is particularly useful for stakeholder groups who still believe every project is critical, which is commonplace among large groups of operationally focused stakeholders in budget-driven organizations.

The vertical axis of the grid illustrates the project's contribution to the strategy (vital, important, and desirable). The horizontal axis illustrates whether it is urgent or nonurgent. Bring peer pressure into play again by encouraging each project's owner to place the project's self-adhesive note on the grid.

Vital and urgent projects are clearly strategic. Important and urgent and vital and nonurgent projects force the group to have a meaningful dialogue, and projects designated as desirable are often forced out of the woodwork as nonstrategic. Use this tool as a last resort for groups that are in denial about what truly matters.

5. Relate Remaining Projects to Strategy Map Objectives
Who: Stakeholder Group Led by the Strategic Planning Leader

In this step, relate the remaining projects to the strategy map objectives they belong with. This approach is similar to the one that relates measures to the strategy map in Chapter 3. Each project's owner or strongest advocate places its Post-it® note on the appropriate objective on the strategy map wall chart. Homeless projects are placed in the parking lot.

A more detailed understanding about scope and relationships among the projects emerges as they are being placed on the map. As a result, several previously uncoordinated projects often get grouped together, which can produce economies of scale, improved synergies, better coordination, and better project performance.

Revise the inventory list to group related projects together

6. Identify New Strategic Project Ideas
Who: Stakeholder Group Led by the Strategic Planning Leader

New project ideas are now explored to *fill gaps* where no existing projects will achieve the objective, and rationalize or replace inappropriate existing projects.

Fill Gaps

Direct stakeholder attention to gaps indicated by objectives with no Post-it® notes attached. Focus discussions on discovering whether the gaps are perceived or real, and brainstorm new project ideas to cover real gaps.

Perceived gaps occur when a note attached to another objective in the same cause-effect chain also covers the gap. Real gaps occur when no notes are attached to an objective, and projects elsewhere in the cause-effect chain don't cover the gap. These gaps may sometimes be disguised by notes that represent projects with only a minor impact on the objective's metric.

Questions that may help to frame this discussion include:
- Will any other projects in the cause-effect chain achieve this objective?
- What can we do to achieve this objective?
- What can we do to move this objective's metric closer to its target? (This reinforces the idea that a good project is one that deliberately moves metrics from their current levels toward the agreed-upon targets.)
- Will these projects have much effect on the objective's metric?

Design Better Projects

Another reason to identify new project ideas is that the stakeholder group may not be comfortable that the existing projects related to an objective will actually produce the necessary changes. This is a difficult and subjective discussion that can be moved along by first reminding the group about all the projects in the objective's cause-effect chain and then asking whether they believe the projects would get the job done. This forces the stakeholder group to develop a position about that question and forces the transfer of ownership to the group. They may redefine the projects, replace some or all of them with new concepts, or confirm that the projects are adequate.

In both cases, explore new project ideas by encouraging stakeholders to brainstorm, recording their ideas on a flip chart, and filtering the ideas against the profile in the same manner used earlier with the existing projects. Stimulate the brainstorming by asking the same questions used in that exercise.

Assess the new projects against the ideal profile in the same way the existing projects were tested. Otherwise, projects that have already failed the test will be rapidly resurrected. Add any new ideas that pass the test to the inventory list.

7. Select Balanced Portfolio Waves and Develop Initial Master Schedule

Who: Stakeholder Group Led by the Strategic Planning Leader

Steps 4–6 have hopefully whittled down the project inventory list to more manageable proportions. Now, it is time to choose which projects will make the vision a reality and the order in which they should be pursued. At this stage of the workshop, the answer is usually becoming self-evident—at least in part—but when it is still unclear, it usually provokes a healthy, passionate debate.

Three or four waves are usually sufficient to assign the projects' implementation priorities without introducing confusing complexities. Figure 5.14 (see next page) provides a typical example. It works because it allows contentious projects to be placed in later waves until their true prioritization becomes clearer. These projects usually either wither on the vine while waiting or ultimately move to an earlier wave.

Discuss each project or group, starting with those that have already

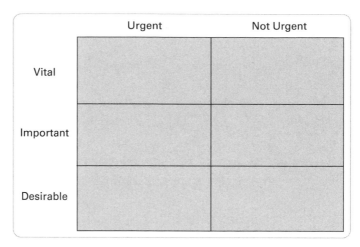

Figure 5.13 Vitally Important Wall Chart

been recognized as clearly strategic and urgent. The following questions can help facilitate the final selection discussion:

- *Location on the strategy map.* Where do projects fit in the natural sequence of related projects, predecessors, and successors?
- *Implementation urgency.* How soon will the outcomes be necessary?
- *Breadth of focus.* Are the projects in one wave too concentrated in one thrust or area of the strategy map?
- *Key resource overload.* How much availability is there for key people? Will they be spread too thinly in one wave?
- *Cash flow.* Are there too many expensive or slow-return projects in any one wave?
- *Areas of impact.* Are the projects in one wave too concentrated in one area of the business (e.g., product line, customers, geography, business unit, process, or technology)?

Implementation Waves	Timing
Wave 1	Let's do these projects right now!
Wave 2	Let's do these projects when Wave 1 resources can be redeployed.
Wave 3	We'll probably do these projects when Wave 2 resources can be redeployed.
Later Waves	Let's reconsider these during the next planning cycle. (The world will probably change before we get here so let's not worry about the details yet.)

Figure 5.14 Typical Implementation Waves

- *Politics.* Do the waves send the right message? Will they embarrass some stakeholders?
- *Restart costs.* Would the cost of stopping and restarting create a false economy? (This pertains to advanced projects that are still needed, even though they may not be urgent.)

Decide which wave to include each project in. Reinforce reality with capacity and profile reminders. Usually, there are still too many Wave 1 projects; if so, try this trick: Unexpectedly introduce a Wave 0. Each Wave 1 project can then be discussed again, or the red-dot/green-dot approach can be used to split current Wave 1 projects between Waves 0 and 1.

Portfolio Wave Wall Chart

Facilitate this wave selection step with the wall chart illustrated in Figure 5.15. The wall chart may be simulated by attaching flip-chart sheets to the conference room wall. Discuss the projects and encourage each project's owner to place its Post-it® note on the chart. The act of moving the note from the earlier chart to its location in the waves begins the final acceptance by the sponsor of his or her project's collectively determined urgency.

This may be a lengthy process, but the payoff is a tightly aligned group

Wave 1	Wave 2	Wave 3	Later Waves	Next Planning Cycle	Stop Work	Dead
Parking Lot						

Figure 5.15 Portfolio Wave Wall Chart

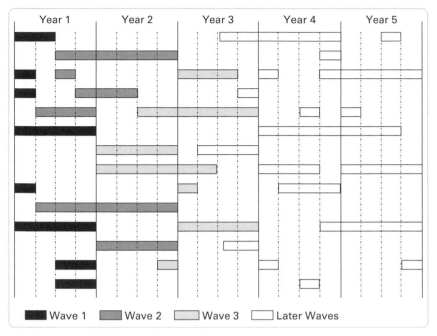

Figure 5.16 Initial Strategy Program Master Schedule

of leaders and a focused portfolio with only a few critical strategic projects. This step can produce earth-shattering insights. One bank CIO never really understood his operations colleagues' passion for a companywide customer relationship management software project, despite the fact that he was the project's official sponsor. In the middle of the ranking discussion, he had an epiphany: "Wow! Now I see why you guys think this project is so important."

Develop Initial Strategy Program Master Schedule

With the strategic projects assigned into waves, develop an initial master schedule for the strategy implementation program. This initial schedule *should not* be developed in any tool whose presentation format implies finality and great accuracy, such as Microsoft Project. A single-page PowerPoint or Visio Gantt chart is usually adequate, but a simple handmade chart made from a roll of plotter paper and colored pens is perhaps a better representation of the schedule's accuracy.

The main purpose of the initial schedule is to provide a sense of the big picture over time. Detailed project plans have not yet been produced, and for many new projects, their durations can only be roughly estimated. Calibrate the time axis in years and quarters, and plot the projects to show which quarter they will likely start and end in. Figure 5.16 provides an example.

8. Assign Interim Sponsors/Managers
Who: Stakeholder Group Led by the Strategic Planning Leader

Many of the chosen projects will be either early-stage projects or altogether new ideas. Unlike existing projects, their descriptions and business cases lack details and documentation. Appoint interim sponsors and managers responsible for preparing proper charters and business cases for their projects. They may not lead the project through later planning and execution phases, but they will be responsible for the initiation phase. Interim sponsors and managers often inherit their roles on a more permanent basis, but sometimes they hand over the reins once a successor is chosen.

9. Disposition of Unselected Projects—Choosing What *Not* to Do
Who: Stakeholder Group Led by the Strategic Planning Leader

This critical decision usually comes toward the end of a very long hard day. Avoid the temptation to leave this step to another time, because doing so dramatically increases the number of seriously wounded projects that come back to life later. Nonstrategic and low-value projects are the enemy of performance and the biggest obstacle to the achievement of the vision. Finish them off now! Kill them while they are seriously wounded, and don't allow them to recover.

This can usually be handled quickly. The facilitator should read through the "pending disposition" list project by project, asking the group what to do with each of them. Again, it can be helpful to have each project's sponsor symbolically place the project's self-adhesive note in the appropriate location

Disposition	Types of Candidate	Project Status	Resources
Stop—not now	Low value, nonstrategic, later waves	Postponed—stop work!	Redeployed
Dead—never	Low value, nonstrategic, later waves		Redeployed
Dead—another strategy	Good idea, but wrong strategy	Canceled—stop work! Reconsider if strategy changes	Redeployed
Operational	Needed by operations (maintain business)	Continue if you can with your existing resources and budget	Paid for by operational department using direct cost savings in business case

Figure 5.17 Disposition of Unselected Existing Projects

on the portfolio wave wall chart or labeled flip-chart sheets. Although unselected new project ideas may be easy to dispose of, existing projects are more difficult. Killed projects can usually be treated in one of the ways described in Figure 5.17.

This is where Buffy the Project Slayer performs the difficult task of killing off unnecessary projects in a way that keeps them dead permanently. The leadership team must play the "Buffy" role to make sure those projects are properly disposed of. Hopefully, the degree of alignment among the leadership team and other stakeholders will be strong enough that the project selection decision sticks. Some stakeholders do not understand that not being chosen means that the project is to be stopped, canceled, indefinitely postponed, unfunded, or otherwise killed until this stage of the process is reached. This can lead to discomfort, second thoughts, and backsliding that should be constantly nipped in the bud.

Portfolio Announcement

The disposition decision is of little value if it is not announced at the first convenient moment. This announcement cannot happen too early—provided it is properly framed in the context of the new strategy, and managers are ready to answer questions from the staff of stopped projects.

Some prefer to announce strategic projects first to allow other project teams to digest the idea that their projects have not been chosen. Official dispositions are then announced later, after the teams have made their inquiries and figured out the consequences of not being chosen.

Although there are times when this approach is understandable, it is sometimes better to avoid dragging out the pain in this manner. Present the announcement in a way that makes it clear that the selected projects are paramount and reassures the affected staff that their energies are being diverted to help these critical projects be successful.

10. Formally Charter Selected Projects
Who: Interim Project Sponsors and Interim Project Managers

Develop charters for each strategic project immediately after the meeting. A project charter is a *brief,* high-level document that describes the project in enough detail to form a team and begin planning activities. A template is provided in Figure 5.18.

Define the project business case in sufficient detail to support meaningful decision making about the project during the planning steps described in Chapters 6–9. Once the business case has been developed, it may become apparent that the stakeholder group made its selection decision based on faulty assumptions. If this is the case, revisit the decision to include the project in the wave. If necessary, reevaluate the entire wave.

Summary

This chapter introduces the first action-oriented component to the *Strategic DNA* by adding a program of high-priority projects to its existing detailed statement of intent and identifying opportunities to reassign resources away from distracting, low-value efforts.

Project Charter			
Project Name:			

Membership:
    Executive Sponsor:
    Project Manager:
    Project Team:			

Overview of Project Purpose:			
Strategy Map Objectives:			
Timing/Phases/Milestones:			
Deliverables:			
Major Activities:			
Project Interdependencies			
Assumptions and Constraints:			
Direct Project Benefits:			
Investment/Cost Assumptions:			
Related Strategic Outcomes:			
Metric	Baseline Value	Impact of Project	Timing of Impact

Figure 5.18 Project Charter Template

6

Implementation Structure Organization
How Will We Organize Ourselves?

B Y THE END OF THE PRECEDING CHAPTER, THE STAKEHOLDER GROUP decided what were the right things to do. Chapter 6 takes the first step toward doing those right things well by helping get the organization ready to do them.

The implementation structure is organized so chosen projects have the best chance of successfully delivering their intended results. To achieve this, it needs to provide good governance, ensure resources are effectively utilized, and provide accurate progress reporting to leaders. While Chapter 7 deals with identifying and assigning participants for *Strategic DNA* components (including the strategic projects), this chapter sets the scene by establishing the overall organizational structure those participants work within and report to.

Governance and Management Oversight

As discussed in Chapter 4, business owners and their representatives are demanding transparent, accountable performance more than ever before. This increased assertiveness takes many forms, as shareholders, parent companies, boards of directors, trustees, government officials, and aldermen demand information, visible progress, and published results.

How tightly should the organization be governed? The answer to this question is different for every organization. Considerations include the organization's culture, historical performance, magnitude of investment, leadership comfort, degree of risk, size of business, and so on.

Projects as Strategic Investments

In Chapter 5, a program of projects was chosen and sequenced in waves to drive the strategy from concept to results. That program is an integrated collection of projects configured to work together in producing measurable strategic results, so the projects can be seen as strategic investments and managed accordingly.

Professional Project Management

Professional project management techniques are widely regarded as best practices for the successful execution of projects. Increasingly, they are applied to projects both large and small. Many project management techniques that were pioneered in major construction, defense, and aerospace programs were previously regarded as too suffocating for most strategic projects. More recently, these techniques have been successfully scaled to suit all types of projects, delivering improved, consistent results and advance warning about problems.

Historically, project anarchy has plagued many organizations unwilling |to control their project managers properly because of nonstandard working and reporting practices. Despite inconsistent performance, they institutionalize their distaste for structure, rigor, and discipline by boasting about their "adaptable, flexible culture"—falsely equating loose methodologies with flexibility, agility, adaptability, creativity, and innovation. These silver-bullet cultures rarely bring the results they promise, but they do allow heads to remain in the sand for a while longer. Fortunately, an increasing demand for focus, transparency, and accountability is obliging many of them to professionalize their project practices.

The Project Culture

The preexisting project culture is a principal influence on the structure of the strategic program's implementation. The structure most likely to produce success may be completely at odds with the existing operational culture; if so, compromises that will erode the chances of success could arise. Operational cultures tend to range from the highly transactional cultures of companies like Citibank, Wendy's, or eBay, to the highly projectized cultures of organizations like NASA, Boeing, or engineering/construction giant Fluor, with an infinite variety of hybrid cultures somewhere in between. Figure 6.1 summarizes the entire continuum.

Figure 6.1 Project Management Culture Continuum

Transactionalized cultures are operationally organized to process a high volume of customer transactions each day. They tend to not think of or collect information in terms of projects. Historically, such organizations may have found it very difficult to execute projects successfully and often underestimated project challenges, applied too little discipline when managing their projects, and considered their budgets to always be the most important thing. In order to ensure that strategic projects will be successful, these businesses must concentrate their limited project-friendly resources and support them with the authority to cut across operational silos.

Projectized cultures, on the other hand, think only in terms of projects, particularly when it comes to charging expenditures. Although this is an effective way to ensure that strategic projects are effectively supported, it can cause strategic projects to suffocate in too much "administrivia." Imagine if a strategic project to win over the hearts and minds of international distributors was as tightly controlled as the project to build the English Channel tunnel or put a man on the moon. Projectized cultures often need to lighten up on their usual project controls.

Why Do It?
To Dress for Success

This chapter's principal goal is to set the scene for a successful implementation by adjusting organizational structures and accountabilities to suit the strategic program and its projects. The implementation structure should be deliberately designed to increase each strategic project's likelihood of success. This means anticipating problems and putting an infrastructure in place that avoids or mitigates them.

The degree of project control must be balanced to optimize the likelihood and degree of success without burdening project teams with unnecessary administrivia. The governance-style spectrum first described in Chapter 4 can be used to guide consideration of this question. Deciding where to position the implementation structure on this spectrum determines the desired level of empowerment and control, which directly affects administrative costs. The decision depends on many variables but all the factors can be condensed to the two curves shown in Figure 6.2. The curves may have a very different shape depending on the needs and current situation of each organization, but the point where they cross is the degree of control where optimum performance is likely.

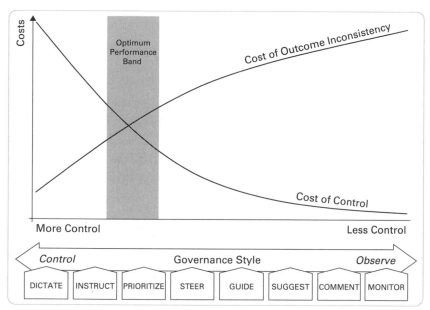

Figure 6.2 Finding an Optimum Governance Style

To Align the Organization with the Task Ahead

The chances of success are increased when the roles, goals, and responsibilities are clearly defined and aligned with the strategy. Conceptually, this means that the implementation structure should parallel that of the strategy map as closely as possible, with the people responsible for the thrusts also overseeing the projects and managers responsible for objectives and targets.

The structure can then be further clarified with documented roles and responsibilities so each person is crystal clear about where his or her individual role fits in with the bigger picture. This is expanded further in Chapters 7, 9, and 10.

To Govern the Strategy Implementation

Management Information

The structure provides a mechanism for leaders to oversee the strategy's implementation. For effective governance, the mechanism needs to provide management with information about the strategic program and its projects such as:

- Visibility of activity

- Visibility of spending
- Visibility of results realization
- Early warning of problems and issues
- Reassurance of progress
- Reassurance of competence
- Visibility of systemic (program-wide) constraints and impacts
- Decision-making support

When an implementation structure is not organized in this fashion, it is invariably forced to react to seemingly unexpected demands for information from uncomfortable owners and leaders. Designing the mechanism to provide sufficient management information proactively keeps the leaders comfortable and out of the implementer's hair!

Leader's Voice

Leaders need and want to have an everyday voice in the management of the implementation. They are, after all, ultimately accountable for its results. The structure provides a forum for these ongoing conversations, a mechanism for influencing activities, and a single point of contact for *ad hoc* inquiries. It should not require leaders to wade through large volumes of details or put unreasonable additional demands on project teams.

Project Start Approvals

Although portfolio waves have already been chosen (in Chapter 5), the decision was usually made on preliminary or incomplete business cases. A more exhaustive business case is usually needed before large-scale efforts begin. The implementation structure provides a mechanism for leaders to confirm a final approval decision before each phase of the project begins. Similarly, as progress is made and resources become available for use on later waves, leaders should be able to confirm project start approval.

Ensure Commitment and Oversee Follow-Through

The implementation structure plays a key role in ensuring people and resources are truly committed to the strategic projects and stay the course until completion. This simply boils down to reminding business-unit leaders about what they committed to do during the previous chapters.

Overseeing the follow-through can be a difficult role, as the scope is hard to predict. When personnel are committed and responsible, the oversight role may simply be data collection and reporting, but frequently a more assertive approach becomes necessary.

To Provide Leadership and Coordination

Corporate strategies rarely affect only one business area. The implementation structure needs to be set up to provide leadership to and coordinate activities in diverse areas across the whole business. This is a critical aspect, as the corporate strategy is really the definition of the CEO's personal objectives, and his performance will be partly evaluated on the strategic program's success. With limited time to spend on hands-on management, the CEO effectively delegates his reputation, credibility, and future to the implementation structure. The same is true for business-unit leaders and their subsidiary strategies. The structure ideally provides effective top-down communication and CEO-like leadership *in absentia*—at least for the day-to-day execution of the strategic projects.

Proactive Sponsors

By now, each project has a sponsor who is aware of and aligned with the intent encoded in the *Strategic DNA*. Sponsors who understand their role and level of accountability tend to be very engaged, effective, and proactive, and they need a supportive mechanism.

Management and Control

A number of very high-profile projects will soon be underway. Project sponsors and managers rightfully become intensely focused on their projects' success, and they may become emotionally invested in them. However, there is also a need to manage and control the projects as a program, coordinate trade-offs and compromises, resolve conflicts, balance tactical priorities, and report on the program as a whole.

Keep Resources Focused—Minimize Distractions

The focus created in Chapter 5 can be easily lost as new ideas or resurrected projects come along to distract workers and leaders. The implementation structure protects the strategy against these distractions—or at the very least, it becomes difficult for distractions to gain momentum and support. The mechanisms should not be overly rigid, however, as there are rare occasions when a new idea rightfully causes the strategy, and the program's project portfolio, to be reassessed.

To Identify Accountability Requirements

This chapter identifies all the accountabilities that have to be assigned to individuals down to the level of the core project teams. Once individuals have been assigned to each role in Chapter 7, the implementation structure clearly identifies who is the go-to person for each responsibility. Project team accountabilities cannot be completely assigned until the projects are planned in detail (see Chapter 8).

What to Do
Establish a Program Team

The program team may be a single person charged with leading the strategy implementation, or it may be a group of people organized into a permanent department (sometimes known as a strategic program management office). Casey and Peck[15] provided useful background about choosing the right setup for a typical project management office. When applied to strategic programs, their more general treatment can be adapted to describe four fundamental roles for a strategic program team: status, skills, standards, and strategies. To accommodate a business's specific current situation, a program team can be configured to include elements of any or all these roles.

Status—A Radar Station Role

The radar station role provides tracking and reporting on the status, progress, and condition of the projects *without directly* influencing them. It satisfies the need for an overview of progress, standardized reporting, and reassurance about expenditures without forcing individual project managers and teams to work a certain way. The radar station's functions include:
- Monitoring progress and status
- Analyzing expenditures
- Assessing risks
- Raising visibility of problems and issues
- Reporting progress and status

Skills—A Resource Pool Role

The resource pool role is particularly useful where there is a shortage of project management knowledge and skills. It satisfies the need for sharing limited resources, finding apolitical managers for interdepartmental projects, conducting specialized recruitment, leveraging high performers, mentoring project managers, and fire-fighting troubled projects. The resource pool's functions include:

- Assigning skilled resources where they are most needed
- Reducing political conflicts of interest
- Improving project staff hiring performance
- Supervising weaker project managers
- Developing project management skill base
- Reducing investment in specialized staff
- Reducing attrition of nonproject skilled resources
- Fixing failing projects

Standards—An Orchestra Conductor Role

The orchestra conductor role provides a center of excellence in project management that becomes a strategic asset for the business. It satisfies the need for standardizing methodologies, applying lessons learned, and predicting performance. The orchestra conductor's functions include:

- Establishing and enforcing standards
- Advising and representing senior management
- Coaching a broader community of project participants
- Overseeing project manager performance
- Protecting consistency of project performance
- Encouraging continual improvement
- Managing program-wide risks
- Helping solve or escalate problems and issues

Strategy—A Quarterback Role

The strategic quarterback role extends the team's roles beyond project management to the strategy itself. It satisfies the need for managing the strategy in a dedicated and decisive way, coordinating activities across multiple divisions or subsidiaries, optimizing corporate resource utilization, and forging a career path for future leaders. The strategic quarterback's functions include:

- Speaking for senior management
- Reducing duplication of projects across business units
- Enforcing commitments at the highest levels
- Providing governance and visibility of the corporate big picture

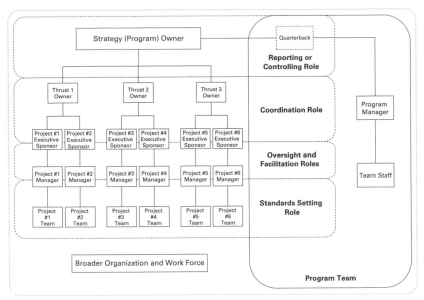

Figure 6.3 Program Implementation Organization Incorporating Program Team

- Standardizing reporting across business units
- Optimizing interbusiness-unit resource deployment
- Facilitating cross-fertilization of cultures, methods, and lessons
- Developing and grooming future executive leaders and rising stars
- Creating effective corporate strategy implementation capability

When the program team has a quarterback mandate, its leader should be a senior executive who is at least the peer of the thrust owners and the CEO's other direct reports. He or she will function as the CEO's representative, make many decisions on behalf of the executive team, personally resolve significant issues, and own the program and its project portfolio. Figure 6.3 illustrates a typical implementation structure.

Manage the Program

When a strong leader makes it his or her personal mission to get the strategy implemented, good things usually result. The program manager coordinates activities across the many projects, protects priorities and master schedules, juggles resource priorities, provides program-wide reporting, and manages the transitions between waves of projects. Program managers may be given the authority to release funds to a project and maintain the project portfolio as business cases are finalized.

Confirmation to Proceed

One of the program manager's key controls is the authority to provide confirmation that a strategic project can proceed to its next phase. The first confirmation becomes necessary once the project's charter and business case, which was initiated in Chapter 5, have been completed. If the business case is viable, the project can proceed to the detailed planning phase, but if it does not appear to be viable, review its place in the program's portfolio.

Configure Roles, Responsibilities, and Accountabilities

The implementation structure is organized to establish roles, responsibilities, and accountabilities for each principal *Strategic DNA* component (illustrated in Figure 6.4). It usually includes the following roles:

- Corporate strategy owner
- Strategic business unit (SBU) strategy owner
- Thrust and relationship owners/thrust target-setters
- Objective owners/target setters
- Metric measurers/reporters
- Project sponsors
- Project managers
- Project teams

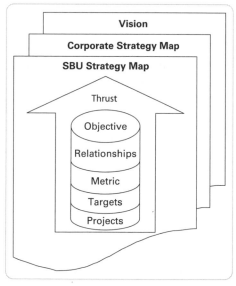

Figure 6.4 Principal Components of Strategic DNA

Component	Owner/Sponsor (Target Setter)	Manager	Measurer or Reporter
Corporate Strategy Map			
SBU Strategy Map			
Thrust 1			
Objective 1			
Achievement Target 1			
Project 1			
Objective 2			
Achievement Target 2			
Project 2			
Etc.			

Figure 6.5 Roles Assignment Matrix

Once individuals are assigned to each accountability (in Chapter 7), there will be clear single points of contact for each component of the *Strategic DNA*.

Roles Assignment Matrix

One of the simplest and most useful tools is the roles assignment matrix. In this table, roles are listed for each component of the *Strategic DNA* (as illustrated in Figure 6.5). While the names need not be assigned until Chapter 7, the table may be used to define the roles as part of the implementation structure. Fields are blacked out in the example where the roles are not necessary.

RACI Chart

The responsible, accountable, consulted, and informed (RACI) chart (see Figure 6.6) takes the clarification of roles to the next level. In it, each function or activity to be performed is listed and cross-referenced with individual participants and the roles they are expected to perform. Roles are described by a simple letter code, as follows:

- Who is *responsible* (R) for performing the function/activity?
- Who is *accountable* (A) for its success or failure?
- Who needs to be *consulted* (C) before any action or decision is made?
- Who needs to be *informed* (I) after the fact?

Dedicated Project Teams

Strategic projects are a significant undertaking, and it should be expected that at least one or two people will be fully dedicated to most projects for more than 50 percent of their working time. If few of the projects require a dedicated manager, how strategic can the program really be?

Most strategic projects require representation from several departments in various capacities. Unfortunately, at the outset of each project, it is not always clear what work needs to be done, and which departments need to participate. The scope of the project team must be defined as part of the project initiation phase. The RACI chart is a useful tool for facilitating and documenting this.

The list of activities to be completed (RACI row headings) emerges as the project is designed. This permits the definition of required roles (RACI columns) and their responsibilities (RACI cells). The RACI chart thus provides a mechanism for managing the discussion about who needs to do what. In this chapter, the RACI chart is aimed at designing the team structure. Actual names can be finalized in Chapter 7, but both frequently happen simultaneously.

Establish Project Decision Gates

The decision gate approach, adapted from Edgett and Cooper's stage gates[16], allows a scalable degree of non-draconian control over a project's entire lifecycle. It is particularly useful when introducing formal project governance in an environment that is not used to being controlled.

Function or Activity to Be Performed	Participants						
	Executive Sponsor	Program Team/Program Manager	Program Team Admin	Engineering Team Member	Manufacturing Team Member	Scheduler	Purchasing Team Member
Approval of Project Business Cases	A	R	C	C	C	C	C
Program Plan Development	I	A	C	C	C	C	C
Technical Approvals	I	A	R	R	R	I	I
Master Purchasing Schedule Development	C	A	C	C	C	R/A	R
Materials Delivery Schedule Development	A	R/A	C	C	C	R	R
Monthly Reporting	I	A	R	R	R	C	C

Figure 6.6 RACI Chart

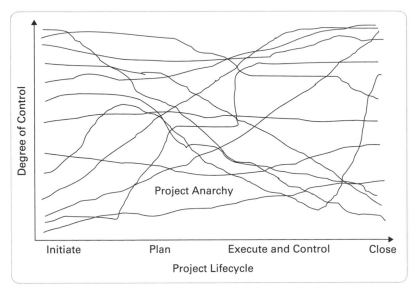

Figure 6.7 Little Control Brings Anarchy

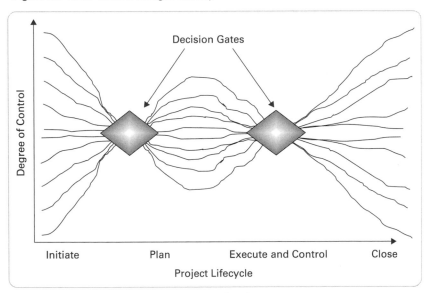

Figure 6.8 Even Few Gates Bring Improved Consistency

Figure 6.7 illustrates the situation in an uncontrolled project anarchy environment. The degree of control over each project plots a unique course during its lifecycle—the random lines on the chart. The course depends on the personal characteristics of the sponsor and manager, the level of discomfort felt by the executive team, the failure to progress, and many

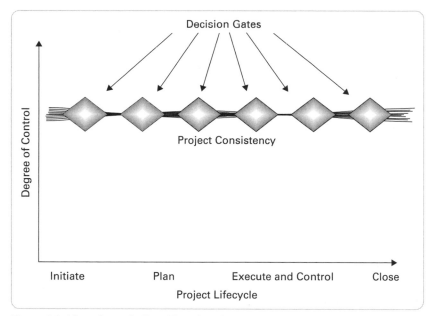

Figure 6.9 More Gates Deliver More Consistency

other factors. The result is total anarchic freedom for the project team and is usually characterized by unknown status, unseen progress, unpredictable performance, and unreliable results.

Figure 6.8 shows how the range of randomness begins to be constrained by the addition of just two decision gates. For example, the first gate might be the introduction of a requirement that a standard project charter form be completed and approved by senior management before anyone can charge time to or spend money on the project. The second gate might be a midterm management review. In between the gates, the individual projects are still able to exhibit varying degrees of control, but the need for satisfying the gates has greatly reduced the range of randomness. This may be an adequate degree of control for some implementations.

Figure 6.9 illustrates how the introduction of more gates steadily reduces the randomness and increases uniformity. No project team is able to deviate too far from the nominal point, as the next gate will soon be upon them. More gates equals more consistency.

Finally, Figure 6.10 demonstrates that even with multiple gates and consistent performance, the actual degree of control can be modified by making each gate tougher or easier to get through. An organization that wants relaxed but consistent project performance may have many easy gates.

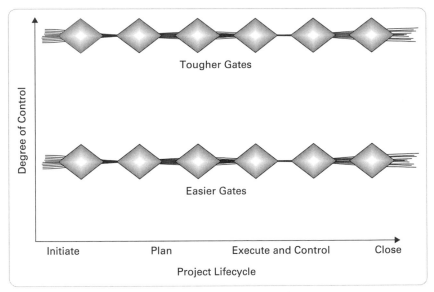

Figure 6.10 Consistency with Variable Degrees of Control

Alternatively, a few very tough gates might be the best recipe for a business that respects the individuality and freedom of its trusted and empowered managers, but at the same time demands high performance from them.

Similarly, projects that follow a standard methodology using mandatory forms and routine management reporting also exhibit a consistent profile. In effect, the forms, methodology, and reports all act as decision gates.

How to Do It
1. Identify Program Role Requirements (Program Jobs)

Who: Leadership Team Led by Strategic Planning Leader

In this first step, a leadership team meeting determines which jobs need to be assigned in order to plan and execute the overall strategic program. Jobs related to individual projects

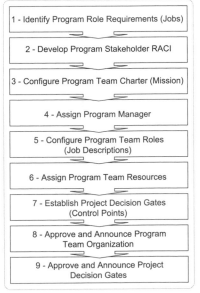

Figure 6.11 Implementation Structure Organization Process

Function or activity to be performed	Participants						
	Job 1	Job 2	Job 3	Job 4	Job 5	Job 6	Job 7
Activity 1							
Activity 2							
Activity 3							
Activity 4							
Activity 5							
Activity 6							

Figure 6.12 RACI Framework

are identified in Chapter 7. The broader stakeholder group need not be engaged in these discussions, as role definitions and organizational changes are typically the responsibility of the leadership team.

The focus of these discussions is on presenting and discussing the management and reporting needs for the whole program, rather than just specific projects. This builds comprehension and alignment on the need for a program team and decision gates. The discussion emphasizes the *whys, whats,* and *hows* of the key program management roles and techniques and prepares the leadership team to perform program governance roles from this point forward.

Once the leadership team has a shared understanding of the reporting needs, use a program stakeholder RACI framework (see Figure 6.12) to define governance, management, and execution jobs for the program. This may be constructed as a brown paper wall chart, but often it is prepared as an Excel spreadsheet that is projected on the wall during the meeting. At this point, focus the emphasis on defining the row and column headings of the RACI chart instead of identifying specific people. This helps contain the level of emotion and reduces jockeying for position.

This step is not as small an undertaking as it may seem. To get to the point where the team agrees on the activities and roles, they must consider and take a position about whether or not to have a program team. If they decide to have one, they must decide how strong it needs to be and what its roles and authority will be. Thought-provoking questions include:

- Will the program team be a single person playing a program management role, or will we need a new organizational entity with a staff and budget?
- Who will the program manager report to?
- Is a strategic quarterback needed?

To speed the discussions in Steps 1 and 2, use a straw-man program stakeholder RACI previously prepared by the strategic planning team.

2. Develop Program Stakeholder RACI
Who: Leadership Team Led by Strategic Planning Leader

Now that the program stakeholder RACI framework has been agreed upon, the discussion moves to role clarification for each job. In this step, the RACI cells' contents are discussed and determined. This essential step is sometimes very quick and often completed concurrently with the previous step, but it helps to think of them as distinct questions.

This step clarifies expectations between the leadership team and those who will perform the program activities. It can inspire questions like, "Does the finance department need to be consulted before that action, or after?" and "Can the program manager have authority for releasing funds, or should the leadership team keep responsibility for that?"

At the end of these first two steps, a draft of a program stakeholder RACI with agreed-upon expectations is complete, but it should not yet identify individual people except one—the program manager. He or she must take ownership of the rest of the activities in this chapter.

3. Configure Program Team Charter (Mission)
Who: Leadership Team

Develop the program team charter using the program stakeholder RACI as a starting point. It defines the mission of the program team including its authority, reporting relationships, responsibilities, and accountabilities. When performing this step, it is sometimes easier to start by defining what the program team is *not* responsible for, or not authorized to do. This step can be delegated to the program manager.

4. Assign Program Manager
Who: Leadership Team

Selecting the right program manager is a critical decision that strongly influences the strategy's success. Program managers are responsible for coordinating the everyday progress of programs and, in the absence of a separate strategic quarterback, they act as the sole point of contact for the program as a whole.

Strategic programs are largely judged by the company they keep, and nowhere is this truer than in the choice of a program manager. The assignment of a program manager can be the leadership team's first opportunity to send a strong message about how serious they are about the new strategy. Appointing a junior or ill-perceived leader tells everyone that the program is not really that special, which plays into the hands of critics and resisters and makes the strategy implementation an uphill struggle. Appointing a respected superstar and taking him or her off other tasks to focus on the strategic program sends the opposite message and gets everyone's attention. It can be a good idea to appoint someone with enough authority to speak for the CEO without having to continually distract him or her.

5. Configure Program Team Roles (Program Job Descriptions)
Who: Program Manager Assisted by Strategic Planning Team

This step takes the definition of program roles and responsibilities to a third level by developing more detailed job descriptions for the program team's staff. Ideally, this step is completed before choosing the right people, so the job descriptions can be used to guide their selection.

The job-description scope and content depends on what type of program team the leadership team would like to see. A purely radar station-type program team may simply need experienced coordinators and bean counters, whereas a strategic quarterback-type program team needs charismatic leaders who can get things done.

6. Assign Program Team Resources
Who: Program Manager in Consultation with the Leadership Team

Select the program team members and start transitioning them from their previous duties. Consider the implementation approach and cascading style chosen in Chapter 4, so business-unit employees who need training for subsequent cascaded *Strategic DNA* programs are included in the team.

7. Establish Project Decision Gates (Control Points)
Who: Program Manager in Consultation with the Leadership Team

The leadership team sometimes establishes the decision-gate scheme before selecting a program manager to implement it, but normally the program manager leads this step with insight from leaders and staff. Decision-gate schemes tend to reflect the culture as much as systemic considerations. Use the following questions to frame the decision-gate discussion:

- What is the track record of successfully delivering such projects?
- What caliber are the project managers likely to be?
- How many control points are desired to govern the program?
- How many control points are needed to manage the projects' progress effectively?
- How much manpower will be available to manage the decision gates?

Figure 6.13 provides an example of a decision-gate scheme used by a large energy company.

Gate	Assessment of	Gate Prerequisites	Outcome
Business needs understood	Conceptual benefits case	• Draft project charter • Preliminary business case • Rough order of magnitude scope and cost • Risk statement • IT impact assessment	• Approval to proceed with project definition
Project defined	Acceptable definition of project	• Complete project charter • Core team identified • Timeline phases identified • Budget estimate (planning)	• Approval to proceed with project planning • Approval of planning budget
Project designed	Acceptable design for project	• Project description • List of deliverables • High-level WBS • Business process impact statement • IT impact statement • Budget estimate (solution)	• Approval to proceed with detailed planning
Project planned	Complete project plan	• Statement of work • Final budget request • Final business case • Complete WBS • Project schedule • Complete team identified • Change management plan • Formal project plan	• Approval to proceed with project execution • Approval of final budget
Mid-project review	Project execution effectiveness	• Project status and progress reports • Project cash flow analysis • Approved change requests • Deliverable sign-off logs	• Approval to continue • Corrective action plan • Project completion forecasts (schedule and expenditures)
Deliverables complete	Project deliverables	• Project deliverables • Deliverable sign-offs • Interim project report • Benefits measurement plan	• Approval to finalize project (or phase)
Benefits realized	Project benefits achievement	• Benefits analysis • Explanation of variation	• Project outcomes statement
Project closed	Project performance	• Lessons learned • Actual expenditures • Project team performance reviews • Final project report	• Project performance assessment • Redeployment of people

Figure 6.13 Sample Project Decision Gate Scheme

8. Approve and Announce Program Team Organization
Who: Leadership Team

Review the program team and decision-gate scheme. This is an opportunity to make minor adjustments while ensuring that leaders own the implementation structure. The leadership team's approval provides a visible vote of confidence and declaration of support for the program team, who have the difficult job of getting old dogs to practice new tricks.

Select a communication media for the announcement that reaches all who need to know. The more people are aware of the program team and its importance, the easier it is to get project managers, project teams, and departmental executives working together effectively. The program team might be announced initially to those who will be involved during the next stage of planning, with broader announcements being reserved for later, when more people need to be aware. In larger organizations, this may require several different forms of announcement made at different times.

9. Approve and Announce Project Decision Gates
Who: Leadership Team and Program Manager

Announce the decision-gate scheme to the project managers and their teams. This may not be broadly announced outside the immediate group that includes the leadership team and preliminary project managers, but the gates should ideally be in place before the project teams are formed in Chapter 7. Frame the gates as being expected when project managers and their teams are initially approached to participate. That way, the old dogs know they will be expected to perform new tricks from the outset!

Summary

The *Strategic DNA* gets its organizational implementation structure in this chapter as roles, responsibilities, and accountabilities are identified for each *Strategic DNA* component (including thrusts, objectives, metrics, targets, and projects).

7

Resource and Accountability Assignment
Who Will Do It, and How Much Can They Spend?

T HE KEY OUTCOMES OF THIS CHAPTER ARE BUSINESS CASES FOR EACH of the projects selected in Chapter 5, a financial budget for the strategy, and the launch of the detailed planning phase for the first wave of projects. The business cases guide the development of the budget, validate the financial feasibility of the strategy, and confirm the decision to proceed with each project. Core project teams are established to develop these business cases; once the decision to proceed is confirmed, they begin detailed project planning activities (see Chapter 8).

Evolving Financial Clarity

Leaders and managers become better informed about the financial business cases for the strategy as the overall *Strategic DNA* lifecycle unfolds. Many of the projects being considered in Chapter 5 were merely ideas, so portfolio selection decisions had to be made based on rough costs and benefits estimates. In this chapter, specialists are assigned to work on projects and leverage their knowledge to prepare business cases that provide more accurate budget estimates. These financials continue to evolve in Chapter 8 (detailed plans including cost baselines), Chapter 10 (actual expenditures and revised forecasts), and Chapter 11 (actual benefits realized).

Strategic DNA Chapter	Type of Estimate/Forecast	Location of Estimate/Forecast	Typical Accuracy
5 Project portfolio selection	Rough order of magnitude	Preliminary project business cases	+75%/-25%
7 Resource and accountability assignment	Budget estimate	Project business cases and program budget	+25%/-10%
8 Project planning	Cost baseline	Project plans	+10%/-5%
10 Project execution and governance	Estimate at completion	Progress reports	+5%/-2%

Figure 7.1 Typical Accuracy of Evolving Project Financials

The accuracy of these estimates typically evolves in the manner depicted in Figure 7.1.

Budgeting for Strategy, Not Strategizing the Budget

Many organizations fall into the trap of letting their departmental budgets dictate their strategic actions. Financial leaders and executives try to avoid uncomfortable discussions by allocating a fair marginal increase or decrease across the whole organization. This is ducking the challenge, as it ensures that areas that need to perform additional strategic actions will be starved of funds, while strategic backwaters will have enough resources to continue supporting nonstrategic efforts. Project chaos will invariably ensue. Figure 7.2 illustrates the typical flow. The budgeting process is independent of the strategic planning effort, so resources can be wasted on project chaos. In effect, the budget directly drives strategic failure!

Concentrate Limited Resources Around the Strategic DNA

Consider instead the alternative illustrated in Figure 7.3. Budgets are not allocated until after *Strategic DNA* characteristics have influenced the strategic program design. The budgeting discussion is now centered around what funds must be allocated to get the program and its projects delivered. Rather than spreading funds thinly across the landscape, the money is concentrated where it can do the most strategic good, thus further increasing the chances of success. Simultaneously, pesky but resilient undead projects are starved of funds, distractions are further reduced, and the message to the work force is reinforced because priority areas receive the lion's share of available discretionary funding. This

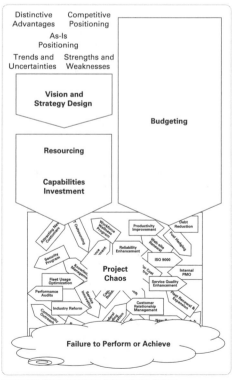

Figure 7.2 Strategic Failure Driven by the Budget

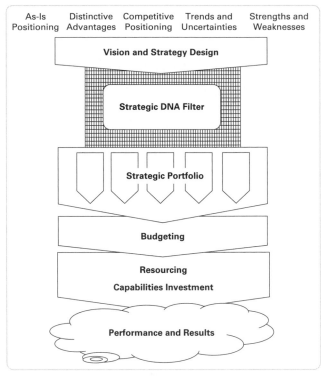

Figure 7.3 Strategically Focused Budgeting

effectively tightens control over what managers may assign resources to and keeps everyone more focused on the strategic intent.

Why Do It?
To Improve Business Case Granularity

The strategic projects included in portfolio waves were selected based on preliminary business cases that may not have been much more than an educated guess supported by a one-page project charter. Before fully committing to dedicating significant financial and human resources to each portfolio wave, the business cases must be further developed until the team has confidence in their feasibility, financial viability, and likelihood of success.

The right people, the right time, and the right money must be assigned to take the business case to the next level. For large public sector projects, this might mean developing terms of reference and may even require public consultations. In most cases, however, it requires a few days of work for a small group of people to develop an overall project design, a list of expected project deliverables and benefits, a target timeline, and a project budget estimate.

Once the business case has sufficient granularity, the leadership team will better understand the financial realities of the strategy. If it is appropriate to do so, the team can confirm the decision to proceed with the first wave's strategic projects.

To Put Your Money Where Your Mouth Is

At this point, resources are allocated to ensure the success of strategic projects, and unselected projects are denied funding so they'll wither on the vine. Now, the work force will perceive the level of seriousness of management, and they will respond accordingly.

To Make the Most of Limited Resources

There are never enough resources to do everything, so available resources must be applied to areas where they can do the most good. The organization can make the most progress possible within its resource limitations by concentrating resources on the right projects and refusing to be distracted by lesser temptations.

Finding the right people to perform the roles required for strategic project success can be daunting. Talented workers are in short supply, and they are usually very busy keeping the business running smoothly. Time and again, good strategies utterly fail because leaders did not assign the resources that could make them successful. Leaders who avoid this pitfall tend to subscribe to the following three schools of thought.

1.   *Have the Most Important Work Done by the Best People*
     The *Strategic DNA* program's portfolio of projects represents the actions the organization will pursue to ensure its ongoing future success. What could possibly matter more? Assigning the best, brightest, and most reliable people maximizes the likelihood of success.

2.   *Do Everything to Increase the Batting Average*
     In Chapter 6, professional project management practices were suggested for increasing the batting average in strategic projects. The batting average school of thought can be extended into the way leaders *think about* staffing their projects.
     •   *"There is nothing more important than our strategy."* You must find ways to free up the best people so they can dedicate enough time to ensure strategic projects are successful.
     •   *"Operational areas will adapt to the redeployment of key people."* The

people remaining in the operational areas are also talented and will relish the opportunity to take up the slack.

- *"The impact of not doing this is worse than the cost of doing it."* If you don't free up the best people, you reduce the chances of success. In the long term, that is far worse than a little operational disruption.
- *"The strategy is the last place we should cut corners."* You cannot understaff the strategy, even if it means robbing from Peter to pay Paul.

3. *Great Project Talent Is Hidden Throughout the Organization*

In Chapter 5, capacity limitations were the basis for establishing the magnitude of the strategic portfolio. Now that it is time to staff those projects, you'll probably discover that the capacity was overestimated, and a shortage of available talent remains. While additional project talent is usually available from subcontractors and consulting firms, there is often an untapped pool within the organization.

Additional project talent can sometimes be found internally by taking a closer look at employees that do not seem to fit their present roles well. Imagine how great project managers would perform in jobs where they were required to just do as they were told, no matter how nonsensical it was. The very characteristics that made them great project managers would cause them to challenge nonsensical ideas, persist when answers don't make sense, point out inconsistencies among published strategies and everyday actions, and suggest alternatives. After a while, they would routinely get poor performance reports, be perceived as not part of the team, and ultimately quit or be fired. Previously unrecognized project talent can sometimes be discovered by looking for people who:

- Annoy their line managers by persistently asking questions they can't answer.
- Express frustration at not being allowed to finish one job before starting a different one.
- Seek to understand why last week's priority no longer matters.
- Refuse to go along with the conventional wisdom.
- Ask why something has to be done *that way*.
- Keep suggesting alternative approaches.
- Aren't seen as team players.

Such people may, of course, be problem employees. Occasionally, however, they are just project talent stuck in the wrong job.

To Promote the Perception of Importance

The strategy's importance should always be consistently reinforced by leadership's behaviors and actions. This team is already convinced of the vision's value and the projects that will make it happen, but the whole work force does not yet share that understanding. As project teams and financial managers are engaged, leaders must begin spreading the word. Mobilization of the work force is addressed in Chapter 9.

Focus Also Means Minimizing Distractions

Concentrating resources on selected projects is the best way to focus everyone on the strategy. However, it is just as important to eliminate or minimize distractions. Actions that are neither essential for ongoing operations nor part of the selected portfolio should not move forward. This point cannot be emphasized strongly enough, as it extends the "Buffy the Project Slayer" mindset to resource assignments.

Judged by the Company It Keeps

Significant undertakings are often judged by the company they keep, a tendency that may be amplified with strategic programs: No matter what leaders might say, people judge the program's value based on who is associated with it. For example, if the program and projects are entrusted to uninspiring managers or executives close to retirement, they may not be taken too seriously. On the other hand, a clear message is delivered if respected troubleshooters, "A-Team" members, and vigorous young change advocates are visibly pulled off other activities to concentrate talent on the strategic program.

To Delegate Accountability to Individuals

More Than Just Lip Service

Accountability, a somewhat diluted and fashionable word, should be assigned to the person who will ultimately deserve the praise or blame for the project's results. To be effective, accountabilities must be balanced, with meaningful potential rewards for success and equally meaningful consequences for failure. Overly draconian consequences can discourage people from taking necessary calculated risks or trying innovative approaches.

Team-Playing Individuals

Until now, *Strategic DNA* has been primarily a team sport. This has been essential, because decisions about the right things to do (and not to do) needed broad-based support. Now, efforts must become more individualized, as the focus shifts to doing those right things properly without losing team spirit.

Strategic projects require many people to be accountable for many actions without losing sight of the collective agenda. It's analogous to an orchestra playing a symphony. Each flutist, violinist, or percussionist is accountable for playing his or her instrument properly, but all must do so within the broader plan conceived by the composer and governed by the conductor.

What to Do
Define Roles

In Chapter 6, the structure for implementing the overall strategic program was worked out and set up. In this chapter, the jobs and the individuals that perform them are identified for both the overall program and each project in the portfolio. This includes:

- Executives accountable for strategic thrusts
- Executives accountable for strategic objectives and their achievement targets
- Executives accountable for each project
- Managers responsible for each project
- Core project teams with the expertise needed to prepare business cases

Role definitions do not need to be too detailed as long as they clarify individual responsibilities (for doing something) and accountabilities (for ensuring something is done correctly.) The roles assignment matrix and RACI charts from Chapter 6 can be used again to define the jobs for each project.

Establish Core Project Teams

Depending on its scope and scale, each project may eventually require the involvement of many people. The specifics of this project team do not become apparent until detailed project plans are prepared, in Chapter 8. In the meantime, a smaller group—the *core* project team—must develop the business plan and increase confidence in the project's feasibility before expensive detailed project planning begins. This core team includes an executive sponsor, a project manager, and representatives from the operational areas most likely to be affected by the project.

Ownership of Business Cases

The core team needs to take ownership of the project's business case.

The team further develops the preliminary business case used to support the prioritization decision to increase confidence that the project's launch is justified. The team must personally validate it, since they are responsible for its planning and execution.

Multi-Functional Project Teams

Most strategic projects cut across departmental lines; to be successful, they require contributions from many different areas of expertise. Getting a range of subject-matter experts to collaborate interdependently can be challenging, which is one reason why strategic projects should be staffed with the best people. The best subject-matter experts are thought leaders who use their knowledge and team spirit to develop a sense of ownership. They play well with others, share their expertise with the team, accept being constructively challenged, build on others' contributions, and are willing to leave their egos at the door. Bringing key thought leaders into the core team ensures they are involved in the project's design and develop an essential sense of ownership.

Dedicated Project Managers

While it may not be desirable or necessary to assign all members of the team to the project full time, the project manager must view his or her strategic project as Job #1. Each project in the portfolio wave needs a manager whose principal mission is to get the project completed. Of course, this is not always possible in the real world, but it should be the target nonetheless.

Who You Gonna Trust?

When establishing the core project teams, the leadership team should never lose sight of the portfolio's critical importance. Remember, these projects make the company's dreams come true. The people who are selected must first justify the project and then successfully implement it. The leadership team should ask:
- Whose judgment can we really trust?
- Who are we most confident will get it done?

Manage Organizational Change Proactively

By definition, strategy is about change. Many strategic portfolios result in a great deal of change for people working in and with the organization. If not properly engaged, those people can develop open and hidden resistance to change. This resistance will frustrate the projects (and the people tasked with them) until they fail. Each project team should anticipate the human factors that stand in the way of success and incorporate the work, time, and resources needed to address them properly in project plans.

This subject is covered in more detail in Chapter 9, but it is introduced here because change-management actions can represent a significant cost component for a project. Building provisions for change management actions into the business case is recommended if change resistance failures or cost overruns are to be avoided.

Develop Project Business Cases

The business case for each project expands on the preliminary business cases and project charters defined in Chapter 5. The core project team provides the additional specialized knowledge needed to better understand the scope, work, resource, and schedule requirements. The team should also develop a more informed statement of the project's benefits.

Costs Based on the Expected Work

The project business case estimates the likely project costs and time period when those costs will become payable. The relationship between cost and scope must be clearly identified to facilitate informed pruning or resequencing of the deliverables when cost estimates or cash flows are unacceptable.

Benefits Stated in Strategic DNA Terms

The business case defines expected project benefits, relates them to strategy map objectives, and quantifies them in the same terms as their related achievement targets. At that point, the project is demonstrably strategic and directly charged with achieving all or part of one or more objectives.

This point is illustrated in Figure 7.4. In this simplified example, the project is expected to deliver all of the cost reductions desired.

Figure 7.4 Project Benefits Related to Strategic DNA

Establish Program Budgets

Individual project business cases can be combined to establish a budget for the program in both cost and benefits terms, including a subdivision for each of the program's portfolio waves. If the projects are expected to result in financial benefits, the benefits budget should be broken down to segregate financial and nonfinancial benefits.

Cash Flow

Combining project business cases to develop a budget for the entire program allows the net cash-flow effects to be quantified. Cash flow was hopefully a consideration when selecting the portfolio waves in Chapter 5. Now that more information is available, a reasonable picture of expected portfolio cash flow can be developed and waves can be adjusted to smooth out deficits. This may need to be revisited after detailed plans are produced in Chapter 8.

Separating Operational and Strategic Budget Pools

It can be helpful to separate completely the organization's discretionary strategic funds from its committed operational funds. This helps managers maintain a distance between daily operations and strategic projects in their minds and explain to the work force why certain departments will receive additional resources.

The separation results in two budget conversations for each department. The first is about the base level of resources needed to support normal daily operations in the coming year, including planned maintenance and anticipated organic growth/decline. The second is about the one-time level of resources needed to support the planned strategic projects and the initial period of any kind of "new normal" the projects will create.

For example, if a customer-service department needs thirty-five people to support 50,000 calls per year, and organic growth is expected to increase the calls to 55,000, the department might reasonably ask for an increase to its base budget to fund three or four additional staff positions. If the program portfolio requires 2,000 hours of effort from that department during the year, it's reasonable to expect that one full-time position should be funded by the project budgets. If the program includes a sales campaign project that is expected to increase the normal level of calls to 75,000, the department could reasonably also expect project budgets to support temporary staff for call-volume impacts during the current year and an increase in the next year's operational budget to accommodate the higher volume on an ongoing basis.

Figure 7.5 illustrates the effects of such an approach. In the current

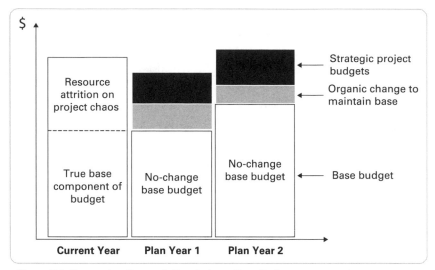

Figure 7.5 Separating Strategic Funds from Core Budgets

year, all department budgets include both the resources truly required to support everyday operations (the "base") and the resources traditionally expended in project chaos. In the first year of the plan, all nonstrategic project work has been eliminated, and related resources have been removed from departmental base budgets. The department's "no-change" base is then adjusted to account for organic change, and additional resources are provided to support strategic projects. In this way, each department's budget becomes aligned with, and naturally reinforces, the *Strategic DNA*.

Initiate Projects

The activities in this chapter conclude the formal initiation of the selected strategic projects. Once complete, each project is sufficiently well defined and justified for the assigned core project teams to begin detailed planning activities. The initiation concludes with the formal approval to proceed and a kickoff meeting that recognizes the core project team's mandate to begin work.

Project Approval Decision Gate

A project approval decision gate provides an opportunity for the leadership team or its delegates to validate that a) necessary information exists, b) the project is sufficiently well defined, c) the project is viable and likely to succeed, and d) sufficient resources have been assigned.

Kickoff Meetings

The kickoff meeting is designed to leave no doubt that an important project is now underway. The executive sponsor and the core team are brought together for the formal launch of the project. The sponsor explains the project's value, addresses issues, and encourages the team to take ownership and start detailed project planning. As the project team begins to tackle the project's challenges, its members will become interdependent.

How to Do It
1. Identify Role and Accountability Requirements (Project Jobs)

Who: Interim Project Sponsors and Interim Project Manager

1 - Identify Role and Accountability Requirements (Project Jobs)

2 - Define Roles and Accountabilities (Project Job Descriptions)

3 - Assign Thrust Owners

4 - Assign Objective Owners (Target Setters)

5 - Assign Project Sponsors

6 - Assign Project Managers and Other Roles

7 - Set Interim Achievement Targets

8 - Develop Business Cases

9 - Develop Preliminary Budget Scheme

10 - Approve and Launch Project Planning Phase

Figure 7.6 Resource and Accountability Assignment Process

In this first step, identify the roles and accountabilities needed to perform the activities suggested in the project charter. This list of jobs for each project should be the column headings on project RACI charts using the same framework illustrated in Figure 6.13. There need not be any names assigned to jobs at this time; the list of activities should be the row headings.

The list of project jobs evolves as the projects are planned in increasing detail. At this time, the charter is the principal information source, and it only provides a general overview of expected activities. This is usually enough to identify at least the core team roles; the RACI can be modified as more details emerge during subsequent project planning.

2. Define Roles and Accountabilities (Project Job Descriptions)
Who: Interim Sponsor and Interim Project Manager

Clarify which roles will participate in each project activity. These roles may expand as detailed project plans are developed in Chapter 8. Performing this step with a RACI chart avoids lengthy text descriptions and prompts healthy discussion of whether each job will be responsible for, accountable for, consulted about, or merely informed of each activity.

3. Assign Thrust Owners
Who: Leadership Team Led by Program Manager

This step, and the next three, can be performed in a single workshop. Figure 7.7 provides a sample agenda.

Thrust owners are senior leaders accountable for the performance of a single strategic thrust. They oversee multiple objectives and the projects intended to achieve them, and ensure achievement targets are integrated and logical. The leader accountable for the overall *Strategic DNA* (e.g., the CEO or equivalent) may prefer to appoint thrust owners personally. If so, he or she will usually choose the most logical executive, such as the CIO for a technology thrust, or the head of marketing for a branding thrust. However, some CEOs prefer to assign counterintuitive thrust owners, simply to ensure that conventional wisdom is challenged and the intuitive leaders stay on their toes.

4. Assign Objective Owners (Target Setters)
Who: Leadership Team or Thrust Owners

Objective owners set interim achievement target levels for their objectives and are accountable for leading corrective action when actual performance does not reach desirable levels (see Chapter 12). They may also be responsible for setting the final target if it was not already established in Chapter 3, and for making sure people are assigned to measure actual performance levels if *that* wasn't already accomplished in Chapter 6.

Like thrust owners, objective owners should be respected leaders who can be trusted to set appropriate targets. They must understand the objective's purpose within

---

Accountabilities Workshop Meeting

Sample Agenda

1. Review Strategy Map and Project Portfolio
2. Review Implementation Structure
3. Discuss and Assign Thrust Owners
4. Discuss and Assign Objectives Owners
5. Review Draft Project RACI Charts
6. Discuss and Assign Project Sponsors
7. Discuss and Assign Project Managers
8. Discuss and Assign or Delegate Assignment of Other Roles

Figure 7.7 Sample Agenda for Accountabilities Workshop Meeting

the broader context of the thrust, be willing to set targets that represent a stretch, and properly understand the magnitude of the task that stretch establishes. Thrust owners sometimes prefer to fulfill this role themselves. Assign an informed executive or senior manager to own each objective.

5. Assign Project Sponsors
Who: Leadership Team and Thrust Owners

When the strategic projects were first selected and organized into portfolio waves, interim project sponsors were assigned to develop project charters and draft roles and accountabilities. Now, it is time to assign staff to own and oversee each project on an ongoing basis. While this may simply be a confirmation of the projects' interim sponsors, the decision may change now that the project is better understood, and thrust owners may prefer to sponsor projects within their respective thrusts.

Project sponsors are the customers of their projects. They often select the project manager who reports to them. They have final authority for the project's goals, oversee its progress, and are ultimately accountable for its success. Assign an informed executive or senior manager to sponsor each project.

6. Assign Project Managers and Other Roles
Who: Leadership Team or Project Sponsor

Now that the project's scope is better understood, there may be several reasons why the interim project manager is no longer the right person for the job. The interim project manager may not have the confidence of the project sponsor, the appropriate skill set, or the time necessary to manage the project successfully. The project manager must never also be the project sponsor, but he must have a proven track record and must be comfortable working with the project sponsor (and vice versa). If in doubt, ask the leadership team, "Who is the single person you trust most to get this done?"

The task of choosing people for other roles is usually delegated to the sponsor and project manager—it is *their* team, after all. However, leaders from the affected business units should also be consulted to ensure that the most capable resources are assigned to core project team roles. After all, they will be expected to supply some of their best and brightest people to the project. At the conclusion of this step, each project manager has a completed RACI (see Figure 7.8).

Function or Activity to Be Performed	Executive Sponsor (Angela S)	Project Manager (Dave K)	HR Liaison (Marilyn B)	Engineering Lead (Manuel R)	Manufacturing Lead (Gabor Z)	Project Support (Darren P)	IT Lead (Rakhal B)
Business Case Development	A	R	C	C	C	C	C
Project Planning	C	A	R	R	R	R	R
Technical Design	I	A	I	R	C	I	R
Manufacturing Planning	C	A	C	C	R	I	C
Staffing	A	C	R	C	C	I	C
Staff Communications	C	A	R	C	C	I	C

Figure 7.8 Completed Project RACI (Simplified)

7. Set Interim Achievement Targets
Who: Objective Owners Consolidated by Strategic Planning Team

Set interim targets by coordinating expectations with the thrust owner, other objective owners in the thrust, and managers of related projects. Design interim targets to set expectations for the rate of change in the metric, and recognize progress toward the final target. Provide the interim targets to the strategic planning team so it may incorporate them into Chapter 3's documentation.

8. Develop Business Cases
Who: Project Manager and Core Project Team

This step requires each element of the project charter to be developed to the next level of detail. The project manager develops the business case in consultation with the newly assigned specialized members of the core project team. The program team and/or the finance department usually provides specialized accounting support. The business case includes the following:

- Executive summary
- Current state assessment and opportunity description
- Related strategy map objective(s) and quantified benefits expectations (including basis of calculation)
- Assumptions and constraints
- Project description, including a list of specific deliverables
- Statement of interdependencies with other projects

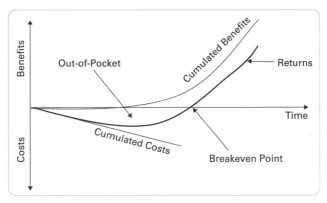

Figure 7.9 Typical Project Business Case

- Statement of principal risks and mitigation strategies
- Estimated staffing requirements
- Other resource requirements
- Intended project timeline
- Projected costs and cash flows
- Cost and benefit analysis and discussion

Business Case Curve

Develop a chart (see Figure 7.9) to present the project's business case over time. The chart establishes benefit/cost timing expectations as a baseline for actual performance comparisons in Chapter 10 and allows project performance to be properly evaluated.

In many situations, the financial benefits may not be readily apparent, but it is usually possible to translate the nonfinancial benefit into financial terms. For example, if the desired benefits are increased customer satisfaction, you must determine what increased customer satisfaction means in terms of additional revenues/profits from customer retention. Similarly, if the benefits are a reduction of staff turnover, you must determine what that means in terms of avoiding recruitment and training costs.

Earned Value Benefits for Nonfinancial Outcomes

If project benefits really cannot be readily translated into dollar terms, the business case inevitably has a leap-of-faith aspect. If that leap is acceptable to the leadership team, the business case can be quantified using an earned value approach.

For example, if the project is expected to cost $100,000, and the

> **Project Approval Meeting**
>
> **Sample Agenda**
>
> 1. Review Strategy Map
> 2. Review Program Portfolio Waves
> 3. Review Project Business Cases
> 4. Address Questions and Concerns
> 5. Review Budget Scheme
> 6. Discuss and Determine Whether to Proceed
> 7. Formally Approve Portfolio Wave

Figure 7.10 Sample Agenda for Project Approval Meeting

benefit is expected to be a 5 percent increase in employee satisfaction, each percentage point can be considered to cost $20,000 (or perhaps less). The key concept in this method is whether the leadership team believes each percentage point is worth $20,000 to the strategy. If they do, when the project achieves a 5 percent growth in employee satisfaction, it can be considered to have earned a value of $100,000. If costs remain on target, it is a success. If the project produces 4 percent growth, it has only produced $80,000 in equivalent value. The business-case chart can then be prepared using earned values as its benefits axis.

9. Develop Preliminary Budget Scheme
Who: Program Team and Finance Department

Armed with the business cases for each project, prepare a preliminary budget scheme for the program and its portfolio waves. Produce the budget by combining the costs and cash-flow projections from each project. This spreadsheet can become quite complex, but it will reveal periods of problematic cash flow and will be helpful in adjusting portfolio waves.

The accumulation of the separate project business cases enables identification of financial and manpower resources and their timing for each department. The additional resource allocations avoid placing an onerous additional burden on operational resources and increase the likelihood that the strategy will be successful. The net effect of this allocation of a strategic pool of financial and manpower resources: Organizational capability will be aligned to the *Strategic DNA*. The budget remains preliminary until after the more detailed estimates are prepared and approved in Chapter 8.

10. Approve and Launch Project Planning Phase
Who: Leadership Team
Project Approval Decision Gate

Review the completed business cases and budget scheme, and finalize the decision to proceed with the first portfolio wave. If possible, preapprove subsequent waves. This project approval decision gate provides final validation of the overall program plan and launches the detailed project planning efforts. This decision is usually made in a working meeting, where well-informed program and project managers brief the leadership team, field

> **Project Kickoff Meeting**
> **Sample Agenda**
> 1. Introductions
> 2. Sponsor Presentation of Business Justification
> 3. Project Manager Presentation of Project Overview
> 4. Project Participation Guidelines and Expectations
> 5. Round Table Reaction to Project Overview (Issues, Concerns)
> 6. Brainstorming of Approaches, Constraints, Obstacles, and Assumptions
> 7. Outline Detailed Planning Activities and Work Assignments

Figure 7.11 Sample Agenda for Project Kickoff Meeting

questions, and resolve outstanding concerns before final approval is given.

Project Kickoff Meeting

Once the projects have been approved, each project manager gathers his or her core team for a formal kickoff meeting to get the detailed project planning phase under way. The whole core project team should attend this meeting (pressure may be needed to ensure their participation). The main goal of the meeting is to help participants understand how important the project is and begin the team-building process. Any additional team members that have already been identified should also be invited.

Summary

Another level of detail is introduced to the *Strategic DNA*, as this chapter assigns and concentrates the organization's limited money, people, and other resources where they can produce the most strategic value.

8

Detailed Project Planning
What Exactly Must Be Done?

WITH RESOURCES NOW FOCUSED ON THE FIRST WAVE OF PROJECTS, it is time to design and plan each of them at a detailed level. In the project charters prepared at the end of Chapter 5, each project was planned in terms of major deliverables and overall timeline. In detailed project planning, the scope and schedule are planned in much more detail to establish who should do what, and when they should do it.

Properly Planned Projects

Both too much and too little project planning can be a recipe for failure. A good project plan is scaled to the project, with an appropriate depth of detail, breadth of communication efforts, and degree of control. If judged properly and neatly integrated into the plan, each aspect increases the chances of success without incurring unnecessary costs. If judged badly or poorly integrated, each aspect increases the chances of failure. Too little planning results in scope, cost, and schedule surprises, and too much planning slows progress and pushes up costs.

Penny Proud, Pound Poor

This is where success gets designed into each project. The problems caused by shortchanged planning far outweigh the savings. Although careful planning may cause the project execution phase to start a little later, it usually heralds an earlier completion, as rework and other problems are minimized.

Special Methodologies and the *Project Management Body of Knowledge*

As discussed in Chapter 6, professional project management is the widely respected best practice for executing projects well. Successful PM methodologies, such as Smart, Agile, Critical Chain, or any other proprietary approach, are usually consistent with the standards codified by the Project Management Institute's Project Management Body of Knowledge (PMBOK® Guide).[17] With the PMBOK as your definitive source, the actual methodology used can be tailored to suit your organization's unique configuration of challenges, people, culture, and resources.

This chapter does not attempt to provide a fixed methodology for planning strategic projects. Feel free to choose whatever methodology suits your environment, as there are hundreds of good books and courses on the subject.[18] The following pages position project planning within the *Strategic DNA* context and highlight key elements of detailed project plans.

Project Management Software

Project management software applications are deliciously dangerous things. Many of them are well designed, but very complex. In the right hands, they deliver a wonderful integrated toolkit that eliminates most of the drudgery and repetition in a project manager's life and simultaneously increases productivity. In the wrong hands, however, they consume massive unnecessary amounts of effort to set up and maintain—energy that would be better spent actually managing the project. When the software user does not fully comprehend the complex interdependencies between the components of a project plan—work breakdown structures (WBSs), activities, networks, calendars, resources, schedules, budgets, costs, and so on—their work becomes an exercise in futility and can turbocharge their problems.

Why Do It?
To Plan Project Work in Detail

At its very core, proper project management is quite simple. It calls for a project team to first plan the work to be done, and then proceed with the work according to the plan. When performed correctly, it can put a man on the moon, but the results are only as good as the work plan. If the work plan is wrong or is missing activities, working to the plan does not produce intended results. Therefore, the key to detailed project planning is making sure that the work is well defined. This demands a good detailed understanding of the project's desired product—its deliverables.

Identify the Work Needed to Produce Deliverables

Many projects seem to involve busily working away on activities that do not seem intended to produce anything. It can be difficult to tell whether such work is adding value. All work on a project should be specifically aimed at producing a project deliverable, even if it is soft and almost intangible (i.e., stakeholder buy-in or customer awareness).

Project work produces two types of deliverables: the project's *intended outcomes* as defined in the project charter, and the *work outputs* that demonstrate completed work. The intended outcomes are the deliverables the project was chartered to produce. The work outputs are internal to the project and usually required as an input to a subsequent piece of work.

A good first-draft project plan can be prepared by defining both types of deliverables and identifying the work needed to produce them. Any work not directly required to produce a deliverable is really not value-added activity—and thus, it should be avoided.

Verifiable Project Deliverables

The plan should allow for work to ensure project deliverables are acceptable to the customer. Recognizing progress, ensuring expectations are met, and formally finishing the project are often neglected aspects of a project's success. Ideally, this means defining specifications or acceptance criteria for the deliverables during the detailed planning effort. If this is not feasible, the plan should at least include provisions for the customer to sign off on each deliverable. For larger interdepartmental projects, requiring a sign-off each time a significant deliverable is handed over to other departments can be effective.

To Establish a Basis for Subsequent Planning

Once defined, the deliverables and work activities are a basis for the rest of project planning (e.g., resource plans identify who will perform the work activities, schedules establish when they should do them, communication plans identify how people will learn what they need to know, and so on).

To Plan Organizational Change

Strategic projects are usually expected to produce lasting positive change in what the business does and how it does it. The most difficult part is getting people to do things differently. These organizational change aspects—thinking differently, using new tools, following different policies, processes and procedures, and/or respecting modified roles and responsibilities—are central to most strategic projects, but often these change aspects are ignored, excluded, underestimated, or starved of resources. Strategic project plans should almost always include organizational change deliverables and their related work activities.

To Mitigate Project Pitfalls and Increase the Batting Average

In hindsight, it always seems that project problems could have been avoided "if only we'd done *x*." This "Duh!" moment happens to even the greatest project managers. However, great project managers encounter fewer problems, and experience far fewer "Duh!" moments, because their work plans deliberately avoid *predictable* problems. Group brainstorming, statistical analyses, and previously collected lessons-learned histories can predict the types of problems that are likely to occur for a certain type of project in a certain environment. If the project manager and the project work team anticipate what is likely to go wrong and take proactive action to avoid it, their batting average of success will be much higher.

Because strategic projects usually include a degree of organizational and process changes, any special attention paid to communication and change-management efforts increases the batting average. Figure 8.1 shows how *Strategic DNA* chapters are deliberately designed to avoid many common pitfalls by emphasizing clarity of purpose, stakeholder engagement, individual and collective alignment, and avoidance of distractions. However, situation-specific mitigation deliverables and actions should also

Common Failure Symptom	Success Symptom	Mitigation by	
		Strategic DNA Chapter	Specific Project Actions
Incomplete or unclear definition of desired end-state	Clearly defined objectives	1-4	Yes
Unclear connections between strategic objectives and actions	Projects aimed at specific objectives	5	Yes
Objectives and plans too complex for broad understanding	Break into understandable chunks—phases and work packages	8	Yes
Inadequate communication of objectives and benefits case	Comprehensive communication plan throughout project lifecycle	9	Yes
Invisible or inconsistent executive support	Visible executive role, consistent all-on-same-page story.	6, 7, 9	Yes
Lack of opportunities to provide input	Interdisciplinary team structure and feedback element in communication plan	All	Yes
Shortage of competent expertise	Justified resource priorities	7, 8	Yes
Unexplained and uncontrolled change to objectives	Justified and formally approved project changes	10	Yes
Too much analysis, too little action	Balanced action-focused analysis	5, 8	Yes
Bending over backwards to avoid conflict—objectives diluted to calm sensibilities	Issues surfaced and proactively addressed	All	Yes

Figure 8.1 Mitigating Common Pitfalls

be included in individual project plans. A plan that deliberately addresses the common symptoms in Figure 8.1 (see previous page) has a much better chance of success.

To Get Ready to Manage Project Changes

Nothing contributes more to failure than an environment where project objectives change quickly, unexpectedly, and significantly. It's hard to score when the goal posts are moved in any game, but it's even more difficult when half the team doesn't even know that it's moved! Rapid, reactive, and uncontrolled changes in key strategic projects suggest that the leadership team does not know what it wants. Effective project plans establish mechanisms for formally managing plan changes and anticipate what work will be involved in the changes.

What to Do
Develop Plans Iteratively

Project plan development should be an iterative process, so the first draft should never be the last. Each step in the planning process improves the project team's knowledge and understanding, fills in some of the blanks, and permits refinement of earlier drafts. For example, if risk analysis reveals that it would be better to contract out some work instead of performing it in-house, the content of the work plan and the procurement budgets should be adjusted to reflect that. Plan iterations steadily stabilize as each section of the project plan is completed, until the completed plan is ready.

Plan in Sections

Like any other significant undertaking, detailed project planning can be broken into several discrete and manageable steps. Each step produces sections, or components, of the final plan. For small projects, each section may be simply one or two paragraphs from an overall project plan document. On larger projects, the development of one section may be a project by itself and may result in a voluminous collection of documents, information and data. Three of these sections form the heart of the project plan. These "big three" baselines are the project scope, the schedule, and the cost estimate.

Good project plans include:
- A definition of deliverables and acceptance criteria
- A statement of work by deliverable
- An assessment of risks and mitigation plans

- A communications plan
- A quality-management plan
- Identification of project roles and responsibilities
- A procurement plan
- A project schedule
- Cost estimates

Define Scope with a Work Breakdown Structure and Deliverable Specifications

One of the most common mistakes encountered on projects of all kinds is planning work independently of the list of deliverables. The work breakdown structure (WBS) is an intuitive method that defines the scope of the project in terms of the deliverables and the work necessary to produce them. As the detailed design of the project, the WBS is a critical foundation for project planning and serves as the reference point against which everything else is planned, executed, and tracked.

In simple terms, a completed WBS resembles a family tree, with the top level representing the major project deliverables and the end of each branch representing the actual work to be done. Each deliverable is decomposed to identify what work must be done to produce it. Each piece of work is in turn subdivided through several stages until each piece of work is manageable. The number of stages depends on the complexity of the work. A fully decomposed manageable piece of work is called a work package. Small projects may have only one or two levels and a handful of work packages, while a major project—such as building a new production plant—might have thousands. All intermediate levels are simply convenient structural checkpoints that help identify and decompose the work; no resources, work, or costs should be assigned to the intermediate levels.

The trick is to take the decomposition to a level that can be effectively managed. Because many strategic projects are broad, multidepartmental initiatives, the rules of thumb shown in Figure 8.2 (see next page) are a good guide for deciding whether the decomposition has gone far enough.

WBS Numbering

There is an established convention for numbering elements of the WBS. Each level is numbered with a period to demonstrate the levels. For example, work package 2.3.5 is the fifth work package of the third element of the second deliverable.

Rule of Thumb	Rationale
Each work package should be assignable to a single and unique individual or department manager who will be accountable for performing the work.	Who owns the responsibility and accountability for progress? Multiple names will usually result in unclear status, disagreements, and finger-pointing.
Don't decompose beyond the department level unless asked to by its manager. It's okay to have multiple activities for one department but ideally, the manager's name will be assigned to all of them.	Managing and assigning work within the department is its manager's job. Decomposing activities within the department is easily perceived as micromanagement and a territorial incursion.
Each work package should represent no more than about two weeks of work.	If you can't get meaningful interim progress reports from participants, at least you can expect it to be finished next week. Eighty hours is long enough to wait for progress.
Each work package should result in the production of a tangible deliverable.	What will be evaluated to determine whether the work has been satisfactorily completed?
Only decompose in detail for the first phase. Later phases need only be decomposed to the level necessary to make meaningful cost and schedule estimates.	Work done in the first phase will likely cause significant changes to the details of the later phases. Too much planning too soon will only have to be redone.
Include work to expand detail of later phases into the structure.	Fleshing out the details of the later phases is additional planning work. There should be a provision for the time and effort required.
Include the project management work—even the progress, review, and update meetings.	Project management and meetings consume a lot of manpower. The plan should include the time and effort required.
Step back. Does it pass the sanity test?	It is probably not reasonable or rational if it does not make intuitive sense.
Each deliverable should be described as a noun.	What thing is going to be delivered? "Final report," "debugged software," "communication strategy document," or even "broadly held understanding."
Each work package should start with a verb.	What work is going to be done? "Write report," "debug software," "prepare communication strategy," or even "explain strategy to work force."
Make the work package level the same as the activities you plan to enter into PM software, unless there is a valid reason not to.	On very large projects, the WBS may only be taken to the level of a subproject, with a separate WBS being developed for each subproject.

Figure 8.2 WBS Development Guidelines

Deliverable Specifications

The specifications define the acceptance criteria for each project deliverable. These characteristics are used to determine whether the deliverable has been satisfactorily completed. Deliverable specifications range in complexity from a lengthy product specification to a simple paragraph of text.

WBS Dictionary

The WBS dictionary is the dataset that defines each work package at the bottom level of the WBS. It describes the work to be accomplished and the acceptance criteria for any work outputs, and it may range from a paragraph of text to a complex procurement contract for subcontracted work.

The WBS and the deliverable specification combine to act as the scope's baseline—the first of the "big three" sections of a project plan.

Address Risks Within the Project Plan

Although risk assessment is usually a consideration throughout project planning activities, it is good practice to make it something you do, rather than something you think about. By identifying, prioritizing, and establishing mitigation strategies early in the planning, many risks can be designed out of the project. The WBS includes activities for monitoring and responding to the actual occurrence of risks that cannot be designed out.

Include Project Management Time and Resources

The second of the plan's "big three" sections is the schedule baseline. Planning the time requirements for the project requires an understanding of each activity's probable duration and constraints imposed by the realistic availabilities of key people and funding.

Two basic approaches are commonly used to plan project schedules. An infinite capacity schedule assumes unlimited availability of resources, and the resource-constrained schedule restricts planned progress with cash, manpower, and other constraints. Although the latter is more common, infinite capacity planning demonstrates what could be achieved if money and time were no object. Planning the project schedule both ways is a useful exercise.

Cost Projects for Realistic Deliverables and Work Plans

The third of the "big three" sections is the project cost baseline. Many organizations are quite relaxed about the internal costs of projects, as their management and accounting systems do little to make projects accountable for the manpower they consume. Many organizations have extensive bureaucratic mechanisms to ensure project managers remain fiscally responsible when considering the purchase of a $100 widget while simultaneously allowing them to run amok with $100,000 of internal labor! Consequently, project costs frequently go unmanaged or are managed in an unbalanced manner, and many projects have business cases that would not make sense if their real costs were compared to the expected benefits.

You can make discussions about project costs more meaningful by estimating project costs in both internal and external dollar terms using

Figure 8.3 Detailed Project Planning Process

the concept of green and blue dollars—green for money to be spent and blue for internal costs to be incurred.

Freeze Project Plan to Control Changes

The "big three" baselines—scope, schedule, and cost estimates—represent the basic project plan. Other components of the plan, such as the communications plan, the purchasing plan, the risk mitigations, and so on, are established individually, and provisions for them are incorporated into the "big three."

Once you have completed this process, freeze the integrated plan as a baseline project design for use in the execution and control phase. Refuse to accept further changes without formal approval, and from this point forward, evaluate proposed changes for their impact on each of the "big three" baselines. If and when you approve the changes, modify the baselines to incorporate them. (See Chapter 10 for more detail.)

How to Do It

Chapters 5, 6, and 7 identified major project deliverables and assigned key roles and responsibili-ties to the core team. Fleshing out the project

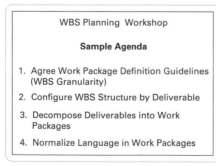

Figure 8.4 Sample Agenda for WBS Planning Workshop

plan starts with definition of the deliverables and work breakdown. This collective effort is made by the planning team, which is a group that includes the core team and some "experts" whose participation increases the plan's quality and broadens the number of people with a sense of ownership for it.

Planning work is conducted in several working sessions. The

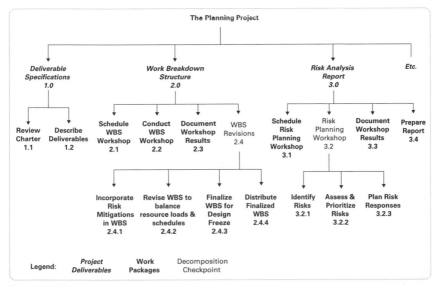

Figure 8.5 A Work Breakdown Structure

natural instinct of the project manager—to go to his cubicle and figure it all out—must be avoided. Doing so does nothing to create or maintain alignment!

1. Define Scope, Deliverables, and Work Breakdown
Who: Project Planning Team Led by Project Manager

A WBS can be produced quickly through a working session (see Figure 8.4) in a room with a large blank wall and a generous supply of Post-it® notes and Sharpie®[19] pens.

Begin the logical decomposition of the WBS by setting up a series of project deliverables on Post-it® notes stuck to the wall. Discuss each deliverable and decide what work needs to be done to produce it and any subdeliverables that are included in it. Write the work and subdeliverables on notes and organize them below the deliverables on the wall. Next, decompose the new notes the same way. Continue the exercise until the decomposition reaches an agreed-upon level of work detail for each deliverable in line with the guidelines listed in Figure 8.2. An example WBS of a small project to prepare a project plan is illustrated in Figure 8.5.

This can be a time-consuming exercise, but it is a worthwhile investment that pays off later, when the plan is almost right the first time. Resist the temptation to break out into subgroups, as it is important to have everyone included in the discussion for the whole plan. If so, everyone retains a sense of ownership, and no one has to catch up later. As the WBS emerges, people move, revise, and replace individual notes. As they do, they provide invaluable input that improves the quality of the WBS and increase their personal buy-in to the eventual plan.

There is a natural but unfortunate tendency to organize the WBS to reflect the sequence of work and the schedule. This is not necessary, as the actual workflow may jump back and forth, from one WBS branch to another, in calendar terms. The WBS's purpose is to decompose the scope of work into manageable pieces. The larger the project is, the more difficult it will be to reflect a schedule in the WBS.

Leave WBS numbering until later, preferably after the risk mitigations have been built in. Computerized project management tools often automatically assign WBS numbers, but these numbers can usually be overridden. If software is used, it may be best to leave the numbering alone until the work packages are entered into the software.

Before moving on to the next steps, verify that work for project management, change control, communication, purchasing, quality control, and governance has been included. Ask an experienced outsider to provide a quick peer review.

2. Evaluate and Mitigate Risks (Rapid Risk Assessment)
Who: Project Planning Team Led by Project Manager

Armed with the project design represented in the WBS, the next step is to take a first look at the risks. While this may be repeated later to address schedule risks and cost risks, early risk planning allows some risks to be designed out of the project. Conduct risk planning in a dedicated workshop (see Figure 8.6), but it can be reinforced by private discussions with individual team members and external subject experts.

Use conventional risk assessment techniques to explore project risks, but take care to avoid becoming unhealthily risk averse and frozen into inaction. By definition, strategy is about change, and risk is as much an opportunity as it is a threat: Zero risk equals zero opportunity!

The following rapid risk

Risk Planning Workshop

Sample Agenda

1. Brainstorm Potential Risk Events
2. Determine Risk Event Severities
3. Prioritize Risk Events
4. Plan Risk Responses
5. Revise WBS and Deliverable Specifications

Figure 8.6 Sample Agenda for Risk Planning Workshop

	Potential Impact			
	Insignificant	**Minor**	**Moderate**	**Major**
Almost Certain	Consider ignoring	Consider addressing	Must address	Must address
Probable	Consider ignoring	Consider addressing	Consider addressing	Must address
Possible	Can ignore	Consider ignoring	Consider addressing	Must address
Very Unlikely	Can ignore	Can ignore	Consider ignoring	Must address

(Left axis label: **Probability of Event Occurring**)

Figure 8.7 Severity Assessment Grid

assessment approach can be used for reasonably large projects and is scalable for smaller ones. This basic qualitative assessment uses the team's expert judgment to build a collective point of view about which risks to address. A more extensive and quantitative risk assessment is usually warranted for large, expensive projects. Recruit a professional risk assessor to conduct an assessment of this nature.

In this step, identify and evaluate the risks to determine their relative seriousness. Prioritize the more serious risks to determine which warrant most attention and mitigation resources. Select an appropriate response for the priority risks, and expand the WBS to accommodate any related additional work.

Brainstormed Risk Identification

A risk is an event that might occur but is not certain. It has a tangible cause and an impact on the quality, scope, schedule, and/or cost of achieving project objectives. Begin the risk-planning meeting with a brainstorming effort to identify all events that could occur. Make a list of the identified events using a flip chart or whiteboard.

Risk Severity (Qualitative) Analysis

Use a wall-chart grid to establish the relative severity of risks (see Figure 8.7). Position each potential risk event on the grid in terms of its relative probability and impact on the project. A calibration for the two axes is suggested in Figures 8.8 and 8.9, and a suggested response is provided in

Likelihood	Probability Characteristic	Probability
Almost certain	It is possible the event will *not* occur	90–100%
Probable	The event will probably occur	50–89%
Possible	The event could occur at some time	10–49%
Very unlikely	The event could only occur in exceptional circumstances	0–9%

Figure 8.8 Suggested Probability Calibration

Consequences	Impact Characteristic
Major	Unacceptable deliverable quality, schedule slippage, or cost overrun
Moderate	Significant quality impact, schedule slippage, or cost overrun
Minor	Some quality impact, schedule slippage, or cost overrun
Insignificant	Insignificant quality impact, schedule slippage, or cost overrun

Figure 8.9 Suggested Impact Calibration

each grid cell. Adjust these calibrations to reflect the magnitude of the project being assessed and the organization's risk tolerance.

Risk Response Planning

Determine the most appropriate response for addressing each risk, and coordinate responses to ensure realistic resource allocations for each response action. Figure 8.10 summarizes the different types of response available.

The key consideration for each risk usually boils down to the following question: "Are the guaranteed costs of incorporating a response in the project design worth paying to avoid the potential impact of the risk event, if it occurred?" This is a subjective but deliberate gamble that is a function of the specific risk and the organization's risk tolerance.

Risk Response Integration

Once the type of response has been identified, the WBS and deliverable specifications must be modified accordingly. This may be as simple as adding another work package to make sure specific quality checks are performed, or it may involve redesigning the project approach or relaxing a deliverable's specifications. In most cases, this can be achieved in the same risk-planning meeting.

Response Type	Action
Avoid	Modify the project design to avoid the risk altogether.
Mitigate	Modify the project design to reduce the impact of the event should it ever occur.
Accept/Ignore	Accept the consequences should the event ever occur.
Transfer	Consciously decide to transfer full or part ownership of the risk to a third party (e.g., buy insurance or subcontract work to a vendor).
Analyze	Conduct further analysis to improve the understanding of the risk.

Figure 8.10 Risk Response Types

3. Identify Resource Requirements
Who: Project Planning Team

In this step, identify resource requirements for each work package. Start by identifying who will be responsible for the work and use his or her expert judgment to estimate labor hours, activity duration, and nonlabor resource needs. Coordinate resource requirements among work packages to ensure consistency and accuracy.

The cost-estimating rule of thumb described in Figure 7.1 illustrates the potential for this resource-estimating activity. Armed with a risk mitigated overall project design and WBS, you can estimate resource requirements with some accuracy. Start by establishing detailed resource estimates (to an accuracy of between 10 percent and –5 percent) for each work package. Include all resources needed to produce the work package deliverable(s) and satisfy their acceptance criteria. In addition to labor hours and purchased items, resource requirements may include other less obvious and indirect items, such as office space chargebacks, meeting facility rentals, tool rentals, external services, and so on.

For larger or hard-to-predict work packages, an adaptation of the Program Evaluation and Review Technique (PERT)[20] estimating method is a useful standby. Originally intended for scheduling, this method lends itself to most types of estimating as well. The method involves making three judgment calls: the worst case scenario, the best case scenario, and the most likely outcome. The following formula can then be used to establish a reasonable estimate:

$$\text{PERT Estimate} = \frac{\text{Worst Case} + \text{Best Case} + (4 \times \text{Most Likely})}{6}$$

4. Prepare Schedules

Who: Project Planning Team (or Scheduler) Led by Project Manager

Scale the degree of scheduling to suit the situation and hire professional schedulers for extremely large or complicated projects. When deciding how much effort to put into scheduling, consider the functions each item must fulfill. Schedules that coordinate among independent risk-sharing partners, authorize supplier progress payments, or validate penalties may require extensive detail. A less extensive schedule is usually adequate to track internal activities and report progress to the leadership team.

Scheduling efforts that start with the end in mind are invariably unrealistic, because everything has to be modified to fit preconceived Gantt charts or externally dictated deadlines. They rarely survive their first contact with reality, during the project execution phase.

Focus the team on capturing the logic of interdependencies among project activities. Use a project network diagram to keep the logic clearly understandable and control changes. For large or complex projects, project management software becomes truly worth the investment, as it keeps a network diagram under control. The simplified network diagram shown in Figure 8.11 shows interdependencies among activities without accounting for time, work duration, calendar, or resource constraints.

Once the logic is captured with a good degree of confidence, apply a timescale to it to develop the project schedule and its most user-friendly representation, the Gantt chart (shown in simplified form in Figure 8.12). Proper development requires the following timing information:

- The project calendar (hours/day, days/week, holiday dates, overtime policy, and so on)
- Dates of mandatory milestones (keep these to a minimum)
- Estimated duration of each activity

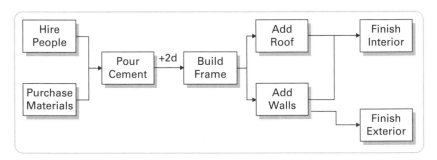

Figure 8.11 Simple Project Network Diagram

- Estimated effort per resource for each activity
- Estimated availability/capacity of labor and nonlabor resources

There are two basic approaches to developing the schedule—the forward pass and the backward pass. Both are automatically applied in modern project management software. Combining the two approaches reveals how much flexibility is available for the timing of each activity.

In the forward pass, the scheduler starts at the beginning of the project and assumes everything will occur as early as it possibly can. The scheduler calculates the earliest possible start and finish for each activity by laying out the activities against a timeline after accommodating the constraints represented by the interdependency logic, necessary workload, limitations of resources, and restrictions of the calendar.

In the backward pass, the scheduler starts at the end date calculated by the forward pass and assumes everything will occur as late as possible. This allows him to calculate the latest possible start and finish for each activity.

The results of the schedule passes invariably indicate the project will take much longer than expected. This is usually because of resource constraints or flaws in interdependency logic. Don't assume these flaws are caused by software foibles: They must be resolved by analyzing and adjusting the

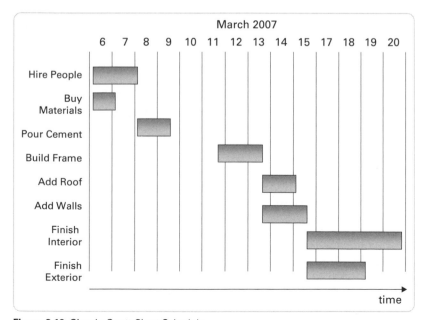

Figure 8.12 Simple Gantt Chart Schedule

project logic. Refine the project plan to make it more realistic by reassigning activities, increasing resources, conducting activities simultaneously instead of sequentially, or even modifying the project design and WBS.

5. Establish Cost Budgets
Who: Project Planning Team Led by Project Manager

Like scheduling, project cost budgeting is a very broad subject. For the purpose of the detailed project plan, cost budgets need only be developed to the depth required to control the project execution properly. Often, cost budgets only need to be detailed enough to confirm earlier business-case decisions and provide a basis against which costs can be tracked. For larger or more complex projects, extensive cost budgets may be needed to manage vendors and clients and permit comprehensive management reporting.

Use the WBS and schedule to develop cost budgets with some accuracy (10 percent to –5 percent), as described in Figure 7.1. The cost budget acts as the cost baseline for change management and progress tracking purposes. Establish a cost budget for each WBS work package by calculating the direct and indirect costs of the labor and nonlabor resources it is expected to consume. In many cases, this involves factoring in indirect overheads, such as employee benefits and office-space charges, in addition to the direct costs of purchased products and services. It is worth taking the time to do this right by involving the project planning team in a cost budget review. Most project managers can relate stories of unexpected—but quite anticipatable—bills that sent an otherwise healthy project over budget.

A simple spreadsheet is often adequate for building a cost budget, but this solution becomes unwieldy when tracking expenditures against the budget over time. Project management software is usually quite adept at building and tracking cost budgets and is an essential tool for complex projects.

6. Establish Procurement Process and Purchasing Requirements
Who: Project Planning Team

If your purchasing department is not already represented on the project planning team, engage that group to initiate the procurement of products and services for the project. Most organizations have a standard methodology for requesting and approving procurement, so project plans often simply need to dovetail with that methodology. Once the scope has been stabilized enough for project design freeze, provide the purchasing department with reliable procurement requirements, specifications, and schedules.

7. Freeze the Project Design with Formal Change Management
Who: Project Manager

When the iterative development of the "big three" baselines has stabilized, freeze the design of the project and start formally managing change. Most organizations have a standard methodology for managing project changes; if not, define it within the project plan. The absence of formal change control is a virulent, and often fatal, project disease!

All that is necessary to implement formal project change management—provided stakeholders are aware of the change methodology—is an official announcement from the project manager that the project design is frozen and can only be modified through a formally approved change request. Include the process and templates for change-request forms in the project plan unless there is an existing methodology for project change management.

8. Design Project Controls
Who: Project Planning Team

In this step, determine how the team will track project progress during the execution phases described in Chapter 10. Much of this is established by the program team in the decision gates of Chapter 6. Many organizations have a standard series of project controls with templates, forms, and datasets that project teams are expected to use and produce. In the absence of such standard controls, establish and communicate expectations to project participants via the project plan documentation. This may involve designing change-request forms and approval processes, scheduling progress review meetings, designing progress-reporting datasets and templates, establishing corrective action processes, and other project control mechanisms.

Summary

The *Strategic DNA* gains further precision as this chapter identifies specific deliverables, work plans, schedules, and costs for each strategic project, and establishes who should produce what, when.

9

Work Team Mobilization

How Do We Get Everyone on Board?

I MAGINE HOW IMPOSSIBLE A HOLLYWOOD WESTERN MOVIE'S CATTLE drive would be if John Wayne had to personally tell each steer which way the herd was going to go. Instead, Big John makes sure the cowboys all know the plan, so they can steer the herd once they get it moving. While modern employees are considerably more intelligent than the average steer, the work force as a whole does share many herdlike traits. Therefore, all of the management "cowboys" must be aligned before getting the employees into motion. Earlier chapters have emphasized the alignment of a management team around a clearly articulated intent and a focused agenda of planned activities. While some of this may have been communicated during planning activities, it is now time to get the complete message out to the rest of the work force, including other stakeholders.

High performance and optimum achievement cannot be realized by a small group of leaders without the support and effort of this broader community. This complex herd exhibits a wide variety of characteristics while pursuing individualized, and sometimes hidden, goals. As illustrated in Figure 4.1, significant forward progress depends on getting a community to pull together in the same direction. Individualist "steers" must be brought back into line whenever the herd slows. A big part of successful mobilization is motivational manipulation tailored for small groups or individuals. A mobilized community will want to accomplish a goal, and it's leadership's job to get them to want to do it.

Why Do It?

Program teams often make the mistake of underestimating the organizational change management and mobilization aspects of a strategy

Stakeholder Characteristic	Stampede Stage				
	Graze	Walk	Trot	Canter	Gallop
Leaders understand what needs to be done		✓	✓	✓	✓
Leaders buy in to the need to do it			✓	✓	✓
All understand what needs to be done				✓	✓
All buy in to the need to do it				✓	✓
All are willing to do their part				✓	✓
All self-identify what they need to do					✓
All do what needs to be done					✓

Figure 9.1 Participant Characteristics During Stampede Stages

implementation. In this chapter, these aspects are directly addressed with an integrated plan designed to broaden alignment, overcome resistance to change, and optimize the chances of the strategic projects producing the desired results. Much of this directly targets the soft stuff that can frustrate strategies.

To Manage and Effect Change

Strategy is all about change, but no amount of strategy design and planning will produce change unless stakeholders are forced to do some new or different things. While strategies may vary considerably, they ultimately result in getting people to:

- Do different things
- Do special things just one time
- Do new things repeatedly
- Do old things differently from now on
- Stop doing things
- Produce new or different things
- Buy new or different things
- Think new or different thoughts from now on

To Start a Good Stampede

Unlike the aligned leadership team, the stakeholder community is too large and diverse to be harnessed together. Instead, they must be mobilized to build momentum and be carefully steered in the desired direction. Leadership teams may think that if they can point to an impending business crisis—a "burning platform"—the community will suddenly accelerate together and make significant progress. This type of stampede can produce significant progress, but like a herd running from a grass fire, its panicky atmosphere often leads to inefficiencies, stress, exhaustion, and resistance to

Stampede Stage	Team Management Culture	Function in Decision Discussions	Role in Decisions
Graze	In a rut	No awareness	Not aware of decisions
Walk	Following instruction	No input	Advised of decisions
Trot	Leadership alignment	Some input	Forewarned of decisions
Canter	Broad mobilization	Influence	Consulted in decision making
Gallop	Engaged interdependence	Empowered	Self-directed decision making

Figure 9.2 Decision Participation During Stampede Stages

subsequent change. Leaders who rely on burning platforms to drive change are eventually perceived as crying wolf.

Instead of startling the stakeholder community into action, it pays to start a *good* stampede by carefully accelerating and guiding the group into a truly effective full gallop. Acceleration to a good stampede can be characterized as moving up through the stages of work force engagement: grazing, walking, trotting, cantering, and galloping (see Figures 9.1 and 9.2).

Grazing—In a Rut

Stakeholders are comfortable with the status quo. They know what is expected and what needs to be done. They collaborate on routine operational activities using known processes with little need for management input. They often have little individual or group enthusiasm, and activities are budget driven.

Walking—Following Instruction

The senior leadership team may have a vision and a plan while relying on a hierarchical command structure to effect change: They tell workers what to do and how to do it. Workers in such a situation may think their instructions will result in additional work or costs, but at the same time they may be reluctant to provide feedback, fearing rejection ("They won't welcome suggestions") or embarrassment ("I guess I don't understand the big picture").

Trotting—Leadership Alignment

Leaders are aligned with common goals. Senior leaders and their managers share a single understanding of the big picture and have become a leadership team. This achievement is significant, because to become aligned, leaders must be realistic, confront painful realities, understand each other's perspectives, and work through a range of issues. Alignment reinforces the clarity in purpose, objectives, and priorities that leaders must communicate if the work force is to reach the next mobilization stage.

Cantering—Broad Mobilization

Stakeholders are mobilized around a common change agenda. The leadership team has successfully communicated a clear and concise vision and strategy and reorganized work assignments and resources accordingly. Stakeholders understand the organization's direction, what it intends to pursue, and why it plans to pursue it. They mostly buy in to the plan and the reasoning, and are willing to do what is necessary—but they may still need to be told exactly what that is.

Galloping—Engaged Interdependence

A full gallop requires more than just mobilized people: It demands mutually reinforcing teams of stakeholders collaborating in informed pursuit of individual and collective goals. These goals visibly and intuitively fit into the bigger picture and matter to them both individually and collectively.

Such interdependence is difficult to achieve. Participants must understand the strategy in terms that matter to them as individuals, as a group, and as an organization. That understanding should be robust enough that with little or no external direction, they will choose to do the right thing and align their thinking with the collective context. Only then will each team perform the right things the right way at the right time, producing organization-wide synergies and optimum performance.

Mutually reinforcing, self-actualizing teams may be of any size and duration. They are easy to recognize. Their participants share a common sense of purpose and high morale, respecting one another's contributions, seeing their individual tasks in the context of the bigger picture, and working with each other.

To Move People from Comfort to Understanding

There is a widely recognized emotional cycle of change[21] that people go through when they are asked to accommodate change. Often illustrated as a "valley of death" (see Figure 9.3), this is a slope that people must go down before they can come up the other side. The valley of death metaphor

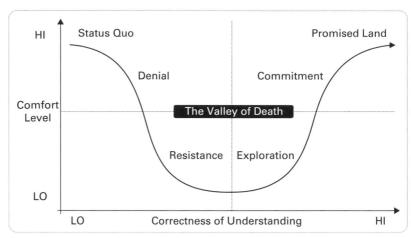

Figure 9.3 Understanding Versus Comfort in the Emotional Cycle of Change

suggests that initially people may refuse to accept the change, but later, they will begin to think the change represents the end of the world. With some sober mental digestion reinforced by early benefits, they hopefully will gradually accept that it won't be all that bad, and eventually they will reach a new normal state that is better than the prechange situation. Leading the work force through this cycle can consume a significant amount of management's time and energy.

To Get Everyone on the Same Page the Leadership Team Is Already On

Hopefully, the alignment-building approach used in Chapters 1 through 8 has resulted in a strategy and program plan that is easy for workers to get behind. This will obviously not be the case if the strategy involves massive layoffs, but for many strategies, the *Strategic DNA* approach will anticipate most concerns and build a plan that makes sense to most people—*once it is explained to them*. Chapters 1 through 8 provide the groundwork for mobilization by:

- Allowing many different constituencies to have their say in the decision-making and design process and have their issues raised and tackled
- Clearly defining strategic objectives and their logical relationships
- Developing maps and other visual aids for concise, clear communication
- Dedicating and concentrating resources
- Postponing or canceling distractions

- Clearly documenting roles, responsibilities, and accountabilities
- Building broad leadership alignment and ownership of the plan

To Deploy Sticks and Carrots

Clear goals, effective leaders, and good communication can only go so far in mobilizing workers to do what is necessary to make the strategy a success. Without rewards linked to performance, the success of the strategy does not intuitively matter to the workers, and they are less likely to go the extra mile. This is readily seen in most large unionized companies and public sector organizations, where reluctance or inability to introduce effective performance management is reflected in the difficulties they experience when implementing strategic changes. It is one reason why they frequently favor the burning-platform approach to mobilization, because in that approach, the consequences for failure are perceived as catastrophic and equally applicable to everyone.

High-performing organizations invariably have a performance component in their work force compensation system. It may be a very detailed system based on evaluations against individual, group, and corporate goals or it may be very high level, such as profit sharing or the employee shareholder model favored by companies like Southwest Airlines and WestJet.

Many organizations also offer nonfinancial rewards linked to performance. Unfortunately, human nature minimizes their effectiveness unless they ultimately offer a route to financial benefits. Fortunately, large unionized companies and public sector businesses are slowly moving more toward performance-based financial compensation.

Rewards for high performers must be balanced with consequences for low performance, whether financial or nonfinancial benefits are used. Mobilization can be significantly frustrated by a perception that nonperforming colleagues share in group rewards. It leaves people thinking, "Why bother?"

Inappropriate rewards can also rapidly undermine a strategy. For instance, a company that rewards its managers with a maximum bonus for staying close to budget could produce an environment that motivates managers to spend their budget whether they need to or not—to the point of paying suppliers in advance to use up the current year's budget! Compensation and financial systems like these effectively undermined one company's strategy of "better, faster, and cheaper."

What to Do
Include *All* Stakeholders in Your Thinking

The effects of strategic projects on *all* stakeholders should be considered when planning mobilization efforts, as any one of them might be capable of frustrating the strategy's progress. In considering mobilization needs, it helps to think of the stakeholders in three segments: participants, "impactees," and those to be influenced.

Project Participants

Project participants are the organization's employees and vendor and partner employees who are directly involved in the project activities. They should take part in the planning as much as possible.

Project Impactees

Many strategic projects introduce changes that affect a broad cross-section of the work force. These employees will be directly impacted by the project. This is particularly true in cascaded strategies, where individual projects might impact the entire company, specific divisions and/or departments, or just a small group of selected individuals. The viewpoints of each group of impactees deserve consideration when planning mobilization.

Stakeholders to Influence

Many other stakeholders may also need to be mobilized, if only to prevent them blocking or resisting the efforts of the participants. This includes the rest of the work force that is not directly involved or impacted and may also include nonemployee stakeholders, such as shareholders, customers, corporate partners, unions, legislators, the public, and so on. They may not be employees or vendors, but if the strategy needs them to do something—even just to think differently—they must be influenced to do it, or better yet, to want to do it. It pays to identify and respect the roles of individuals and stakeholders and consider appropriate communication actions when planning the mobilization program. Several examples are provided in Figure 9.4.

Assess Change Readiness

The question "How hard will it be to get our workers to do this?" keeps many leaders awake at night. Identifying how resistant the organization is likely to be to the implied change is an essential step for framing appropriate

Strategy Needs	Stakeholders to be Influenced	Stakeholder Action Needed
Regulatory adjustments	Civil servants and legislators	To pass/approve the desired changes
Plant relocation	Employee's families	To consider relocating
City infrastructure improvements	Taxpayers	To support different spending priorities or new taxes

Figure 9.4 Examples of External Stakeholders to be Influenced

Aspect	Characteristics
Responsible leadership	Overall ownership, public commitment, inspiration, personal involvement, leadership teamwork, resource commitment, education investment, empowerment
Common perceived need	Overall need, openness to change, common opinion, competitive pressures, internal pressures, individual understanding, perceived importance, prioritization
Clearly comprehended vision	Vision communication, business objectives, overall outcome, customer outcome, stakeholder outcome, personal outcome, personal impact, specific goals, excitement
Mobilized stakeholders	Stakeholder recognition, alliance building, buy-in of key players, matrix building, individual roles and responsibilities, work force commitment, appropriate resources, teamwork, ad hoc sharing, workload adjustment, perception of change agents, overcoming resistance
Supportive infrastructure	Recognized impact, business process alignment, HR system integration, work force retraining, information availability, information accuracy, IT change management, legal system adaptability, regulatory constraints
Progress management	Measures and goals, management methodology, project design, stakeholder integration, progress measurement, progress reporting, progress communication, record of success
Multiterm perspective	Change project initiation, plan horizons, rapid results visibility, pilot projects, adaptability, change implementation effectiveness, recognition of magnitude, open communication, tension and stress, group comfort, individual resistance, risk of instability

Figure 9.5 Change Readiness Characteristics

communication and mobilization plans. A single overall change-readiness assessment (sometimes inversely described as change resistance) is usually sufficient, but for strategies with dramatic, controversial, or unpopular impacts, it can be worth building a more detailed picture of change readiness at the divisional, departmental, or project level.

The most comprehensive form of assessment is the company-wide change readiness survey, which is appropriate when the surveying activity contributes to mobilization by demonstrating management's desire to consult the work force. Most leadership teams prefer to rely on a foundation of management evaluation of change readiness instead of surveying the whole company.

The characteristics identified in Figure 9.5 (see previous page) can be included in either a company-wide survey or a management team evaluation.

Communicate
Communicate the Plan and Leadership's Commitment to It

Explaining the plan, its priority, and leadership's commitment to it are all important aspects of work force mobilization. In earlier chapters, leaders demonstrated commitment by canceling or postponing nonstrategic actions and reassigning funding and respected workers to strategic projects. The activities and outcomes in this chapter reinforce this demonstration.

Raise Awareness

Another key aspect of work force mobilization is raising awareness of the strategy and its details. The more workers understand what is being done and why, the easier it is to encourage them to get on the same page, buy into the plan, and support the strategic projects.

Set Clear Expectations

People need to understand what is expected of them. This does not only apply to the strategic projects but also to the effects of their outcomes. What will they be expected to do differently in the future?

Sell the Idea

In earlier times, it was enough to tell employees what you wanted. In the modern knowledge economy, people need to know why you want it. Part of selling the idea is making sure employees know why the leadership team thinks the strategy is the right thing to do, and telling them what's in it for them.

Communication Planning
Needs

Communication needs are identified by considering the following questions:

- Who do we need to communicate with?
- What do we need them to understand?
- Why do we need them to understand it?
- What would be the impact on program success if they don't understand?

Type	They Need to Understand	Communication Goal
Hearts and minds	The justification and design of the strategy as a whole	Get them on board
Education	The new world the strategic program will create and the role they'll play	Help them fully understand
Team briefings	Where and why the project contributes to the overall strategic ambition	Properly frame project plans
Training	New ways of working that will be produced by the strategy	Show them how it will be done in the future, and why
Exploratory	Detailed implications of the change on personal environment and activities	Internalization
Management interventions	Why what they are doing is considered inappropriate	Corrective action

Figure 9.6 Types of Communications Needs

- When do we need them to understand it?

Outside of project-specific needs, which are ideally addressed during detailed planning in Chapter 8, there are several types of communication needs that targeted actions can address. These are described in Figure 9.6.

Coordination between the projects helps when identifying the program's communication needs. Some will be common to several projects and might be more effectively tackled for the program as a whole. Communication needs and plans developed for each project during Chapter 8 act as an input to this analysis.

Target Groups

Communication needs vary depending on the recipient. Work-team members, the work force as a whole, and other stakeholders can be organized into groups sharing common needs, so communications can be effectively targeted, developed, and delivered. Figure 9.7 (see next page) illustrates the many influences to consider when defining the target groups. In theory, for a complex strategy in a large organization, there could be as many different groups as there are people. In practice, the more granular the grouping, the more customized the communication, and the more likely the strategy will succeed.

Prioritization

In a perfect world, communication actions would be tailored to the individual and repeated until understanding is validated. In practice,

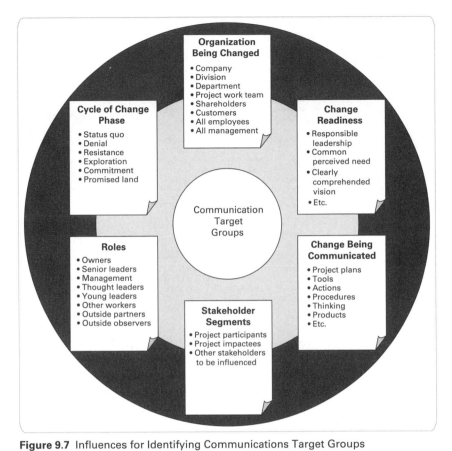

Figure 9.7 Influences for Identifying Communications Target Groups

program and project teams focus their limited communication resources where they can contribute most to the success of the program. This is achieved by prioritizing identified needs, targeting communications resources to the most critical ones, and relying on indirect communications for the rest.

Actions

Specific communications actions can be designed to address specific needs. In broad terms, there are two types: direct and indirect communications.

- *Direct communications* transmit necessary information to a target group directly. They should also provide opportunities to clarify and validate the information. Direct communications usually include training, meetings, and briefings supported by more detailed documentation (see Figure 9.8).

Type	Typical Facilitator	Target Groups	Content
Rallies and open-day events	Leadership team	Large distributed groups brought together in person	General explanations and explorations
Off-site workshops	Leadership team	Management groups	In-depth explanations and explorations
Executive briefings	Individual executives	Smaller groups of stakeholders	Detailed overviews
Executive road-show	Individual executives	Multiple distributed groups of workers or other stakeholders	Detailed overviews
Departmental briefings	Individual executives	Department staff	Specific overviews
Staff meetings	Department managers	Department staff	Specific Impacts
Face-to-face dialogues	Change leaders	Individual stakeholders	Personal Impacts
Reports and white papers	Change leaders	Selected stakeholders	In depth explanations
Newsletters and notice boards	Change leaders	Broad stakeholders	General overviews and specific points
Internet and intranet websites	Change leaders	Broad stakeholders	General overviews and specific points
Broadcast e-mails	Change leaders	Broad stakeholders	Specific points
Conference calls	Leadership team	Smaller distributed groups	In-depth explanations and explorations
Progress review meetings	Change leaders	Selected stakeholders	In-depth discussion of progress
Staff performance targets	Individual manager	Individual employees	Personal expectations
Staff performance appraisals	Individual manager	Individual employees	Personal performance
Informal dialogues	Individual stakeholders	Individual stakeholders	Explorations
Problem-solving systems	Individual stakeholders	Change leaders	Specific points

Figure 9.8 Common Types of Communications Actions

- *Indirect communications* include the self-analyzing common sense of the individual, everyday dialogues with managers and colleagues, the motivational influence of published achievement targets and performance incentives, and the self-evident implications of reassigned resourcing priorities.

Communication Action Timing

The emotional cycle of change and the related evolving role of leadership imply that communication needs must be addressed in sequence over time. It is pointless to try to convey project value to someone who has yet to understand the strategy as a whole.

Evolving Leadership Styles and Roles

A clear implication of the emotional cycle of change is that a leader's

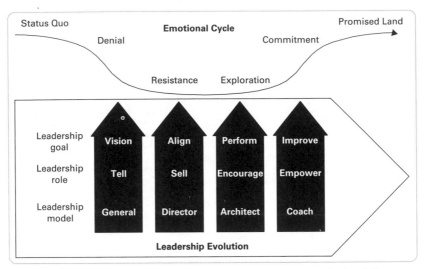

Figure 9.9 Evolution of Leadership Needs during the Emotional Cycle of Change

role evolves as workers develop their understanding of each change. When leaders are involved in multiple changes at any one time, they are often called upon to play many different roles simultaneously. Figure 9.9 illustrates the following roles: tell, sell, encourage, and empower.

Tell

While workers are in the denial stage of the cycle, leaders behave like military generals: They tell them what to do, what to think, and why their agenda is good.

Sell

During the resistance stage, leaders behave like theater directors, selling the change and its impact to the workers and persuading them about its value.

Encourage

At the exploration stage, leaders behave like change architects. As their understanding increases, workers begin exploring the change and look to these gurus for confirmation and encouragement.

Empower

Finally, workers reach the commitment stage where they get the idea of the change but still need encouragement for their efforts and praise for their achievements. The leader now only needs to perform a coaching role.

In effect, the leader's role begins as a champion for change, providing clear, realistic, and rational instructions. Subsequently, they provide more emotional and political guidance, calibrate shared hopes for results, point to early wins, and eventually celebrate completion and announce rewards.

Change leaders aren't necessarily found among the leadership, management, and project teams. They may also include respected thought leaders and young stars (assertive, passionate advocates of change). Once identified, change leaders must be educated about their role, so they understand what is expected of them and when. For example, if they are still telling when they should be coaching, their efforts can become counterproductive.

Rewards Scheme

Corporate policies, employment contracts, and collective agreements tend to be the main constraints as you align the rewards and consequences with the strategy. Unless part of the strategy is to change those constraints, they will become the framework for the rewards scheme.

Although personal rewards are satisfying to individuals, they should be balanced with group rewards based on the achievement of team, department, divisional, and/or corporate goals. This tempers the single-minded pursuit of individual rewards to the detriment of group objectives.

Performance rewards are usually related to business-unit operations. To be aligned with the strategy, the scheme must reward two streams of strategic ambition:
- Participation in required progress towards an achievement target
- Participation in the successful progress of a strategic project

Both streams of strategic ambition should be included in the basis for team and individual performance goals.

Performance Goals Aligned with Strategic DNA *Achievement Targets*

This continues the cascading that began in Chapter 4 between the corporate level and the business units. Achievement targets can be cascaded through multiple levels of the organization until they are ultimately translated into individual goals. This shares out accountability for desired performance changes among those expected to produce it. Perhaps the most

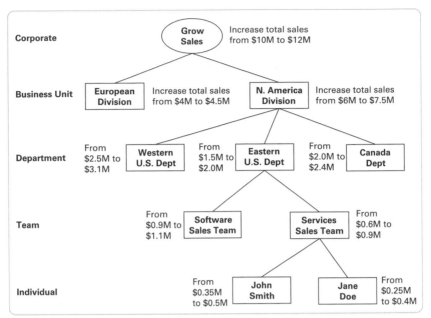

Figure 9.10 Cascading Achievement Targets to the Individual Level

intuitive example of this is cascading a sales growth target into individual sales quotas (see Figure 9.10).

For example, if a company with sales of $10 million wants to increase to $12 million in the course of a year, a $2 million stretch is desired. Because of the organization's underlying business situation, $1.5 of the $2 million is assigned to its North American business unit. The business unit allocates $0.5 million to its eastern U.S. sales department, which in turn expects $0.3 million to come from its services sales team. The manager of the services sales team adjusts the quotas of his salespeople, John and Jane, to provide each with an individual performance goal. If the rewards scheme links some of their bonuses to their team or department goals, their motivation will be balanced. If not, they, or their manager, may react inappropriately when someone misses a target.

Figure 9.11 Work Team Mobilization Process

Many achievement targets should not be cascaded to the individual level. If people feel they have little control over a target, they can be demotivated by it. Unless the target can be meaningfully shared out, it is best kept at collective levels. Individuals may still find that part of their performance recognition is based on that target, but the reward/consequence impact should be leveled out across the broader group.

Performance Goals Aligned with Strategic Projects

For many project participants, achievement targets are less intuitive than just success or failure of the projects. Occasionally, even a successful project does not produce desired results, perhaps because it was based on a flawed hypothesis, or because external factors intervened—the operation was a success, but the patient died anyway. In this situation, if a worker's rewards were based solely on the target, he or she would be denied recognition of successful project work, possibly unfairly so. Similarly, if project participants are only rewarded based on the performance of the projects they are immediately tasked with, they may be less inclined to collaborate effectively with people working on other strategic projects. These are compelling reasons for including elements of both in individual performance goals.

Integrated Mobilization Program

Many visions are branded with a catchy name and an identity: Dell Computer's "The Dell Effect," Philips Electronics's "Sense and Simplicity," and GE's "Imagination at Work" campaigns are good examples. Workers become mobilized around a brand when mobilization activities are implemented in a coordinated and brand-building manner.

Broad mobilization requires a consistent and constantly reinforced message delivered by educated leadership in consort with a communication plan and rewards scheme. Integrating these delivery vehicles into a mobilization program and giving that program the stature of a strategic project ensures that it will receive appropriate attention and enhances the probability of its success.

How to Do It
1. Identify Change Management Needs
Who: Leadership Team or Selected Managers Led by Program Team

The first step in getting the project work teams mobilized is identifying change resistance so plans can be designed to overcome it. Change-readiness

```
┌─────────────────────────────────────────────┐
│                                             │
│     Change-Readiness Assessment Meeting     │
│                                             │
│               Sample Agenda                 │
│                                             │
│   1.  Identify Change-Readiness Characteristics │
│   2.  Review Program Portfolio              │
│   3.  Identify Organizational Impacts       │
│   4.  Evaluate Readiness Characteristics    │
│   5.  Identify Intervention Needs           │
│   6.  Repeat Items 4 and 5 for Each Organization │
│   7.  Document for Use in Step 3            │
│                                             │
└─────────────────────────────────────────────┘
```

Figure 9.12 Sample Agenda for Change-Readiness Assessment Meeting

assessments use surveys or management evaluation to identify probable areas and aspects of resistance.

Effective management evaluations reflect a joint assessment by either the leadership team or a selected group of respected managers. Conduct the assessment as a dialogue in a change-readiness meeting (see Figure 9.12) and formulate a collective opinion about where to concentrate communication and mobilization interventions. Prior to the meeting, prepare a series of discussion points to characterize each aspect of change readiness. During the meeting, discuss each characteristic until you develop a shared opinion and identify related change-management needs. Tabulate and document the results to provide input for the rest of this chapter.

Whenever the leadership team believes the divisions, departments, or project work teams have significantly different change-readiness profiles, the activity should be repeated for each, usually with different participants.

2. Educate Leaders About Their Roles
Who: Leadership Team and Program Team

This step sets expectations for the change leader's roles in a successful strategy. The program team identifies core change leaders, and the leadership team includes additional thought leaders and young stars.

Once change leaders have been identified, establish expectations for their evolving role in the context of the strategic program and each of the strategic projects. This expands on any change-leadership roles and responsibilities identified in the RACI charts of Chapters 6 and 7 by applying the additional insight of the change-management needs captured in the previous step. This work can usually be done by the program manager for the overall strategy and by each project manager for specific projects. Expectations can be added to the RACI charts, but they should be organized to reflect the evolution of the roles during the change-cycle phases.

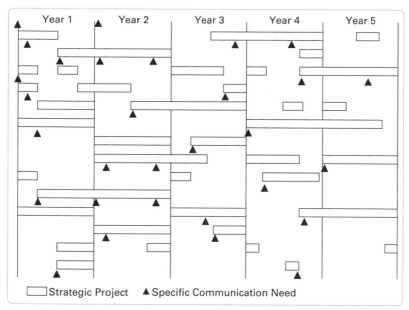

Figure 9.13 Master Schedule Showing Specific Communication Needs

Many leaders will be identified for broad impact strategies, but fewer may be necessary for narrowly focused strategies (or those in smaller businesses). If they already understand their change-management roles, leaders' education needs may be as simple as a briefing about the strategy (performed by the leadership team, program manager, or a direct supervisor) and copies of supporting documentation. If extensive leader education is needed, add a separate strategic project to the program to develop and deliver the necessary training. Extensive leadership education is addressed in the next step.

3. Identify Communication Needs
Who: Program Team and Project Planning Teams

Identify who needs to be told what, and when. Define target groups for the overall strategy and for each strategic project in meetings dedicated to the discussion.

Communication Needs Priorities

Prioritize needs in the context of why the target groups need to understand, and the impact on the strategy if they do not understand. Low priority needs with little or no impact on success can be left to general indirect communication actions. High-priority needs ultimately undermine, frustrate, or threaten the strategy if they are left unaddressed. Tackle them with direct communication actions.

Communication Needs Scheduling

Schedule high-priority communication needs using the overall program master schedule first developed in Chapter 5 and individual project schedules as guides (see Figure 9.13). Aim for a schedule that develops target groups' understanding as the program progresses. Leadership role education can be scheduled in a similar manner to develop leadership capabilities before they are needed. The schedule is used in Step 5 to sequence mobilization actions.

4. Align Rewards and Consequences Scheme

Who: Finance/Human Resource Departments Led by Program Team

Well-designed rewards schemes can be realigned by simply changing the targets. Define new targets by using focused discussions to establish the content and structure of the required information.

If the scheme has been hard-coded to support an earlier strategy, it should be changed, because the scheme's alignment with the strategy is crucial to success. This tends to be a complex and challenging undertaking that should be treated as an early project in the integrated mobilization program.

5. Develop Integrated Mobilization Program

Who: Program Team

Develop the integrated mobilization program using the defined leadership roles and expectations, prioritized communication needs and schedules, and strategically aligned rewards scheme. The first activity in this step is to decide how to satisfy specific needs. Choose what type of message to develop and convey to address the specific need, and then select appropriate delivery methods. Plan other mobilization actions at the same time, including any necessary leadership education and rewards system realignment.

Combine actions together as a coordinated series of mobilization projects, with schedule requirements derived directly from the overall program master schedule (see Figures 9.13 and 9.14). Expect to adjust the

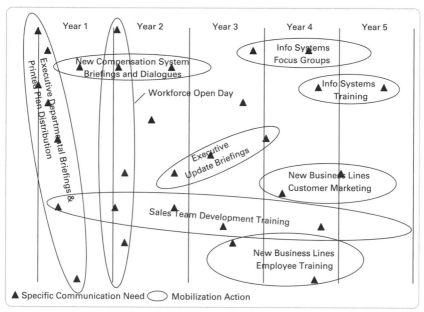

Figure 9.14 Planning the Mobilization Projects

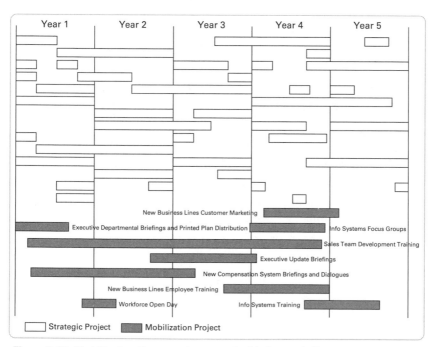

Figure 9.15 Mobilization Program Integrated with Strategic Program

projects and their schedules whenever the program master schedule changes. Finally, incorporate the integrated mobilization program within the master schedule to present a complete program plan (see Figure 9.15).

Adding communication projects to the program can reduce the organization's capacity to pursue other strategic projects. The portfolio waves may need to be revisited to rebalance the workload within the capacity.

6. Develop Team and Individual Performance Goals
Who: Management Team and Project Teams Led by Program Team

With the rewards scheme as a framework, use the *Strategic DNA* to develop timed performance goals that encourage optimal performance. Identify specific team goals, individual involvement in strategic changes, and goal-setting responsibilities (these may already have been defined in Chapter 4).

Setting Performance Goals from Strategic DNA *Achievement Targets*

Decompose achievement targets to establish a challenging but attainable stretch for teams and individuals. Take care that each individual's share of the targets is reasonable, fairly assigned, and encouraging, not demoralizing. The key questions to ponder when setting performance goals are:

- Which achievement targets should we cascade to teams and individuals?
- How deep should we cascade each target into the organization?
- What proportion of the desired stretch should we assign to each team or individual?

Decisions about which targets to cascade, and how deep to cascade them, should be made by the strategy owner (e.g., the CEO) in consultation with the leadership team. In larger organizations, the program team may be asked to prepare a draft scheme at the business-unit level (for starters). Discuss this "sharing out" of the stretch with representatives from human resources, finance, and all other appropriate leaders, and then review it with the leadership team. Once it is approved, work with business-unit leaders to cascade the stretch within their organizations. Repeat this for each level until the stretch has been cascaded to the desired level.

Setting Performance Goals for Strategic DNA *Projects*

Performance goals for strategic projects should be challenging, reasonable, and fair, and they should reflect the time an employee spends working on a project. For example, a 5 percent time commitment to a successful project cannot reasonably account for 50 percent of a person's bonus! The key decisions are:

- Whose performance rewards should be affected by the project's success?
- How will success be defined?
- How will performance be evaluated?

The first question depends on the individual's degree of involvement in the project. A manager who chooses to assign one of her best people to a project despite the consequences to her own department may have been the difference between success and failure. In most cases, rewards are only linked to project success for workers who are actively involved in them. The overall thinking is simplified by only providing project-based rewards to people who have been assigned a minimum amount (or more) of project work.

The answers to the questions about defining success and evaluating performance largely depend on the project's culture (see Chapter 6). Well-developed project cultures have established methods for gauging project performance and tracking individual activity. They may use recognized project measures (such as the earned value method) to evaluate performance, information systems to manipulate data, and respected project management offices to pass judgment. Intermediate cultures may measure the completion of deliverables against the schedule and/or the budget, but usually the focus is on one or the other. Undeveloped project cultures generally use the subjective opinion of the sponsor to judge project results and that of the project manager to judge individual performance.

7. Implement Mobilization Program
Who: Program Team and Project Teams

The next chapter deals with the execution and governance of the strategic program, including the mobilization projects. Treat mobilization projects the same as any other strategic project. Implement the mobilization program immediately when its activities need to be completed to enable strategic projects (e.g., if leaders must be educated about their roles before they perform them). Early mobilization activities can attract the best people to work in the program and project teams.

Summary

This chapter engages the work force and incorporates it into the *Strategic DNA* by ensuring workers can see where they will contribute, and why their contributions matter. Worker motivations have been connected to project plans, budgets, accountabilities, the implementation structure, metrics, targets, objectives, and so on, and the *Strategic DNA* has now reached its full depth. Strategic projects can now be carried out with a better chance of success.

10

Project Execution and Control

Where Should We Be? Where Are We?
What Are We Doing About the Difference?

T HE MOST EXPERIENCED STRATEGIC PLANNERS IN THE WORLD ARE
probably those in the military who often repeat von Moltke's maxim,
"No plan survives its first contact with the enemy." In theory, the
perfect project plan anticipates all the work needed to produce all the
deliverables. If the project team does nothing but work according to the plan,
the deliverables should be readily produced. In practice, of course, no plan
is perfect; something always obstructs progress, whether it is unanticipated
work, unpredictable human factors, or a flawed hypothesis. Monitoring
progress and taking corrective actions when necessary is essential if intended
results are to be reliably and fully realized. Even the self-actualizing efforts of
the galloping teams described in Chapter 9 require constant reinforcement
from formal progress measurement and accountability.

It is remarkable how often investments in strategic planning are wasted
by failing to routinely monitor progress and proactively adjust for reality.
In this chapter, project execution and control activities are arranged as a
repeating process that oversees and controls the progress of each strategic
project and the *Strategic DNA* program as a whole. It can be scaled to suit
the program's complexity and the organization's culture. Use it diligently to
achieve steady and manageable progress.

In mature project cultures, established project execution and control
processes can usually be applied to strategic projects, but they may be too
complex and cumbersome. If, for example, a construction company were to
control an organizational change project using the same tools and techniques
it uses to build bridges, it may find its strategic project suffocated by too
much administrative accounting and too many meetings.

Immature project cultures, on the other hand, need to get more serious about the way they control strategic projects. The progress reporting, problem identification, and corrective action management processes described in this chapter provide enough control and oversight to increase their success.

At the end of the day, project control boils down to repeatedly asking three questions about each of the projects and the overall program:

- Where should we be?
- Where are we?
- What are we doing about the difference?

Depending on the specific situation, there are many ways to ask each question, but the intent behind the questions remains the same. Only a project manager who can definitively answer those three questions for every item in the project plan is truly in control.

Why Do It?
To Work the Plan—Project Execution

Project execution is the act of performing the project work by following the plan. For the project manager, this means making sure people perform the planned work and produce the desired deliverables. The project manager coordinates the people and other resources necessary to perform the work and makes sure external managers provide the support anticipated in the plan.

To Monitor Progress and React—Project Control

Project control is the act of evaluating whether the project is progressing as planned, and taking appropriate action when it is not. For the project manager and his team, this means comparing actual progress against the plan (i.e., the completion of the work packages and project deliverables) to identify variances and then reacting to them.

Progress Versus Status

It can be very helpful to focus on the project's *progress* rather than its *status*. Even though they may seem to be the same, emotionally they can be quite different. Discussions about status tend to seem negative, even if things are where they should be. Progress discussions offer a more positive and less intimidating dialogue, especially when the status is bad but progress is being made. By concentrating on progress, a project team can focus on

, the immediate past and future, rather than reopening old wounds every time status is discussed.

Adjust the Plan for Reality

One essential aspect of project control is adjusting the work to accommodate emerging realities. As each new reality is identified, it is distilled down to two root causes: Either the plan was incorrect or incomplete and needs to be changed, or something isn't going as expected and corrective action is needed.

Release Further Funding, Resources, and Commitments

On larger or longer projects, the assignment of resources and other commitments may be phased or staged to control the manpower or cash flow being consumed. Progress monitoring allows management to release appropriately timed additional resources.

To Report Progress and Celebrate Success

Progress monitoring is often used to celebrate successful completion of project work or deliverables. This provides reassurance for project customers and morale-boosting reinforcement for team members—particularly when it is connected to performance rewards.

To Systematically Avoid 90-Percentitis

Have you ever participated in a conversation like this?

Boss: *"Where's that activity at?"*
Worker: *"It's 90 percent complete."*
Boss: *"But you said that last month, and the month before."*
Worker: *"Well, it's still 90 percent complete."*

The boss is thinking that there has been no progress for the last two months, and the worker is being disrespectful and ensuring that the boss has no idea what the status of the activity really is. It's the same as saying, "It's none of your business!"

When monitoring project performance, work in progress should not be recognized until it is completed. Activities can remain 90 percent complete for a very long time. This avoids credit being taken or implied for incomplete work and forces project planners to plan their projects with enough detail to track progress meaningfully. For example, if planners know there can be no progress recognition for a six-month-long activity until it has been completed, they will break it into shorter pieces of work that can be recognized earlier. The result is more control, visibility, and transparency.

This is less of a problem in organizations that have properly planned projects and employee time-tracking systems integrated with computerized project software. These organizations can measure and compare actual, planned, and budgeted hours. For example, an organization can use earned value analysis to forecast the number of additional hours a project may be expected to consume. They might forecast that an activity will probably consume 10 percent more hours than planned, which means that it's really only 38.5 percent complete! Unless this degree of data collection and analysis is available, it is best to keep progress binary—"done" or "not yet done"; 100 percent or 0 percent; or yes or no.

What to Do
Two-Tier Monitoring and Reporting

The project execution and control process involves two tiers of monitoring and reporting. The first tier is that of each strategic project and the second tier is that of the *Strategic DNA* program as a whole.

Strategic Project Monitoring and Reporting

Project work activities need to be monitored routinely, and actual progress should be reported against the plan. This proactively reassures the project sponsor and other managers that it is under control and provides early visibility of developing problems.

Strategic DNA *Program Monitoring and Reporting*

Combining individual project progress reports with routine program monitoring provides an overall view of program progress against the master schedule.

Summarizing Planned Performance Highlights

Establishing clear progress expectations for each project and the program as a whole limits lengthy progress reports to project sponsors and the management team. These expectations can be extracted as highlights from the business cases, detailed project plans, and performance goals established in Chapters 7, 8, and 9.

Anticipated Question	Progress Expectation
How is the overall project progressing?	Overall project schedule
When is the phase supposed to end?	Scheduled completion of project phases
When are specific key activities supposed to be finished?	Specific schedule milestones established for high profile project activities or groups of activities
When should project customers expect to receive the deliverables?	Scheduled acceptance of significant project deliverables
How fast are expenditures supposed to be made?	Project cost cash-flow schedule
How good a job are we doing as a team?	Deliverable quality metrics
Does it look like we'll get that bonus?	Scheduled expectations for changes to specific measurable team/individual performance goals

Figure 10.1 Design Progress Expectations to Answer Anticipated Questions

Well-developed project cultures may have an established and comprehensive mechanism for doing this, such as an earned value reporting system or detailed project management software reporting. Less well-developed project cultures often use a project schedule Gantt chart to set and monitor progress expectations against the schedule. This method tends to illustrate only one part of the story, and leaves a lot of room for project teams to manipulate the appearance of progress.

The project charter, detailed project plans, and team/individual performance goals are the principal inputs for choosing progress expectations. They should anticipate and answer key questions (Figure 10.1 provides examples).

A summarized list of scheduled expectations offers simplicity and clarity and permits a dashboard approach to progress measurement. For example, Figure 10.2 (see next page) provides a simplified illustration of progress expectation highlights for a fictional aircraft design project. The expectations focus the attention of the project team and communicate progress up the chain of command. Summarized expectations do not replace the manager's detailed internal progress monitoring; instead, they provide a framework for conveying an overview of the progress. When printed for any one project, the list should be two pages or less, because a reader's attention frequently wanes by the second page!

Keeping Records

Records of completed work and accepted deliverables should be kept and compared against plans and performance goals to evaluate progress, identify variances, and eventually celebrate success.

Expectation/Milestone	Expected Value	Planned Date	Contact
Project plan approval	Complete	March 1st 2007	A. Ball
Master lines freeze	Complete	June 15th 2007	R. Wilson
Initial wing design	Complete	August 3rd 2008	R. Charlton
Initial fuselage design	Complete	July 27th 2008	N. Stiles
Initial systems design	Complete	November 1st 2008	G. Hurst
Component designs approved	300	June 1st 2007	R. Moore
	2000	December 1st 2007	R. Moore
	4000	May 17th 2008	R. Moore
	6000	October 1st 2008	R. Moore
	100%	November 1st 2008	R. Moore
Hours charged	100,000	March 6th 2007	G. Banks
	200,000	June 30th 2008	G. Banks
	270,000	November 1st 2008	G. Banks
QC changes per design	<2 changes	Ongoing	M. Peters
Average design approval time	<5 days	Ongoing	R. Hunt
Planned activities behind schedule	<5%	Ongoing	R. Moore
Overtime rate	<5% of total hours	Ongoing	G. Banks
Estimate at completion	$43,250,000	Ongoing	R. Moore

Figure 10.2 Summarized Program Progress Expectations

Data Collection and Processing

The degree of data collection depends on the degree of reporting and control required by the project manager, project sponsor, program manager, and management team. At minimum, five master lists should be maintained. These lists can be used to compare and record results as the project progresses.

- All planned work activities and their completion dates.
- All planned deliverables and their customer-acceptance dates.
- All planned expenditures and the amounts actually paid out.
- All problems and issues and their resolution dates.
- All change requests and their disposition/integration dates.

In most organizations today, sophisticated project management software is used to compile, manipulate, and report this information, but unfortunately many project personnel are not comfortable with these tools. For many smaller projects, simply keeping these lists on paper or in a spreadsheet can require considerably less effort and are still adequate for control and reporting purposes.

Deliverable Signoffs and Project Closing

For project deliverables, the project customer's formal acceptance and

Project Deliverables Sign-Off Sheet

Project Deliverable	Project WBS	Date Delivered	Customer Signature

Figure 10.3 Deliverables Signoff Sheet

signoff confirms that the work associated with the deliverable has been completed. It forces the customer to evaluate the deliverable against the stated requirements, other agreed-upon specifications, and previously unstated expectations. An example of a simple signoff sheet is illustrated in Figure 10.3.

Each project should be formally closed once the project customer has accepted all its deliverables. It is customary to review, document, and implement any lessons learned on the project as part of the project's closeout activities. Once the project is finally closed, its resources may be made available to other projects. For people, this usually means a return to home departments, but nonhuman resources like office space and equipment are usually made available for redeployment by the program team. When the program includes multiple waves of projects (as described in Chapter 5), the close of one project may be the trigger to begin another.

Managing Project Changes

Any decision that alters a project's charter or plan is a change. A project change modifies work or deliverables. Most of them have scope, schedule, or cost impacts because they modify specifications, add new tasks, agree to a later finish, or approve additional expenditures. All proposed changes should be formally reviewed, approved, and integrated into the plan. If they are not formally managed in this way, the team may trying to do something the plan doesn't call for. Such unnecessary work reduces progress in other areas.

Project changes may be requested for many reasons and by anyone involved or impacted by the project. Some of the most common changes are requested:

- As problems or issues emerge.
- As the true nature of the project and its deliverables is understood.
- As the program master schedule or funding priority is adjusted.

Sometimes, it may not be obvious that the action represents a project change. For example, RACI responsibilities may need to be modified, form designs may need to be altered, or rules may need to be adjusted.

Project change management can be an enormous issue for organizations with complex operational projects. They may have whole departments and budgets set aside to deal with it. As a result, their tools and processes may be too structured, overly complicated, and inappropriate for use on their strategic program. These types of methodologies may need to be scaled down for strategic projects.

Formal project changes can be the project manager's best friend—provided the change mechanism is not too onerous. Ideally, the change mechanism should allow the project manager to resist unimportant adjustments and reduce the volume of minor requests. It should ensure that control remains with the team, and that budgets and schedules are adjusted to accommodate additional work. Without formal change management, the team may be at the mercy of undocumented and everchanging expectations, be expected to do additional work without more time or resources, and have different understandings of what they are trying to achieve.

Strategic DNA Project—Change Request

To:　　　　(Project Manager)
From:　　　(Change Requestor)
CC:　　　　(Change Approval Authorities)
Date:

Discussion:
Narrative description of change and reason why it is necessary

Proposed Change to Scope

WBS	Scope Was	Scope Will Be
1.1.1		
1.1.2		
2.1.5		
4.5.3		

Expected Schedule Impact

WBS	Schedule Was	Schedule Will Be
1.1.1		
2.1.5		
4.5.3		
4.5.8		

Expected Cost Impact

WBS	Item	Cost Was	Cost Will Be
1.1.1			
2.1.5			
4.5.3			

Expected Contract Impact

Clause	Contract Was	Contract Will Be

Change Approvals

	Name	Signature	Date
Project Manager			
Other Approval Authority			
Project Sponsor			

Figure 10.4 Change Request Form

Change Requests

The most effective way to manage project changes is to document each suggested change with a standard change request form that is appropriately scaled to program needs and used by all the strategic projects. The form and its supporting attachments should define the suggested change in sufficient detail to support its review and potential approval. Figure 10.4 illustrates a basic change request form.

Change Orders

Once approved, the change request becomes a change order that dictates the project plan's modification. It either becomes an attachment to the existing project plan, or the plan is revised to include the content of the change order. This modifies the baseline against which progress is measured and makes the plan properly reflect the agreed-upon intention.

Program Changes and Strategic DNA *Changes*

Some changes may be identified that impact the overall program or even the design of the *Strategic DNA*. Program changes to the project priorities, portfolio waves, budgets, master schedule, and so on are addressed in this chapter in a manner similar to that used for project changes, but they may result in coordinated changes to multiple projects. Changes to the fundamental *Strategic DNA* are even more complex, as they may result in adjustments to the vision, strategy map, achievement targets, cascaded objectives, or any other component—as well as the entire program. These are addressed in Chapter 12, but the need for them may be identified and requested during this chapter.

Assessing Progress

Progress is assessed by comparing the data collected about actual progress to the expected progress anticipated in the plan. This identifies any variances that have not already been both explained and accommodated in the project plan and reveals problems and issues that remain to be addressed. The comparison looks for three types of variances:

- Failure of corrective actions performed to combat previously identified variances.
- Newly identified variances between actual results and planned results.
- Variances between forecast and planned results.

Var #	WBS	Variance Description	Identified Date	Problem or Issue	Corrective Action Plan	Disposition
001	1.2.4	Forecast at completion over budget by $15,000	1 Mar 2007	P4 and S3	S3	Cost baseline change approved (S3) and implemented
002	3.7.2	Research activity taking too long	4 Mar 2007	P5	P5	Corrected

Figure 10.5 Basic Variance Log

Variance Logs

Variances can be logged in a simple spreadsheet. As illustrated in Figure 10.5, the log can track the relationships between variances, the problems and issues that caused them, the corrective actions designed to resolve them, and their ultimate disposition. The log provides structure for project review meetings and other discussions.

Challenges—Problems and Issues

Analyzing variances identifies emerging problems or issues. It can be very helpful to think of problems and issues as two distinct challenges.

- A *problem* is a challenge that can be addressed using available resources. The project team can fix a problem by itself.
- An *issue* is a challenge that cannot be addressed without involving additional resources. The project team cannot fix an issue by itself and must secure external decisions, actions, and/or resources.

Impact Assessments

Impact assessment is analogous to the risk analysis performed during Chapter 8, but now that the project execution is underway, some of the risks may have turned into actual challenges, and additional risks may have emerged. When assessing their impact, apply the same analysis and response planning techniques described in Chapter 8.

The project team's expert judgment can often identify and explore new problems, issues, and risks, but sometimes structured risk analysis is needed. The analysis prioritizes problems and issues for their urgency and impact on the plan.

P/I #	WBS	Problem/Issue Description	Identified Date	Var #	Corrective Action Plan	Disposition
S3	1.2.4	Contract design labor rate higher than planned	1 Mar 2007	001	• Try to renegotiate rate • Request cost baseline change	Cost baseline change approved (S3) and implemented
P4	1.2.4	Contract design labor requirements may be too high			• See if we can reduce requirements • Decided not possible	Addressed by S3
P5	3.7.2	Research activity taking longer than expected because of very broad search requirements	4 Mar 2007	002	• See if search requirements are too broad • Revise search requirements	Corrected

Figure 10.6 Basic Problem and Issue Log

To justify expensive corrective actions, the project team may need a more detailed estimate of the problem or issue's impact on the deliverables, cost, and schedule. The project risk management discipline offers many specialized methods for evaluating problem/issue impact, including expected monetary values, decision trees, sensitivity analysis, and Monte Carlo simulations,[22] that can be adapted for use in these situations.

Once they have been fully explored, project problems and issues are documented and cross-referenced in the variance log to highlight areas where multiple variances are caused by the same problem or issue. A separate problem and issue log (see Figure 10.6 on previous page) may be maintained, or the variance log may be arranged so it can perform both functions.

Independent Reviews

For large or long projects, the plan should include one or more independent reviews. The review, which is conducted by a respected independent outsider, provides a sanity check of project progress and clarifies previously unclear or unknown problems and issues. It provides a fresh perspective for project teams who may no longer be able to see the forest because of all the trees they're trying to fix. Independent reviews are a particularly good idea for troubled projects.

The independent reviewer may not necessarily be an outside consultant, but ideally he or she should have not been involved in the project at any point. Independence is a key asset, because he or she does not have a predetermined opinion about the project, its plan, or its performance. An outside reviewer is generally more effective in highly politicized situations.

Taking Corrective Action

Once a problem or issue has been identified, corrective actions are planned to fix or mitigate its effects unless those effects can be accepted as part of a new reality. Most corrective actions are designed to address challenges that have caused actual variances, and they tend to be very reactive. They can be proactive if they are aimed at a forecasted variance or newly identified risk. The biggest danger comes when they are taken in desperation or panic. Significant corrective actions should not be planned, led, or performed by the people who feel the pain the most.

Corrective Action Plans

A corrective action plan is a short-term mini-project designed to address an identified problem or issue. Most of the time, corrective action plans can be described as a short list of tasks assigned to specific people with urgent deadlines. They can often be simply documented as meeting-minute action items that must be completed before the next scheduled meeting.

On very large projects, some corrective actions may be quite large. If they involve many tasks, or are not short term in nature, they are managed as a separate project, with proper plans, baselines, and controls.

Corrective Project Changes

Most problems and issues can be corrected by one-time interventions to eliminate or modify a root cause, but some eventually require that a project change be implemented to accommodate a new reality in the project plan.

Corrective Action Teams

In rare circumstances, innovative problem solvers may find themselves in a corrective action team (CAT) on a semipermanent basis. A CAT usually includes decision-empowered representatives from each involved department. It is established when the complexity and volume of corrective actions disrupt everyday operations.

Reporting Progress

Project and Program Progress Reports

The progress report is a *brief* document intended to provide the management team with an overview of project progress and any problems or issues that are ongoing. It is based on the planned performance highlights and issued by the project manager at regular intervals. A similar report is prepared for the program as a whole by compiling reports from each active strategic project.

The progress report format must be intuitive and easy to prepare. Progress reports are usually similar in design to operational reports, but they should be different enough to emphasize the unique priority of strategic projects. These are brief, succinct documents—ideally one or two pages long—with detailed supporting information available on request rather than automatically attached. The report includes the summarized information listed in Figure 10.7 on the following page.

Information	Why
Work completed during the last period including closed problems and issues	How far we've come and how many difficulties we've overcome
Summarized progress expectations met in the last period	Promises we've kept
Current value of key team/individual performance goals	Keep the carrot in sight
Project team progress recognition and rewards	Motivate team members
The number of planned project activities currently behind schedule	How late/early we really are
The total number of planned project activities not yet completed	How much remains to be done
The forecast project completion date and the planned completion date	How late/early we will ultimately be
The estimated cost at completion and the budgeted cost at completion	How much more/less it will ultimately cost
The number and highlights of problems and issues currently being worked	How many difficulties are being tackled
The number and highlights of changes approved in the last period	How much the project has changed
The number and highlights of changes currently in the approval process	How stable the project is
The project manager's explanatory notes and requests for support	The chance to ask for help or more resources

Figure 10.7 Progress Report Content

Don't Use Meeting Minutes

Project review meeting minutes are often used as progress reports because they are perceived as killing two birds with one stone. Unfortunately, meeting minutes rarely achieve both tasks adequately. They usually include confusing discussion notes that provide unnecessary, and potentially embarrassing, information, and they lack the statistics managers like to see. When minutes are repeatedly used as progress reports, project team members often resort to predistribution sanitization, which helps no one. Separating a proper progress report from the meeting minutes leaves the minutes dedicated to their real purpose: capturing and communicating discussions and decisions.

Personnel Performance Evaluations

Progress reporting provides staff evaluation systems with the necessary information to confer recognition. When a formal performance compensation system is being used, relevant evaluations are made for each performance evaluation period and at the end of the project. Progress reports provide an opportunity for the project manager to draw attention to outstanding work. As long as it's prudently done, these evaluations can positively impact motivation. Outstanding performance should always be recognized in the final project report.

Project Team Celebrations

The team celebration is a highly symbolic mechanism for reporting and recognizing progress. Many project teams only celebrate the ends of their projects, but celebrating the achievement of project phases or major deliverables can also be very effective. This may be as simple and inexpensive as a lunchtime pizza meeting.

How to Do It

The process outlined in the following steps provides a two-tier approach for controlling strategic projects and the overall *Strategic DNA* program. The first step is completed at the launch of projects for each wave. Steps 2, 3, and 4 are everyday project execution activities, and Steps 5 through 9 are *project* progress evaluation and reporting activities. Their repetition frequency is established by the reporting scheme (see Chapter 11). Steps 10 through 13 are *program* progress evaluation and reporting activities. The leadership team decides the frequency of their repetition.

1. Establish Progress Expectations

Who: Program Manager and Project Managers

Perform this first step for each of the projects and the program as a whole. Establish progress expectations by analyzing the project and program plans and consulting with the leadership team to ensure *key highlights* are included.

For projects, establish progress expectations by talking to the project sponsor, program manager, leadership team members, and other key team members. The project sponsor should have the final say about which expectations to report progress against.

Create a list of progress expectations that includes those of the individual projects and also the program's master schedule. This final list is usually the

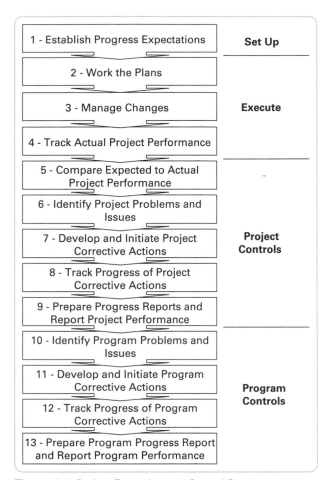

Figure 10.8 Project Execution and Control Process

result of a dialogue between the program manager and—depending on how the program has been organized—the CEO, the strategic quarterback, or the entire leadership team.

2. Work the Plans
Who: Program Team and Project Teams

As the activities defined in program and project plans proceed, they produce the tangible and intangible deliverables the projects were intended to create. These deliverables may be hard, such as products and documents, or soft, such as improved employee engagement.

Task	Who	Usual Forum
Request project changes	Project team members and other stakeholders	Change request form
Evaluate potential impact of change	Project team members	Request review meeting
Approval/refusal decision	Project manager and project sponsor	Change approval meeting
Change integration	Project manager and project team members	Project plan updates

Figure 10.9 Principal Project Change Tasks

3. Manage Changes
Who: Program Team and Project Teams

Project change management is an ongoing effort. In complex programs, it may even represent a separate process with dedicated resources and teams. It can be scaled up or down, but it typically involves performing the tasks described in Figure 10.9.

4. Track Actual Project Performance
Who: Project Manager

This step sets up a process for routinely recording successfully completed work and the customer's accepted deliverables. If project management software is used, the records of actual work completion are usually kept in its database. If not, the simplest manual method is to check off completed work activities and deliverables in a paper copy of the project plan; unfortunately, this method does not lend itself to manipulation for reporting. When not using project management software, keep an Excel spreadsheet list of the project activities, deliverables, and other progress expectations, with completion dates recorded in one of the columns.

5. Compare Expected to Actual Project Performance
Who: Project Manager and Project Team

This step formalizes the comparison of actual progress against the project plan. Routine analysis ensures that less intuitive variances are identified and daily analyses are substantiated with periodic formal comparisons—often in preparation for routinely scheduled project review meetings.

Some low-impact variances can be safely ignored, but most should be logged for further analysis and action. Maintain a separate log for these unless using a project management software that manages variances.

WBS	Project Activity	Planned Completion	Actual Completion	Schedule Variance	Cost Estimate	Actual Cost	Cost Variance
1.1	Lay Foundation	01-Sep-07	03-Sep-07	2	$4,100.00	$4,190.00	–$90.00
1.2	Build Frame	30-Sep-07	29-Sep-07	–1	$12,300.00	$13,200.00	–$900.00
1.3	Build Walls	15-Oct-07	18-Oct-07	3	$8,700.00	$8,100.00	$600.00
1.4	Install Windows/Doors	30-Oct-07	30-Oct-07	0	$16,550.00	$16,700.00	–$150.00
2.1	Paint	15-Nov-07	16-Nov-07	1	$4,450.00	$4,550.00	–$100.00

Total Cost Variance   –$640.00

Figure 10.10 Simple Progress Comparison in Microsoft Excel

Compare Actuals Against Plan

Evaluate whether project activities are being completed on schedule and budget. Project management software packages usually provide a report specifically designed to review actual completion against planned completion. If you are using Excel to track and compare, it is relatively simple to track progress and highlight actual variances (see example in Figure 10.10). Results shown in this way are readily understood.

Review Earlier Variance Corrections

Review the progress and impact of corrective actions that were initiated in previous periods. Have those actions had the desired effect? Has the previously identified variance been successfully addressed, or are additional corrective actions needed? Can the variance be closed out?

Successful completed corrective actions and the lessons learned from them should be closed, logged as closed, and remain closed. There is usually little to be gained from reopening old wounds, and there is much to be lost in the recurring embarrassment and discomfort of the people involved. Unless an earlier variance is being used to warn of an underlying trend, consign it to the historical file.

Identify New Variances

Next, identify newly discovered variances from the last reporting period. These usually result from the new actual data captured in Step 4, but they can also arise from earlier errors, counterproductive corrective actions, or the impact of newly approved changes to the plan. Most variances are identified by systematically comparing actual progress against the cost and schedule baseline. In some situations, scope variances appear when a project's product fails to achieve one of its specifications, usually resulting in a change. Add new variances to the log with references to any supporting information so corrective actions may be planned in Step 7.

Anticipate Forecast Variances

Anticipate future variances by looking at current trends that point to their future likelihood. This form of project risk identification looks ahead to reporting periods into the future and proactively corrects emerging variances. Nipping a problem in the bud this way is generally less expensive and time consuming than trying to correct a problem that has already developed. A useful rule of thumb is to look ahead about three reporting periods.

The team's ability to anticipate problems is usually a function of the depth of the performance data available for analysis. For example, organizations with work force time-tracking systems get an early warning when resource consumption exceeds expectations, but those without time-tracking measures may never discover that excess time was used. Even those that collect little data can anticipate delays.

This type of analysis is helped by looking at trends, by assessing whether targets are realistic, and most powerfully, by simply asking whether assigned resources and prerequisite deliverables will be in place at the new activity's start date.

6. Identify Project Problems and Issues

Who: Project Manager, Project Team, and, When Absolutely Necessary, the Project Sponsor and Program Manager

Regular project review meetings (see Figure 10.11) provide a structure for identifying problems, reviewing actual progress, providing positive feedback, discussing variances, and assigning corrective actions.

Discuss the variances logged in Step 5 to identify underlying root causes and quantify the impact these problems and issues might have on the project if they are not addressed.

Other problems and issues might also be identified or tabled by a team member without originating in the variance analysis. These often have a longer-term perspective—"If we

> **Project Review Meeting**
>
> **Sample Agenda**
>
> 1. Review and Recognize Planned Progress
> 2. Review Corrective Action Progress
> 3. Explore and Discuss New Variances
> 4. Explore and Discuss New Problems and Issues
> 5. Assign Impact Assessment Tasks
> 6. Schedule Corrective Action Planning Sessions

Figure 10.11 Sample Agenda for Project Review Meeting

don't address this problem now, we'll eventually get a variance." Some of the challenges identified are not certain to occur, and therefore, they may be considered new project risks. The probability of them occurring may be less than 100 percent, but some may have significant impact if they do come to pass.

> Program Review Meeting
>
> **Sample Agenda**
>
> 1. Review Progress on Each Project
> 2. Review and Recognize Overall Progress
> 3. Review Corrective Action Progress
> 4. Identify and Discuss New Problems and Issues
> 5. Assign Impact Assessment Tasks
> 6. Schedule Corrective Action Planning Sessions

Figure 10.12 Sample Agenda for Program Review Meeting

The final element of the review meeting is to assign people to assess the potential impact of the identified challenges and plan actions to correct them. These task assignments usually result in detailed discussions among smaller subgroups of the team. On smaller projects or ones with few challenges, the impact assessment and corrective action planning may be conducted during the review meeting.

Assess Impacts

Like the risks discussed in Chapter 8, the potential impact of variances, problems, and issues range from the insignificant to outright showstoppers. There are many approaches for assessing potential impacts, and the first task is to select the right approach, which may range from a straightforward judgment call to a detailed series of what-if scenarios using the project management software.

Avoid Having Sponsor Involved in Project Team's Review

Occasionally, the project sponsor may demand to be involved in the review meeting. This is understandable if the project is high profile or troubled, but the most common causes are far less reasonable—either a tendency to micromanage or a lack of trust of the project manager. Having the sponsor involved in the review undermines the authority of the project manager and should be avoided. The sponsor will be briefed on the outcome of the review meeting in Step 9.

Independent Project Reviews

Independent project reviews are either preplanned activities that provide reassuring second opinions or *ad hoc* activities initiated for troubled projects. For troubled projects, independent reviews are initiated by the project sponsor or the leadership team he reports to. Provide a clear terms of reference document to the independent reviewer and the project manager (unless the project manager wrote up the document in the first place).

Independent reviewers usually apply their own methodology, but the team should support the process. Explaining the real reasons for a troubled project review avoids a vote-of-no-confidence perception. Any recommendations made by the independent reviewer should, once approved by the sponsor, be included in the following corrective action planning step (Step 7).

7. Develop and Initiate Project Corrective Actions
Who: Project Team Led by Project Manager

Plan a series of corrective actions for each problem or issue. This corrective action planning session involves all who have a stake in the challenge. Corrective actions are frequently planned for all challenges in a single meeting that involves most of the core team. Hold dedicated working sessions for large or highly specialized challenges, or whenever outside people need to be involved in planning corrective actions for a particular issue.

Use the following questions to frame corrective action planning discussions and formalize discussion outcomes in a dedicated plan document, a change request, meeting minutes, or the problem log.

- What is the problem, why is it a problem, and how big is the variance?
- Can we mitigate or fix the problem, or should we change the project plan?
- What approaches could we try to mitigate or fix the problem?
- Which of the alternatives seem feasible?
- Which alternatives should we try first?
- Who needs to do what tasks, and in what sequence do they need to do them?
- Who will be the accountable leader for the action plan or for preparing the change request?
- When should each task be completed?

- Are any additional resources needed?
- What will be the impact of diverting those resources, and can we afford it?

8. Track Progress of Project Corrective Actions
Who: Corrective Action Leaders and Task Assignees

This step records the leadership, facilitation, and performance of the corrective action plan's tasks. Intervene when necessary to keep the correction on track, and be ready to report progress at subsequent project review meetings (see Step 6). Corrective action plans are usually very short-term undertakings, and the tracking may simply involve checking off each task as it is completed on a printed copy of the planning meeting minutes. Larger projects may produce corrective action plans that are substantial enough to be treated as a project in their own right. In that case, prepare a proper project plan and track its progress as if it were *one of the strategic projects*.

9. Prepare Progress Reports and Report Project Performance
Who: Project Managers

In many organizations, progress briefings are provided only when sponsors specifically request them. As a result, projects often make less progress than expected, and sponsors may feel that they only get informed when they express concern—which doesn't exactly instill confidence. Steer clear of this by communicating progress regularly and systematically in a standard format at predetermined intervals.

Avoid any temptation to eliminate the formal progress report. A brief progress report describes the project situation in terms of where the project should stand, where it actually stands, and what is being done to address the difference. The degree of detail and statistical content should be just enough to meet the recipient's expectations. Include notes on the progress report that anticipate questions, escalate issues, or request additional support. Review the report with the project sponsor and program manager before distributing it to the leadership team and other recipients.

Unless report recipients are geographically distributed, it is usually better to distribute the report as hard copy instead of as an e-mail attachment or web page. Delivering the paper provides a reason to meet each recipient face-to-face, giving the project a human face and providing an opportunity to discuss any outstanding points. E-mail is impersonal and frequently gets lost in inbox clutter, and attachments often remain unopened. Publishing the report to a Web page does not ensure the recipient will see it, and as a result, recipients may remain uninformed about things they need to know. Going to the trouble of personal delivery reinforces the document's value and ensures a communication exchange.

10. Identify Program Problems and Issues
Who: Program Team and Project Managers

This step, which mirrors the activity carried out for each project in Step 6, usually includes a routine program review meeting. It uses the same tools and methods but looks across all the projects in the program as a whole. The step starts with identifying program challenges by summarizing projects' problems and issues. Look for commonality and underlying trends, and document problems in a program problem log.

The program team may identify additional problems or issues. These are often related to balancing resources among the projects or measuring the impact of one project's challenges on another project. Occasionally, program problems are related to the cumulative impact of multiple projects on specific achievement targets, and some may even be related to the integration and coordination of *Strategic DNA* changes across multiple projects. Examples are provided in Figure 10.13.

Problem or Issue	Example
Cumulative effect of problems/issues on different projects	Overall program cost or schedule variance
Problems/issues common to multiple projects	Human resources are slow to provide new or reassigned people
Balancing resources across project portfolio	Delays in earlier project means something will have to be postponed to protect overall cash flow
	Redesign of one project means engineers can't be redeployed to other project
Impact between projects	Newly implemented software will not be ready to support forthcoming sales force re-engineering
Shared achievement targets being missed	Sales force growth, process training, and product rationalization projects are not producing quicker sales pipeline flow
Integrate Strategic DNA change	Decision to acquire competitor will have to be reflected in multiple project plans and coordinated

Figure 10.13 Typical Program Problems

11. Develop and Initiate Program Corrective Actions
Who: Program Team

Perform this step using the same method the project teams followed in Step 7. Hold corrective-action planning sessions to address identified problems or issues. Produce program change requests and corrective-action plans, and assign tasks. Project managers affected by the challenge should participate in the planning sessions for two reasons: to ensure corrective actions work for their projects, and to commit their resources to work on the tasks.

12. Track Progress of Program Corrective Actions
Who: Corrective Action Leaders and Task Assignees

As in Step 8, perform, track, and facilitate corrective actions and report them at subsequent review meetings.

13. Prepare Program Progress Report and Report Program Performance
Who: Program Manager

In this last step of the repeating project execution and control cycle, prepare a program progress report similar to the project report from Step 9. Compile the report using the project reports, a problem/issue log, and program review meeting minutes. The main difference between the program and project versions of the report is that the program report provides a very high-level overview of each project's progress. Project progress reports may be attached as appendices to the program progress report.

Deliver the progress report to the CEO and the leadership team in person, before anyone else sees it. Many CEOs prefer to be briefed privately before the update meeting, so they will be prepared to perform an appropriate role in the meeting. Schedule update meetings routinely just before distributing the progress report.

Summary

The *Strategic DNA* implementation gathers momentum as this chapter keeps the organization's attention energized on planned actions. Now that the projects are underway, activity is systematically monitored and proactive interventions are made where needed.

11

Results Realization Measurement
Are We There Yet?

F YOU'RE NOT GOING TO ROUTINELY MEASURE AND COMMUNICATE results, there really isn't any point in establishing objectives and targets in the first place! Periodic measurement gives leaders early warning about flaws in their hypotheses, so their plans can be adjusted. It lets them see if good things are starting to happen, and if objectives are being achieved. Many organizations don't see the signs of impending disaster because they're not even looking for them.

In Chapter 10, the progress of the strategic projects was monitored for work realization and production of deliverables. This process measures the realization of results for the individual projects but in many cases, project results do not reveal whether the *Strategic DNA* objectives are actually being achieved. In a perfect world, it should be possible to design projects that directly drive relevant performance metrics toward their achievement targets. Unfortunately, in practice, strategies often depend on a hypothesis to turn those project results into strategic results—such as the hypothesis that a "successful" surgery would save a patient's life. Therefore, in addition to giving credence to Chapter 10's project measurement efforts (the surgery's results), it is also necessary to monitor the strategic performance metrics (the patient's vital signs) to find out if hypotheses are being confirmed.

For example, management may believe that providing a sales force with more extensive training earlier will improve sales of new products in their first six months. Perhaps the training project was successful, and the sales force was properly trained before the products' launch, but did that really result in improved sales during the products' first six months?

Unfortunately, even organizations that do monitor results often collect and analyze far too many metrics. They lose sight of the specific answers they need because key information is obscured by an overwhelming clutter of unimportant data. The challenge is to gather and analyze just enough performance data to reveal answers to specific questions about the strategy's progress. Results realization measurement should not be allowed to become a research project!

One Size Doesn't Fit All

Result realization measurement methods vary greatly depending on what industry, strategy, and metric is being measured, so it is impossible to develop a universal approach. Many industries have developed methods to suit their particular environment, such as statistical process control in manufacturing, community perceptions and crime statistics in policing, economic value-added in financial services, and capability model maturity integration in software systems. These methods should have been reflected in the metrics you selected in Chapter 3 but, whatever the focus, the metrics still must be measured, the data must be transformed into usable information, and the information must be communicated to those who need to know about it; this chapter describes a general approach.

Why Do It?
To Provide Intelligence Information

The gathering and analysis of achievement target data produces information about the progress of the strategy. This information can then be provided to various levels of management and employees to guide their actions and decision making.

To See If the Strategy Is Being Successful

The primary motivation for monitoring strategic results is to see if the strategy is successful: Even if the *Strategic DNA* program and its projects are progressing according to plan, is the plan actually moving the organization toward its vision? It is too easy for people to confuse successful progress with successful achievement. A project may look and feel successful, but the real situation can only be understood after progress is measured and communicated against achievement targets. Will the patient survive?

To Avoid Surprises

Deep down, all managers love predictability. If a situation can be predicted confidently, management can concentrate its resources in the right place (correcting predicted underperformance) instead of wasting them in the wrong places (areas that don't need correction). In the same vein, managers hate embarrassing surprises, especially when they know the problem could have been addressed if they'd had sufficient warning. Strategy realization surprises can usually be avoided by concentrating on metrics that indicate future success or validate strategic hypotheses.

To Identify Questionable Hypotheses

Reviewing achievement target progress permits analysis of whether strategic hypotheses are being proven or brought into question by actual results. Overall, a strategy is built around a large number of hypotheses, each of which may or may not be correct. The principal hypotheses are the relationships among objectives, which are documented as connections on the strategy map and phrases in the strategy narrative.

Many other hypotheses may also be implied throughout the *Strategic DNA* lifecycle wherever managers make assumptions or decisions (e.g., the scale or timing of achievement targets, the business-unit allocations of shared targets, the size of the project portfolio, or the skill level of people assigned to a project). With so many management hypotheses capable of influencing success, the early identification of questionable ones is a necessary first step for a continuously improving strategic program.

To Initiate Adjustments to the Strategy and Program Plan

Tactically, the main reason for measuring results realization is to take corrective action when reality does not meet expectations. Organizations that fail to do so are usually completely surprised when their strategies suddenly fall apart. Those that measure results realization can anticipate emerging problems and can usually adjust their plans to compensate for such developments. Their continuously improving strategies never fail suddenly, and rarely fail completely.

To Reinforce Desired Objectives and Behaviors

Measuring results realization reinforces the objectives and desired behaviors. The use of measurement to motivate behavior, which was discussed in Chapter 3, is one of the principal reasons to have achievement targets. Their purpose is invalidated if an organization fails to measure and communicate the results actually produced by everyone's hard work.

Routine measurement and reporting continuously reminds people of their targets and encourages them to focus their energies in the right place. This continuous pressure—even if it is very gentle or only implied—positively modifies employee behavior. Failing to provide this constant reminder can result in achievement targets that are hidden behind everyday concerns, where they lose their importance and ultimately are forgotten as "last year's problem."

To Calculate Rewards and Consequences

Chapter 9 stressed the rewards scheme's value for setting expectations and mobilizing the work force. Rewards cannot be calculated or delivered to workers unless the realization of results is measured. Being provided with a goal, doing their best to achieve it, and then receiving neither reward nor consequence is terribly demoralizing to workers, particularly if it's all because management never got around to measuring the results!

Rewards close the loop for the diligent worker. When they strive to achieve management's goals, they are rewarded for their additional efforts. In turn, they derive satisfaction from seeing underperforming colleagues receive less—and rightly so.

To Build Credibility
To Demonstrate That Management Is Walking the Talk

Many management teams could benefit from increased credibility among employees, owners, and other stakeholders. This is especially true in situations when performance management is being implemented for the first time, or in situations where leaders have a track record of not walking the talk. In both cases, management can demonstrate their commitment by measuring the results that have been produced so far, communicating those results, and acting appropriately.

To Demonstrate the Value of the Strategy and the Strategic DNA Program

Clear communication of results demonstrates the value of the overall program to its stakeholders. This demonstration is especially important during the first implementation lifecycle in larger organizations that subsequently intend to cascade the Strategic DNA approach to their business units. Visible progress convinces people that the program is worth implementing on a larger scale: "It's working over there, so I can't wait to do it here, too!"

What to Do
Establish Management Report Scheme and Formats

Results realization measurement is most valuable when people who need to know about actual performance know about it early enough to take appropriate actions.

Management reports should provide appropriate and timely information to the right people. If a report provides too much information—especially about things its reader doesn't need to know—it confuses the message, creates work that adds no value, and can lead to important information being overlooked or ignored. It is extremely difficult (if not impossible) to provide each reader with a report tailored to his or her individual needs. But with careful thought, it is possible to design a scheme of focused, tailored, and concise report formats that provide meaningful and consistent information to management decision makers.

Information, Not Data

Reports should provide meaningful information, and not simply raw data. It is usually enough to provide five pieces of information about a performance metric:

- The target value for the current reporting period
- The actual value for the current period
- Any shift in variances over previous periods
- Explanatory notes from the metric's owner
- Existing corrective actions that are currently being pursued

Providing more information than this encourages data-diving, time-wasting, and micromanaging behaviors. It can also lead to an excessive focus on unchangeable historical data that is nothing more than crying over spilt milk.

Explanatory notes help a reader digest the information by explaining assumptions and constraints that frame the underlying data. The notes identify any unexpected factors that have influenced results and explain what the information means for the business and its strategy.

Reporting Scheme

The reporting scheme establishes overall reporting standards, including distribution and confidentiality philosophies, preferred media, update intervals, and so on (i.e., who, what, when, and where). It provides a framework and guidelines for the design of report formats and processes, and considerably reduces unnecessary and iterative discussions during their development. The reporting scheme accommodates the reporting expectations, communication goals, and rewards scheme for all organizational levels. It also establishes the scope and frequency of progress review meetings.

Some organizations prefer management reports to be broadly available online and in real time, but that may result in an information overload for staff. Others prefer to keep many reports restricted to hard copy only. Doing so makes it easier to keep information confidential and also increases the information's value, particularly when it is delivered in a personalized way. Unfortunately, a downside of hard-copy reporting is that in some cases, people who need the information never get it. The method of distribution should be tailored to each report's content, frequency, and purpose.

Multilevel cascaded strategies introduce another layer of complexity to

Report Type	Contents	Frequency	Distribution
Annual report	• Corporate thrust metrics • Divisional thrust metrics • Selected corporate performance metrics • Selected divisional performance metrics	Annual (January 1st)	Shareholders, all staff
Mid-year review	• Corporate thrust metrics • Divisional thrust metrics • All corporate performance metrics • All divisional program review reports	Annual (July 1st)	Strategy owner, board, division heads, and program team
Progress update (compensation system)	• All relevant performance metrics	Semi-annual	All variable compensation staff
Corporate overview	• Divisional thrust metric trends • Corporate thrust metric trends	Quarterly	Strategy owner, board, division heads, and program team
Corporate program	• Corporate thrust metrics • All corporate performance metrics	Monthly	Strategy owner, board, division heads, and program team
Division overview	• Division thrust metrics • Division financial & customer performance metrics	Quarterly	Strategy owner, division head, division leaders, project sponsors, and program team
Division program review	• All division performance metrics • All division project progress reports	Quarterly	Division head, division leaders, project sponsors, and program team
Thrust update	• Thrust metric • Thrust performance metrics	Monthly	Thrust owner, involved managers, involved project sponsors, and program team
Project impact review	• Related performance metrics • Project progress report	Monthly	Thrust owner, project sponsor, project manager, project team, and program team
Project portfolio progress	• Selected project progress metrics	Weekly	Project sponsors, project managers, and program team

Figure 11.1 Management Reports for Cascaded Strategic DNA Programs

the reporting scheme—a need to combine results realized across business-unit strategies for use at the corporate level. For example, monthly business-unit staff turnover results may need to be consolidated into a quarterly corporate report. Software automation should be used for such complex schemes. Figure 11.1 provides an example.

Tabular Scorecard Reports

The most popular report is a simple table that presents key information

Strategic DNA Quarterly Management Report

Thrust 4 – Sales Growth   **Period**: May 2007

Performance Results

Performance Metric	Targets		Actual Result	Notes
	End	Current		
Net Profit	$153M	$104M	$91M	Delays to launch of Super Widget product
Average Transaction Margin	22.0%	16.0%	14.2%	Assumptions re logistics cost/price ratio appear optimistic
Manufacturing Cost/Price	11.0%	18.0%	18.5%	Plant recalibration project expected to accelerate improvement
Average Rework Cost Per Unit	$2.25	$4.25	$4.16	
Employee Engagement	87	74	63	Data from Feb 07 Survey

Key Trends

PROFIT

MFG COST/PRICE

Figure 11.2 Basic Management Report

for each metric. The table is used as a scorecard to provide an at-a-glance overview of results realized in specific areas of the *Strategic DNA*. Scorecards can be produced for each level of the *Strategic DNA* that provide drill-down capability, even in the absence of a sophisticated information system. However, Herculean Excel[23] efforts are required if reporting software is not used. Many measurement implementations have relied on this method during their initial cycles. Figure 11.2 (see previous page) provides an example of a formal performance scorecard.

Scorecards may have many blank spaces when first introduced because either interim targets have not been set or actual performance data is not available. There is a natural tendency for reporting staff to modify the format to eliminate blank metrics, thereby avoiding uncomfortable questions from report recipients. Vigorously resist this tendency, as visibility of the blanks encourages leaders to force targets to be set and to collect actual data.

Charts and Diagrams

Charts and diagrams are a popular method for presenting performance data. Although they may take longer to set up than tabular scorecards, they usually take little time to update each period, lend themselves to automation, and communicate information very clearly. Choosing the wrong type of chart or calibrating the axes incorrectly can emphasize the wrong information, and you might miss important performance insights as a result. A chart that implies more accuracy than the data can really support can also be very misleading. Figure 11.3 explains the most common types of charts.

When choosing the type of chart, consider the audience, what it will use the information for, the message the chart is intended to convey, and the appropriate distribution media.

Figure 11.4 provides an example of a well-chosen chart type. The chart describes how many retail stores in each geographic region exceeded, met, or failed to meet sales targets in a given period. The stacked vertical bar provides a crisp overview of the information.

Business Intelligence Software and Dashboards

Performance measurement processes need to be defined and refined before they are automated. Premature automation is a common reason why strategic performance projects fail. In the last ten years, many business

Chart Type	Typical Usage
Histograms	How frequently each value occurs during a single reporting period; communicates patterns of variation
Pareto	A histogram organized to indicate the order of importance of the values being presented
Pie	Contributions made by different components of a whole at a single time or during a single reporting period
Vertical bar	How values change over time
Stacked vertical bar	How values and their constituent components change over time or by group
Vertical line	How a group of values (or several groups) change over a longer time period
Horizontal bar	Comparison of values at a single time or during a single reporting period
Clustered bar	How groups of related values change over several reporting periods
Scatter diagram	Relationships between the two variables plotted on each axis; very useful for exploring relationship insights.
Control charts	The quality and repeatability of results produced by a process; variations of the control chart can illustrate averages, counts, ranges, nonconformities, subgroups, standard deviations, time, proportions, and rates

Figure 11.3 Common Types of Charts and Diagrams

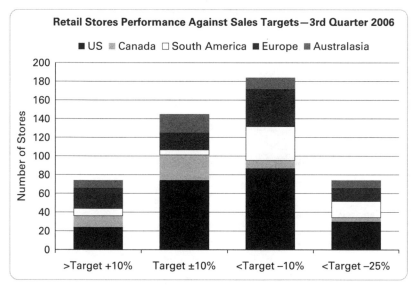

Figure 11.4 Stacked Bar for Groups

intelligence systems have been introduced that are available as modules within enterprise-wide business systems or as modestly priced standalone solutions. These products provide managers with high-level dashboards that oversee performance and allow them to drill down in particular areas of interest. In the right hands, they provide consistent reports and charts while delivering highly flexible, *ad hoc* reporting. In the wrong hands, they consume large amounts of effort to set up and maintain, dazzle micromanagers with a world of fascinating minor details, overwhelm staff with volumes of information, obscure the effects of disconnected decisions and actions, and—perhaps most importantly—distract leaders from the real issues.

Many business intelligence systems are capable of drawing data from any operational database. When selecting business intelligence software, review the alternatives against comprehensive requirements. Simply extending existing integrated operational systems to manage the strategy may be the wrong decision. It could make it more difficult to one day adopt a strategy that replaces those existing operational systems. The right solution is one that most closely satisfies the complete requirements.

Develop Measurement Processes

Before any measurement and analysis can be performed, a process (see Figure 11.5) must be developed to gather and treat the data and communicate the resulting information for each performance metric identified in Chapter 3 (also Chapter 4 for cascaded strategies). Each metric may require a unique process, but they are normally repeated variations of a short list of boilerplate processes. Factors to consider when designing measurement processes include:

- Data sources and data collection
- Calculation algorithms
- Measurement and reporting frequencies
- Measurement responsibilities and accountabilities

Process Stage	Work
Gathering	Collecting data from their sources, standardizing their formats and units of measure, and entering them into a form or computer tool
Validating	Reviewing the entered data to identify data collection or entry errors and validate the data makes sense (the sanity test)
Treating	Compiling multiple data elements together and applying the calculation algorithm
Identifying	Assessing the information, comparing it against expected results and explaining any variances caused by the measurement process
Communicating	Compiling information into management reports, distributing reports to those who need the information, and confirming the information has been received and reviewed by those individuals
Analyzing and reacting (Chapter 12)	Reviewing management reports, interpreting the meaning of the information, assessing variances not caused by the measurement process, deciding where action is needed, and then taking those actions

Figure 11.5 Typical Measurement Process Stages

- Audit mechanisms
- Measurement process implementation

Data Sources and Data Collection

The data needed to produce performance metric information is usually collected from a variety of sources. It is rarely available in a single form (or media). Data may have to be manually entered, captured directly from operational systems, transferred from networked storage, or calculated from other data before being combined into meaningful information. The procedures for collecting data from their sources vary greatly and can rarely be fully automated. Even the highest performing organizations use manual methods until processes are stable enough for automation. This avoids investment in measurement technologies until methods are proven and an acquisition specification can be written from an informed perspective.

Business intelligence software makes the combination of data from multiple sources much easier through data warehouses, user-defined reporting tools, and vendor-neutral data exchange formats, such as ODBC. These technologies are available for companies of all sizes, but larger organizations may find they already have them in their toolkit.

Calculation Algorithms

Unless it is already available in raw data form, each performance metric needs a calculation algorithm or formula. The algorithm consists of a set of well-defined mathematical functions organized into a procedure that calculates an output from a specific set of inputs. Many algorithms are clear, absolute, and readily agreed upon by the stakeholders concerned (e.g., "sales in dollars divided by number of products delivered equals average product sale price"), but many may be open to debate (e.g., how should "sales per employee" count temporary and subcontractor employees, or employees who leave halfway through the period?).

Measurement and Reporting Frequencies

Measurement frequencies should be appropriate to the metric being measured, as not all things need to be measured at the same intervals. Some should be measured daily, while others should be updated quarterly or annually. There are several considerations when selecting the most appropriate interval for a performance metric.

- The frequency the data will actually be available.

- The cost of measuring and calculating it.
- The interval before significant changes would become apparent.
- The frequency with which management reviewers would like to see it.
- The achievement target intervals established in Chapter 3.

The reporting frequency for a metric may be quite different from its measurement frequency. For example, "sales per day" data may be collected on a daily basis, but only reported as an average in a monthly report. Translating measurement frequencies into reviewer-friendly information in this way is a simple example of how data can be turned into information.

Reporting frequencies are designed to reveal warning signs early enough to take necessary action, but they shouldn't be so frequent that they are distracting. As a general rule, higher-level managers need reports less frequently. However, specific reports may be needed more frequently. For example, an executive who is sponsoring several projects aimed at a specific objective may wish to review the objective's performance metric with the project managers on a monthly basis.

Measurement Responsibilities and Accountabilities

The measurement process identifies responsibilities and accountabilities for gathering, validating, and treating data, and for analyzing, communicating, and reacting to the information it generates. Preliminary responsibilities established in Chapter 3 may need to be adjusted once the measurement process for each metric becomes clearer. The preliminary owner assigned to lead the design of the metric is replaced by an appropriate operational owner at this stage.

Audit Mechanisms

Establish an audit mechanism that periodically tests the quality of the process and the information it produces to increase confidence in the performance metric. The audit mechanism's method, scale, and frequency depends on several factors:
- Data reliability
- Quality controls
- The metric's importance
- The information's significance at a given time

The most rigorous method is a formal audit by an independent third party.

Measurement Process Implementation

Once they are defined, the processes and reporting formats must still be implemented before they produce information. This implementation is usually managed as a discrete strategic project. Because it enables the systematic review of performance, it is urgent enough to be included in the first wave.

The process implementation project may be large in scope and may be expensive, particularly if it involves the simultaneous introduction of new software. It typically involves people from many business units and departments and requires strong support from the organization's information technology department. Much of what the project seeks to accomplish may require going into unknown territory, so it's usually prudent to conduct a limited-scope pilot before the full-scale attempt is launched.

Strategic Performance Variance Identification

With the measurement process producing data, it becomes possible to pinpoint variances between actual performance and the expectations of the interim achievement targets. Even assuming the projects have been progressing as planned, you must still find out if the measured results reached their interim targets and if the objectives are being achieved.

Management reports identify all three aspects of the variance needed for the analysis, change identification, and action planning in Chapter 12.

- Is there a performance gap?
- Is there a performance trend?
- Are there any assumptions, constraints, or unexpected developments in the measurement process that might explain it?

Strategic Performance Gap (Variance) Identification

A performance variance, which is often called a gap, can be either bad (a shortfall) or somewhat good (a surplus). Surpluses are relatively rare and usually not problematic, but in some cases they may be time consuming and unexpectedly costly (for example, Sony Corporation's surplus of sales orders for its PlayStation 3). Both types of variances are identified for later analysis.

The basic method for analyzing whether strategic performance is progressing as expected is comparing actual results against expected results for the reporting period. This reveals any gaps and provides management with an opportunity to take corrective action when necessary. The gap identification can be readily automated with user-friendly reporting highlights (e.g., green ticks and red crosses).

Gap identification relies on both the interim targets set in Chapter 3 and the actual data collected in this chapter. In the absence of either, the management report shows a blank or error message, and no later analysis will be possible.

Strategic Performance Trend (Relative) Identification

A performance trend is revealed by plotting actual performance over several reporting periods. Once the information is available for several periods, every performance metric can be said to have a trend; they are typically of little value until at least three periods have elapsed.

However, it is not enough to simply measure whether achievement is improving. It is also essential to identify whether it is improving *as much as it needs to*. It is quite common to find that although a metric's performance may be improving, the gap is actually deteriorating. This relative trend matters most when you are analyzing the strategic performance.

Trends may be expressed in many ways depending on what is being measured (e.g., improving, deteriorating, early, late, overachieving, or underachieving), but changing trends usually offer the most opportunity for management action to make a difference. That's because a changing trend may indicate the relative success of earlier actions or new factors that must be addressed. For example, when the performance of sales against targets that had previously been improving begins deteriorating, managers can analyze the root causes and take action to stop the deterioration.

Measurement Explanations

Management naturally attempts to correct variances included on reports (Chapter 12). Since these can be caused by the measurement process, they should be questioned before the reports are distributed; otherwise, they could be a total waste of time. Process-induced variances can be caused by invalid assumptions, unanticipated constraints, or some other new development.

The Excel Hero

The amount of work involved in measuring and reporting results is often unclear during the first implementation of the *Strategic DNA* approach. The work may eventually become the responsibility of an existing support function (e.g., information technology or finance) or even a dedicated performance-measurement department, but leadership teams generally expect the program team to perform this work initially.

In practice, one member of the program team takes on the critical, thankless, and complex task of coordinating the participants, gathering data, processing it into information, and reporting the results. The copious spreadsheets this team member produces may result in him or her becoming known as an "Excel Hero." The Hero's star shines brightly until the overwhelming workload forces him or her to burn out or leave. The Excel Hero is only a temporary measure, and leaders are wise to not depend on them for too long.

How to Do It

The results realization measurement process outlined in the following steps produces various management reports at routine intervals. Their formats, intervals, and distribution are driven by their purpose. Steps 1 through 3 design the reporting scheme and the processes to measure and report the results. Steps 4 through 7 validate and refine the designs, and Steps 8 through 12 represent the routine measuring and reporting of realized results.

Responsibilities for each step typically vary depending on an organization's size and culture. Some may create dedicated performance-measurement departments, and others might initially depend on an Excel Hero. Because the program team usually performs these activities during the first implementation, this model is used in the generic process below.

1. Develop Reporting Scheme and Frequencies
Who: Program Team Validated by the Leadership Team

This step depends on the media chosen to communicate results. Widespread communication demands broadcast (e.g., a website or video) or digital (e.g., application software) automation, while confidential or limited communication requires secure software, paper, or in-person media.

Reporting Scheme Development

Define the reporting scheme through discussions with selected leaders—especially the strategy owner and the thrust owners. The scheme should reflect their expectations: what do they want to see, how often they want to see it, who else should see it, and so on.

Build a draft scheme using the interim target intervals, master schedule, mobilization program, and variable compensation schemes as overall guides. Use the draft scheme to guide validation discussions with the leadership team.

Establish Desired Reporting Frequencies

Reporting frequencies become clear during scheme development discussions and are typically preset to calendar intervals (e.g., quarterly overviews, monthly updates, and weekly progress reports). Ensure that the desired frequency is clearly defined and documented for each performance metric and its constituent data elements. This ensures that the frequency of measurement is directly related to reporting expectations for each metric and is consistent with interim target intervals, measurement processes,

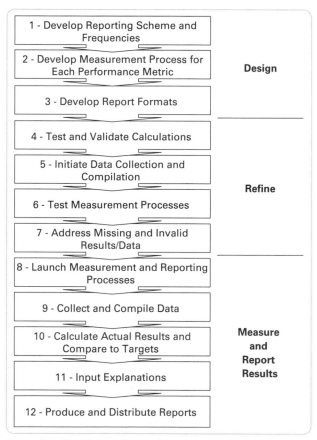

Figure 11.6 Results Realization Measurement Process

management reports, compensation schemes, the mobilization program, and the master schedule. It keeps the cost of measurement under control by ensuring that each metric is neither measured too often nor too frequently.

2. Establish Measurement Process for Each Performance Metric
Who: Program Team

Perform this step for each performance metric destined to appear on management reports. This includes all the metrics identified in Chapter 3 and may also include selected project metrics identified in Chapters 8 and 10. In practice, processes for related metrics can usually be defined simultaneously, and similar types of metrics may use the same basic process with the addition of tailored data sources and calculation algorithms.

Seek advice and agreement from the metric's owners, the information's expected users, the people responsible for producing the performance that is being measured, the people responsible for the source data, and the information systems staff who must provide or process the data.

The work is often so extensive that it needs to be organized, managed, and resourced as one of the strategic projects. The amount of work involved in this step depends on the following factors:

- Number of metrics to be measured
- Desired frequency of measurement
- Quantity of data elements needed to calculate each metric
- Number and type of sources for the data
- Proportion of data sourced externally
- Trustworthiness of the data
- Complexity of the calculations
- Methods chosen to process data into information

For smaller efforts, assign a team member to lead the measurement process design. That person can then convene working meetings with all involved parties to flesh out the details.

Inconsistencies occasionally become apparent between the frequency that the measurement process can produce the information and the desired intervals established in Step 1. If the measurement process is expensive, it may not be cost effective to report it frequently. Identify and resolve these inconsistencies before the process is implemented to avoid costly modifications later.

Assign responsibilities to individuals or department managers for the process stages identified in Figure 11.5 (at minimum). This may have been included in the resource assignments in Chapter 6, but if not, responsibilities should be assigned within the measurement process. Although some of the stages can be automated through information technology, specific people still need to be responsible for them.

3. Develop Report Formats
Who: Program Team Validated by the Leadership Team and Report Users

Develop draft formats for each report required by the scheme (e.g., Thrust 1 Summary Report). The initial decision is whether to use a scorecard, one or more charts, or a predefined dashboard view to present the data. This is driven by the reporting scheme, the report's intended purpose, and the technologies that are available. Once that decision has been made, a format can be drafted and validated in discussions with involved leaders and intended users. Report formats should include the basic results realization information, highlighted results where analysis and action may be needed, and provisions for additional explanations.

4. Test and Validate Calculations
Who: Program Team or Information Systems Department

Test the calculations by implementing the algorithm and producing real information for each performance metric. Doing this in an information system requires interconnecting the data sources and programming mathematical formulae into the system. Doing it manually (or semimanually using Excel) requires physical data gathering and calculations. In either case, this step may become large and expensive if many metrics are involved. Control costs by building and testing complex calculations in a low-cost format, such as Excel. Once proven, the calculations can be implemented in more costly systems that make the information more widely available.

The principal aims of the test are to validate that the algorithm produces the correct results and that the technology works. Once the results pass this sanity test, the algorithm may be incorporated into the final reporting system. If the metrics have never previously been measured, the test will also produce a performance baseline.

In a typical environment, coordinated efforts are needed to test and implement the calculation algorithm. Operational people will produce the data and validate calculation results, systems people will carry out data collection and calculation functionality, and metric owners and report users will confirm they can work with the output. Consult the metric owners if the calculation provides first-time information to find out if the achievement targets are now unrealistic.

5. Initiate Data Collection and Compilation
Who: Program Team or Its Excel Hero

This step is not always necessary, especially in cases when source data is being collected and results are being calculated. However, it is always necessary when measurement processes include manual activities, or data gaps have to be filled. This process may involve counting, subjective analysis, surveys, and so on. Coordinate with operational managers to ensure their staff performs the work with the required frequency. When manually compiling multiple data sources, initiate a scheduled procedure to bring together the data from the various sources.

6. Test Measurement Processes
Who: Program Team

Next, it's critical to test the processes to ensure they can produce the management reports. Perform a dry run for each report in the scheme, which may require coordination of many people's activities and a review of technology performance. Try to avoid the temptation to skip this step and go straight to report production and distribution. This may be a viable alternative for small-scale implementations, but for complex, large-scale ones, there will be many first-time errors. Running a proper test allows problems to be fixed before the broader community sees the results. Failing to do this can erode confidence in the measurement processes and demoralize employees whose compensation may depend on them.

7. Address Missing and Invalid Results/Data
Who: Leadership Team Led by the Program Team

The dry run highlights performance metrics with unavailable or invalid results. Most of these errors are caused by a lack of availability of source data elements. Others are caused by mistakes in the calculation algorithm or measurement process that did not become apparent during the earlier calculation testing. A few will be because underlying assumptions were flawed.

If source data is absent, renew efforts to make it available, preferably before the reports are launched. Reports with blank fields can still be launched to focus management's attention on the need to make the absent data available. Unless the reports are intended for use outside the organization, there are few circumstances where it would be beneficial to change the report simply to eliminate the blanks.

If mistakes exist, correct or adjust the measurement process so reports are as accurate as possible. Use relationships with the leadership team to ensure everyone treats this debugging effort as a high priority. Leaders will be less informed about the progress of their strategy without it!

If there are flawed assumptions, the test results have brought the measurement's logic into question. This is a valid learning experience, as your results are showing that you're measuring the wrong things. Summarize these results and their meaning and present them to the leadership team so they can modify the achievement targets or, if appropriate, select a different performance metric altogether. Take care when deciding to change a performance metric, as doing so can call into question the projects, budgets, resource assignments, and so on that may have been derived from the original metric. This type of change should be managed using the *Strategic DNA* change described in Chapter 12.

8. Launch Measurement and Reporting Processes
Who: Program Team

Measurement processes may be launched into production once they have been tested and debugged (to the extent possible in the available time.) Don't wait until the reports are perfect before launching them, because it can take months to address all the challenges. However, make sure the reports are meaningful and valid before launch.

The launch makes the collection, compilation, calculation, comparison, and communication of strategic results a routine recurring activity for all involved. Steps 9 through 12 describe the main activities for distributing them at routine scheduled intervals.

9. Collect and Compile Data
Who: Program Team and Operational Staff

This recurring step is the operationalization of the work done for the first time in Step 5. In fully automated processes, the data is collected by various operational information systems and then compiled by a business intelligence system. In manual processes, the data is collected by the operational staff responsible for it or by the program team itself.

10. Calculate Actual Results and Compare to Targets
Who: Program Team (Excel Hero) and Operational Staff

In this recurring step, calculate actual results using the algorithms tested in Steps 4 and 6 and compare them against the achievement targets set in Chapter 3. The work may be done manually or automatically, but in initial cycles, a hybrid approach is often adopted that uses Microsoft Excel or equivalent tools. The program team will again shoulder this burden until it can be assigned to appropriate operational staff.

In the hybrid approach, the targets are maintained in one table and actual data is loaded into a separate table as it becomes available. At predetermined intervals, the actual data is used to calculate the results for comparison against the appropriate target. Present the results in a previously established format (e.g., an Excel spreadsheet or chart). This task creates Excel Heroes, as the quality of the results relies on those Heroes' personal determination.

The comparisons reveal any variances—whether good or bad—and allow trends to be observed. To identify whether the expectations are being achieved, compare the actual performance trend to the expected trend codified in the interim achievement targets. This way, management can judge whether performance is improving *enough*.

11. Input Explanations
Who: Program Team and Operational Managers (Explainers) Responsible for Performance

In Chapter 12, the actual results, variances, and trends will be reviewed by the management team. This step provides additional input for that evaluation.

Let explainers know when results significantly deviate from the targets, thus giving them the opportunity to input their explanations. In fully automated implementations, this can be accomplished through messaging or responsibility coding, but unfortunately, leaders tend to review results before explanations are posted.

Avoid making excuses, because it won't help management's assessment of the variance. Focus explanations by providing additional information that can help decision makers avoid taking inappropriate actions. Explanations may identify previously unanticipated operational influences or variances within process accuracy limits, and they may also suggest potential solutions. Examples of reasonable explanations include:

- "The production plant was closed for twelve days because of the hurricane."
- "Our competitor's new product seems to have a greater market share than we assumed. The assumption may need to be revised up from the 14 percent listed in the plan."
- "This month's data is not yet available, so results should really be compared to last month's target."
- "The result is 6 percent below target, but the measurement process has a plus or minus 8 percent accuracy rate."

12. Produce and Distribute Reports

Who: Program Team

This step involves the routine production and distribution of the formal management reports, and it may be fully automated with business intelligence software. Reports are produced and distributed according to the requirements laid out in the reporting scheme—either digitally or in hard-copy form. Other documents, such as project progress reports, may be appended or linked to the management reports.

Summary

This chapter broadens the implementation activity to monitor whether the *Strategic DNA* objectives are actually being achieved. It connects actual performance to *Strategic DNA* targets and advises management of progress and variances.

12

Learning Analysis and Feedback

What Went Wrong? What Went Right?
What Should We Change?

ANY ORGANIZATIONS CONSIDER THEIR STRATEGIC PLANS TO BE major undertakings that, once approved, become mandatory and unquestionable texts of almost biblical proportions. This can be dangerous: When results fail to live up to expectations, such plans prove impossible to change, so many bury their heads in the sand in the hope the problems will simply go away. Sometimes, this occurs because senior management is expected to be infallible (and thus their plans must be perfect), or because the effort was so difficult that they're reluctant to revisit it. Plans usually don't survive first contact because they are based on assumptions, hypotheses, estimates, and educated guesses, and reality rarely behaves exactly as predicted. Strategic plans should neither be carved in granite nor cemented in place. If they are, they will eventually be ignored altogether.

It is better to think of the strategic plan as a governing master plan that slowly evolves to adapt to reality. If it changes too quickly, it loses credibility, but it needs to be flexible enough to react when foundational assumptions and hypotheses are challenged. A plan that continuously improves in this way sets the *current* direction for the organization. It's analogous to a ship's compass heading that is slowly adjusted to compensate for external effects, like crosswinds and ocean currents.

In Chapter 11, the overall progress of the strategy implementation was measured, explained, and reported against expectations established by the objectives, hypotheses, and achievement targets. In this chapter, those reports are reviewed to determine what went right (so successes may be celebrated)

247

and what went wrong (so adjustments can be made). When executed well, this chapter turns the *Strategic DNA* lifecycle into a learning loop of continuous improvement. Your journey will be adjusted by changes to the vision, strategy, targets, project portfolio, resource allocations, and so on.

Why Do It?

The overall reason for analyzing performance results is to turn the information provided by results measurements into the knowledge and insight needed for management to react appropriately to them.

To Validate the Logic of the *Strategic DNA*

The core *Strategic DNA* logic is codified as the lines connecting the objectives on the strategy map, the achievement targets, and the choice of which projects to pursue, but many other hypotheses and assumptions are generated throughout the *Strategic DNA* lifecycle. Some of these are well documented, such as the assumptions stated in a project charter, but evolving decisions and actions imply many more (e.g., "Let's assign Joe to that project, because even *he* can do that.").

By analyzing the results measured in Chapter 11, management can determine whether the strategy is being as successful *as expected*. The *Strategic DNA* logic is confirmed when results achieved are consistent with expectations. When they are not consistent, analysis can sometimes reveal that the logic is invalid, thus providing an opportunity to adjust it and make it more realistic.

There can be very many reasons for invalid logic. The two most common are erroneous and usually optimistic assumptions and unanticipated impacts from external forces. For example, in the case described in Chapter 11—where early sales force training did not result in the level of improved sales that was expected—analysis may reveal the hypothesis was overly optimistic, that the arrival of an unexpected new competitor offset the training gains, or perhaps both.

The compilation and comparison of results performed in Chapter 11 may already point to questionable hypotheses. The analysis in this chapter confirms whether those hypotheses are actually flawed.

Understand When Successful Projects Fail to Produce Intended Results

Another aspect of the analysis is to understand why successful projects have failed to produce the expected results. In this case, the hypothesis dictates that conducting a specific project will produce the results desired.

To Identify and React to Unsuccessful Strategies as Early as Possible

Timely collection and analysis of results provides early indications of unsuccessful strategies (failing projects, invalid hypothesis, flawed assumptions, missing actions, and so on) and permits corrective actions to be taken. These early actions may not always be able to correct for flawed logic, but they might make it possible to stop the bleeding before it becomes life threatening.

Failure to follow through with this exercise means unsuccessful strategies are usually not discovered until far too late, after damage has been done. Early identification permits management to adjust the strategy and program plan in a reasoned manner, instead of the panic that usually ensues when it is too late to take action.

To Fine-Tune the *Strategic DNA* for Optimum Results

Systematic, ongoing identification of flawed logic and failing strategies enables continuous improvement by allowing management to tackle minor problems before they grow into major disasters. Continuous fine-tuning might even head off situations where an otherwise achievable strategy must be completely abandoned and replaced.

To Celebrate Successes and Improve the Quality of the Next Strategy

The analysis recognizes areas where the strategy has been completely successful. As discussed in Chapter 11, it can be used to calibrate rewards, demonstrate credibility for the methodology, and provide positive lessons learned about what worked, and why it worked. Understanding what worked (and why) is just as essential as understanding what didn't work when developing subsequent or cascaded strategies.

Celebrating success impacts subsequent strategies positively in both explicit and implicit ways. Explicitly, understanding what works and why permits success criteria to be deliberately built into the plans for subsequent strategies. Implicitly, celebrating success through recognition and rewards reinforces successful practices and encourages others to emulate recognition-earning behaviors in the future.

What to Do
Identify Priority Performance Variances

Variance analysis asks, "Is action needed, and if so, what action is needed?" There are usually so many variances that management cannot reasonably respond to all of them. The first stage of the analysis identifies which variances matter most. Prioritizing the variances allows corrective action efforts to be concentrated where they are needed most and where they can do the most good.

Preliminary Variance and Trend Analysis

Performance gaps have previously been identified by the comparisons in Chapter 11, and some explanations may have been suggested by those who are knowledgeable about the specifics. Most performance metrics do not track exactly to enshrined expectations—this is normal—but this does not necessarily mean there is an underlying problem. These variances may be anomalies caused by natural, temporary influences, or they may be indicators of a real problem.

The most reliable approach for identifying real problems is monitoring the metric over several reporting periods to determine whether the performance has an undesirable trend. The trend approach reduces the statistical likelihood that the variance is caused by temporary factors, but it also delays management's response for the reporting periods that pass as the trend develops. In their analysis, management makes case-by-case decisions about the potential impacts, or costs of waiting to respond, and balances them with the costs and risks of taking potentially unnecessary corrective action.

Therefore, management must decide which variances to respond to immediately, when to wait until a trend is established, and when to ignore them as anomalies. While the explanations offered in Chapter 11 may provide a guide, variances can be prioritized based on their magnitude, the certainty of the trend, and their impact, which is often closely related to the location of the metric's related objective on the strategy map.

Performance Root-Cause Analysis

Priority variances are analyzed and investigated to see if their root cause can be determined. Root-cause analysis can also help clarify a variance's significance when the preliminary analysis is unable to determine whether

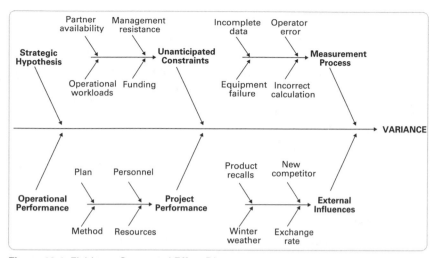

Figure 12.1 Fishbone Cause and Effect Diagram

it should be treated as a priority or when management is unsure whether to wait to respond.

There are many different ways of performing root-cause analysis, and the most appropriate method depends on the situation, the type of metric being measured, and the time and resources available. Most of these methods evolved out of the quality control discipline; they include such tools as statistical charting, process flowcharts, "fishbone" cause-and-effect diagrams, and business system models. Statistical tools are particularly useful when multiple data points are available. For single data point variances, fishbone diagrams are usually best, but process diagrams may also be of value.

With a fishbone approach, the analysis first identifies all factors that could have directly caused the performance variance. Each of those potential causes is then analyzed to identify what factors might in turn cause them to fail to perform: The *cause* at the first level becomes the effect of causes at the second level. This is repeated at several levels and can be illustrated by positioning lines from each of the potential causes to the variance, resulting in a diagram that resembles the bones of a fish (see Figure 12.1).

Once the diagram has been completed, investigations can be made to reveal whether each factor caused some or all of the variance. The investigations often result in the addition of more layers of potential causes to the diagram. Fishbone diagrams can rapidly become large and complex, but they are reusable for later variances in the same metric and easily adapted to variances in other metrics.

In the process diagram method, the analysis uses traditional process diagrams to map the process that produces the performance. The measurement process was already documented in Chapter 11, but sometimes the operational processes that produce the results must be mapped for the first time at this juncture. The cause(s) of the variance may be found in either the measurement process or the operational process, so both must be considered in the process diagram method. Hopefully, the measurement process was already excluded as the root cause in Chapter 11. Once the process has been defined, investigations can be made to determine which procedure or decision in the process is the cause of the variance.

Real-Time Distributed Analysis

Real-time distributed analysis of variances is possible if the implementation is managed with performance management/business intelligence software. Those accountable for setting targets (assigned in Chapter 7) and measuring actual results (Chapter 11) can be clearly identified in the software. The system can then draw their attention to variances when they first become apparent. This is usually done either with colored indicators on a personalized dashboard or via automatically generated messages. Once alerted, individuals can investigate, analyze, and report the corrective actions they plan to take. Such software may also provide functionality for managing corrective actions.

Strategic DNA Validity Analysis

Strategic DNA validity analysis examines priority variances to establish whether they point to errors in the *Strategic DNA* itself. This analysis asks whether the actual results that emerge confirm the *Strategic DNA*'s logic (relationships, hypotheses, and assumptions). The analysis is usually performed most effectively when the analyst plays a devil's advocate role, first by assuming the *Strategic DNA* is in error, and then by systematically reviewing the assumptions and hypotheses until the flaw is revealed. Figure 12.2 describes some common symptoms and flaws.

Strategic DNA Changes

The close integration of the *Strategic DNA* components means that any change can have a broad impact. Thus, changes should not be made lightly. A change to an early component, such as the relationship between two objectives, can call into question its foundational achievement targets,

Symptom	Possible Strategic DNA Flaws
Unsuccessful projects and unachieved targets	• Invalid assumptions about management focus, resource levels, or staff capabilities • Overly optimistic project charters or plans • External risks unanticipated (and risk actually occurred)
Successful project(s) but metric does not improve as expected	• Hypothesis that certain actions will produce desired results is incorrect • Calibration of cause-effect is overly optimistic • Achievement targets too ambitious—bar set too high • Performance elsewhere has offset performance gain (assumption of performance elsewhere is invalid) • Project goals too modest—bar set too low • Project scope did not include important changes/results • Project portfolio too modest (important projects not selected) • Multiple related projects not all successful • Preceding thrusts have not built sufficient platform for success (hypotheses were overly optimistic) • Assumptions about contribution of external factors not valid or overlooked
Preceding objective's target met but succeeding objective metric does not track as expected	• Hypothesis codified as relationship on strategy map is invalid • Additional preceding objective missing/overlooked • Response of succeeding metric is negated by unexpected factors • Assumptions about contribution of external factors not valid or overlooked
Subsidiary performance successful but corporate targets unachieved	• Hypotheses codified as cascaded objectives and targets are invalid or overly optimistic • Subsidiary performance offset by performance loss elsewhere (assumption of performance elsewhere is invalid)

Figure 12.2 Common Strategic DNA Flaws

project plans, resource allocations, measurement processes, and so on. In large-scale cascaded implementations, a corporate-level change may require extensive rework of many divisional *Strategic DNA* components.

Even when analysis has identified a flaw in the logic, the cost of changing the *Strategic DNA* must be balanced against the benefits. In some cases, the identified flaw is merely one of calibration (e.g., results are tracking slower than expected, or achievement targets are overly ambitious), and the cost of implementing the change might significantly exceed the benefits.

Using the slower tracking situation as an example, management must decide whether adjusting project plans and achievement targets is worthwhile, or if it would be better to leave them alone and accept the slower results as an explained variance. These situations should be evaluated individually, as there is no real rule of thumb. In many cases, the evaluation can be based on whether the slower tracking results have a wide-ranging negative effect on other objectives, targets, and projects. If slower results make subsequent targets and projects seem to underperform when they aren't, it is probably worth making the change. Otherwise, targets may collectively become perceived as meaningless. Slower results with a modest localized effect are often acceptable.

There are times when coordinated changes should be made to the *Strategic DNA*, but it should only occur through a formal process that is not too easy to accomplish. A formal change mechanism for evaluating and implementing changes discourages people from proposing too many minor

<table>
<tr><td colspan="7">Strategic DNA Change Notice</td><td>Ref</td><td></td></tr>
</table>

Initiating Variance

Strategic Objective and Performance Metric	Targets		Actual Result	Explanations
	End	**Current**		

Analysis

Variance Analysis

Stage	Preliminary Analysis	Initial Response	Source Process	Impact	Response	Priority
Status	Critical Significant Minor Unknown	Correct Investigate Monitor Ignore	Measurement Operational Unknown	Critical Significant Minor Unknown	Integrate Escalate Correct Improve Monitor Ignore	Extreme High Routine Low Close

Root Causes:

Reference Documentation

Lessons:

Lesson	Action for Future Avoidance

Figure 12.3 Variance and Change Notice Template

changes. A simplified template for a formal variance/change notice is provided in Figure 12.3. The form performs the dual purpose of tracking both the variance analysis and any proposed change resulting from that analysis.

Most *Strategic DNA* changes fall into one of the following types: vision changes, strategy map changes, achievement target changes, or program changes.

Strategic DNA Change Notice		Ref	

Planning

Action Type	✓	Corrective Action Plan			
		#	Action	Assigned to	Due Date
Corrective action		1			
Corrective project		2			
DNA change		3			
Monitor		4			
Ignore		5			
Close					

Proposed Strategic DNA Changes:

Strategic DNA Components	ID #	Details of Proposed Change

Notes:

Approvals

Status	Name	Signature	Date
Initiator			
Analysis go-ahead			
Action planning go-ahead			
Escalate to program team			
Implementation go-ahead			
Implementation complete			
Close-out			

Figure 12.3 *Continued...*

Vision Changes

Vision changes are significant and potentially quite risky because they have wide-ranging impact on the *Strategic DNA*, including the strategy map, achievement targets, and project portfolio. They also have the potential to reduce the credibility of the leadership team and program team in the eyes of management and the work force. The vision evolves naturally with the business environment, but in most cases, it shouldn't evolve too quickly!

Learning analysis rarely causes vision changes, but it can happen. If it does occur, it may be a response to newly recognized factors that were not considered when the original vision was formulated. In one example, a Latin American insurance company had to rework its vision when large European competitors suddenly entered its markets, a change that was unexpected because of the limited potential for profit in those markets.

Strategy Map Changes

Strategy changes are more common and include any modification of the strategy map that results in a revised strategy. Such changes may be small or large, and they can include one or more of the following:

- Revised wording for thrust or objective
- Addition or deletion of thrusts
- Addition or deletion of objectives
- Addition or deletion of relationships

For example, if it becomes apparent that an original hypothesis that improved sales force training would result in increased sales is inadequate because competitors are taking away market share, the strategy may need to be adjusted. In this case, an additional objective, such as "maintain competitiveness in all market segments," might need to be added to the strategy map as a second enabler.

Adding or deleting thrusts is a serious change that can undermine confidence in the strategy or the leadership team. It should only be considered when it is proven to be a strong response to a rapidly changing business environment.

Achievement Target Changes

Achievement target changes are common. They become necessary when awareness grows that original targets are far too easy to achieve, impossible to measure, completely unrealistic, or not motivating any significant performance improvements. Such changes usually either raise or lower the bar for a performance metric, but sometimes a completely different performance metric must be adopted.

Program (Project Portfolio) Changes

Program changes are another common type of change. They may be changes to the desired outcomes of a single project, or they may be changes to the broader implementation program.

Changing desired project outcomes causes the project's charter to be revised and results in an updated project plan and schedule. Specific changes within a project are implemented using the mechanisms discussed in Chapter 10.

Program changes can be much more complex, as they can affect the implementation structure, resource and accountability assignments, definition of decision gates, the outcomes expected from multiple projects, the addition or removal of projects, or the content and timing of the implementation waves.

Strategic DNA Change Log

Logging *Strategic DNA* changes helps keep the overall program under control. The log's form depends on the nature of the program. It can range from a simple spreadsheet to a complex real-time database that is available online to all participants. At a minimum, it provides a summary of proposed changes to the *Strategic DNA*. The log can also be used more broadly to track all variances, including those that do not require changes to any *Strategic DNA* components. Figure 12.4 illustrates a basic log.

Change #	Description	Requester	Status
1	Change staff engagement thrust to staff retention	R Charlton	Rejected
2	Add objective "maintain competitiveness in all market segments"	N Stiles	Implemented
3	Delay sales force training project until Wave 3	N Stiles	Rejected
4	Revise new product sales targets	G Banks	Implemented
5	Expand scope of market research project to include South America	G Cohen	Approved
6	Revise program RACIs to include divisional representatives	R Charlton	Implemented
7	Increase pace and budget for Wave 1 projects	N Stiles	Analysis
8	Add project to Wave 2 to identify and invest in product updates	N Stiles	Requested
9	Revise plant overhead ratio calculation algorithms	R Moore	Requested

Figure 12.4 Strategic DNA Change Log

#	Symptom	Lesson	Suggestion for Next Time
1	Sales force training didn't increase market share as expected	Other (external) factors offset gains from training	Don't assume external factors will stay constant; assess whether external factors will also be changing during the strategy timeline
2	Projects routinely start up too slowly	Managers are slow to release key staff to external projects	Enhance forcefulness/strength of communications with managers or allow more time for project start-up
3	High proportion of information missing on progress reports	It takes longer than expected to automatically produce performance results	Use already available information as proxies until right information becomes available
4	Business unit resisting the program	BU failed to fully participate and is not committed to success	Do not allow rogue leader to prevent his BU from participating—insist all participate, and don't move forward until this problem is addressed

Figure 12.5 Lessons Learned Log

Identify and Log Lessons Learned

The analysis of trends, variance root causes, and *Strategic DNA* validity together reveal reasons why actual performance did not meet expectations. Even successful corrective actions or *Strategic DNA* changes may not prevent an organization from making the same mistake again in the future.

Further analysis of performance variances and invalid logic can reveal lessons. Validity analysis asks what is wrong, and lessons-learned analysis asks why it was wrong in the first place. Once identified, lessons can be logged and made available to guide the next cycle of decision making. Policies, processes, and procedures can also be modified when appropriate to prevent the lesson from being relearned in the future.

The lessons log can be a spreadsheet or paper document, but it is best to make them broadly available on an intranet page or other shared repository. Figure 12.5 provides an example of a simple spreadsheet log.

System Modeling

Larger businesses sometimes find it useful to develop a more extensive model of their business against which strategic performance can be analyzed, allowing lessons to be learned more systematically and ultimately producing a calibrated model of the entire business to guide future strategy design. The examples below show how system models may be either relatively simple or very complex.

Strategic Hypothesis Listing

The strategic hypothesis listing is perhaps the simplest model of the system. It is a cumulative listing of the hypotheses and other assumptions documented on the strategy map, in the achievement targets, in project charters, and elsewhere. The status of each hypothesis is adjusted as actual results are analyzed to identify whether they are still untested, proven, questionable, or incorrect.

Business and Financial Drivers Model

Some sophisticated businesses develop a statistical understanding of their fundamental business and financial drivers. Together, these produce a model of the business and how it interacts with its business environment. An insurance company, for example, might identify "level of fear" as one of its business drivers—an earthquake would increase the level of fear in the immediate area and result in a greater demand for its property and life insurance products. Similarly, an aircraft manufacturer might identify "interest rates" as a financial driver, because lower rates make their high-value products more affordable.

Well-developed models of business and financial drivers can be calibrated over time as hypotheses are tested. Once calibrated, these models provide an understanding of the sensitivity of the business, so strategic actions can be targeted on specific drivers. Proven models encourage a high degree of confidence that specific strategies will produce desired results and allow exploration of what-if scenarios when designing strategies.

How to Do It

The actual process used to analyze and respond to results should closely reflect the management's everyday culture. Highly formal organizations probably already use a similar process to what is described here. Their existing processes can usually be readily adapted to satisfy learning analysis and feedback needs. Informal organizations may not be as disciplined, preferring instead to learn and adapt on the fly. These organizations usually benefit from a little additional discipline because it helps them retain focus, but too much can undermine their core cultural strengths. How much formal structure should be introduced here—as with processes in previous chapters—is for each organization to decide, but the thinking represented by this process should be included in all cases.

Formal tracking mechanisms document the analysis and decisions made about each variance. In a nonautomated environment, the most straightforward method is to prepare a standard tracking form for each variance and keep a spreadsheet log of the forms that have been created.

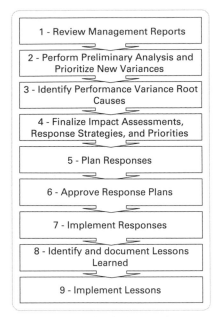

The form can be designed to evolve into a *Strategic DNA* change document if appropriate. Individual fields are completed at each stage of the process to record the results of analyses and decisions. The template provided in Figure 12.3 illustrates this approach, with separate sections for the analysis phase, the planning phase, and approvals. The analysis section tracks the analysis of the variance, and the planning section is only used when the variance requires corrective action.

Organizations learn from both their failures and successes. This section emphasizes looking for failures, but you should also take every opportunity to celebrate success, declare victory, and learn what to replicate next time before investigating the next failure.

Figure 12.6 Learning Analysis and Feedback Process

1. Review Management Reports
Who: Management Team

The management reports compare actual results to expected results for the same period and highlight variances and trends and provide explanations, if they are known. Each manager contributes to the learning analysis and feedback process by reviewing the reports and becoming informed of progress and aware of performance variances. Discuss the results with the people involved in producing them and participate in subsequent decision making.

Look for successful completion of any particularly difficult or significant achievement targets or projects, and initiate appropriate steps to recognize and publicize success. Steps 2 through 7 can be bypassed for the successes, but Steps 8 and 9 still apply.

2. Perform Preliminary Analysis and Prioritize New Variances
Who: Program Team, Responsible Managers, and Selected Specialists

This step is typically performed as part of the regularly scheduled strategy progress meetings established in the reporting scheme (see Figure 11.1). With appropriate technologies, it can be conducted in real time. Figure 12.7 provides an agenda for a typical progress meeting, with this step representing Part 1 of the meeting. There may be a hierarchy of meetings to review progress by thrust, business unit, or overall strategy.

In the meeting, briefly discuss each new variance in the context of the strategy and determine its likely impact if it remains unaddressed. This preliminary impact analysis

> **Strategy Progress Review Meeting**
>
> **Sample Agenda**
>
> Part 1—New Variances
>
> 1. Review New Variances
> 2. Identify Preliminary Impacts and Priorities
> 3. Determine Actions to Be Taken
> 4. Assign Analysis Tasks
>
> Part 2—Analyzed Variances
>
> 5. Review Analyzed Variances
> 6. Categorize Impacts and Response Strategies
> 7. Set Priorities and Assign Action Tasks
> 8. Schedule Action Planning Sessions
>
> Part 3—Action Plan Approval
>
> 9. Review and Approve Corrective Action Plans

Figure 12.7 Sample Agenda for Strategy Progress Review Meeting

needs to be substantiated with more detail, but triaging it now reduces the number of detailed investigations that will be necessary. The *Strategic DNA* logic connections and the area of the strategy map that is affected by the variance will guide the preliminary analysis. Each variance can then be allocated a preliminary impact category, such as:

- *Critical*—The variance appears to undermine the entire strategy.
- *Significant*—The variance will probably have a significant impact.
- *Minor*—The variance will probably not have a significant impact.
- *Unknown*—There is insufficient data to form an opinion.

Once the preliminary impact category has been identified, establish relative priorities for each variance and decide what actions to take. The actions usually fall into the following general types of action:

- *Correct*—Take corrective action immediately.
- *Investigate*—Perform a root-cause analysis.
- *Monitor*—Await additional data to establish a trend.
- *Ignore*—No further action is required.

The final step is to assign specific next steps to individual managers or employees and establish completion deadlines. Settle on the time, place, and participation for the corrective action planning sessions before ending the progress review meeting.

Each variance in the first two categories will be subjected to the rest of the learning analysis and feedback process. Prepare a variance/change notice for each that includes preliminary priorities and actions. Steps 3 and 4 of the process can be bypassed for the first type, as the root cause is self-evident and corrective action is definitely required.

3. Identify Performance Variance Root Causes
Who: Responsible Managers and Selected Specialists

Conduct a detailed analysis to identify the root cause of the variance (i.e., the real reason for the underperformance). In Chapter 11, the measurement process may have been eliminated as the cause of the variance, but the detailed analysis double checks it before looking further. Once the measurement process is eliminated, focus the analysis on the operational processes whose outputs form part of the metric. Tailor the analysis to the type of metric being measured by selecting the most appropriate method (e.g., statistical, fishbone, or process diagram).

Communicate root-cause analysis results to the program team and involved leaders to help them make decisions. The source process can now be indicated, and the root cause can be described on the variance/change notice.

4. Finalize Impact Assessments, Response Strategies, and Priorities
Who: Program Team, Accountable Leaders, and Responsible Managers

Armed with the findings of the root-cause analysis, the leaders can make an informed assessment of the variance's probable impact. This can often be done during scheduled progress review meetings (Part 2 in Figure 12.7), but sometimes the variance is important enough to warrant a separate decision-making meeting.

The leaders and the managers responsible for the performance being measured participate in the assessment discussions. They discuss the variance and its root cause(s) in the context of the overall strategy and decide:

- How serious the impact is likely to be
- Whether it is worthwhile to address the root cause
- Whether the root cause can be addressed
- How to respond to the variance
- How urgently to respond
- Who should prepare the corrective action plan
- When corrective action planning should be performed
- Who needs to approve the corrective action plan

Response Types	
Type	**Response**
Integrate	Accept root cause and adjust Strategic DNA to accommodate revised hypotheses or assumptions
Escalate	Refer variance to higher level in the organization with recommendations for action
Correct	Take action to correct root cause and recover lost progress
Improve	Take action to correct or minimize root cause and reduce lost progress
Monitor	Take no corrective action at this time but monitor variance trend
Ignore	Accept variance and ignore root cause

Figure 12.8 Variance Response Types

Response Priorities	
Priority	**Response**
Extreme	Variance is very urgent. Stop other work if necessary to address root cause.
High	Variance is urgent. Address root cause as soon as resources can be made available.
Routine	Variance is not urgent. Address rootcause when resources become available.
Low	Variance is unimportant. Address root cause when available resources are under utilized.
Close	Variance is non-issue. Close out log record and take no further action.

Figure 12.9 Variance Response Priorities

Review meetings often have to deal with many variances, so a categorization approach may be helpful. The simplest method is to revisit and finalize the preliminary impact category assigned in Step 2. Standard categories can also facilitate priority setting and identification of response types while streamlining the assignment of tasks and ensuring expectations are clearly understood. Figures 12.8 and 12.9 contain example schemes for these categories, as reflected in the sample variance/change notice (see

Figure 12.3). Record category assignments, responsibilities, and schedule expectations on the variance/change notice.

5. Plan Responses
Who: Corrective Action Manager and Involved Specialists

Assemble involved managers and subject-matter experts to determine how to correct the variance's root cause.

Corrective Actions

The corrective action plan usually includes a short list of necessary actions, each of which is individually assigned with clear schedule expectations. Describe planned actions on the variance/change notice.

Corrective Projects

Occasionally, a full project is needed to correct the variance. These projects tend to compete for the same resources as the strategic projects and as such, they should be managed carefully. Prepare a charter for each corrective project and record the need for the project in the action plan section of the variance/change notice. The charter then becomes part of a proposed change to the project portfolio. Defer detailed project planning until the proposed project has been approved and integrated into the portfolio.

Other Strategic DNA *Changes*

Some root causes require revision of other components of the *Strategic DNA*. These might include changes to the strategy map, achievement targets, project portfolio, resource assignments, roles and responsibilities, and so on. Record the proposed changes in the planning section of the variance/change notice. Once approved, the program team will implement the *Strategic DNA* changes.

6. Approve Response Plans
Who: Accountable Leaders and Program Team

Corrective action plans are often preapproved at the time responsibilities are assigned, but if the plans are costly or complex, leaders may prefer to review them before committing to their implementation. In this latter case, the corrective action plan is reviewed and approved at the next meeting (Part 3 in Figure 12.7).

Discuss the action plan's appropriateness before approving its implementation. This can be relatively straightforward, but for corrective projects and other *Strategic DNA* changes, meeting participants may not have the authority to approve the implementation. For example, the participants in a review meeting may believe the strategy map should be revised, but the entire stakeholder group might need to be involved in that approval discussion. In these cases, escalate the change to the program team as a proposed *Strategic DNA* change. Add the change to the change log, determine who needs to participate in its review, and facilitate the process.

Document the status on the variance/change notice, and do not implement corrective actions unless the variance/change notice has been approved.

7. Implement Responses
Who: Corrective Action Manager and Involved Specialists

Once the plan has been approved, validate that employees assigned to specific tasks are ready and able to perform them, and then facilitate their efforts.

The program team is usually responsible for implementing *Strategic DNA* component changes, but its role is normally one of coordination and facilitation. The team should not preempt the intellectual ownership of the component by making change implementation decisions. For example, in the case of a proposed change to relationships on the strategy map, the program team should resist the urge simply to make the change unless it has authorization to do so. It may take longer to reconvene the entire stakeholder group, but proceeding with a change without obtaining approval from the entire stakeholder group can result in a total loss of alignment.

When implementing corrective actions or *Strategic DNA* changes, properly coordinate changes in work priorities with project and departmental managers. When a corrective action requires an employee to stop what he or she is doing and do something else instead, his or her manager must be involved in changing the work assignments.

8. Identify and Document Lessons Learned
Who: All Participants Led by the Program Manager

Document lessons learned as soon as they are identified so they don't get lost. It is not always feasible to assess lessons from each variance, but try to identify some from significant variances—especially those that result in corrective projects or *Strategic DNA* changes.

Although lessons sometimes appear as an unexpected bolt of insight, they can be identified systematically through a brief brainstorming activity at the final action team meeting or at the next scheduled review meeting. Facilitate the discussion by asking, "What can we learn from this variance?" Document lessons on the source variance/change notice, and centralize them in a lessons log that is available to all. Any blanks in the notice's lessons section should prompt the same question.

Don't forget to draw lessons from significant successes, too! These conversations are pleasant to facilitate and produce tremendous value. Facilitate the discussion with a friendlier take on the initial question: "What can we learn from this *success*?"

9. Implement Lessons
Who: Program Manager or Accountable Leader

Once a lesson has been identified, follow up immediately by asking, "What needs to be done to avoid relearning this lesson in the future?" Specific actions—usually policy, process, or procedure revisions—can then be assigned to individual employees to institutionalize the lesson.

Summary

The final chapter learns lessons from implementation results to continuously improve the *Strategic DNA* and the organization's related capabilities. The *Strategic DNA* is fine-tuned as its hypotheses and assumptions are validated or disproven.

In Conclusion

BY THE END OF THE FINAL CHAPTER, THE STRATEGY IS BEING IMPLE-
mented through focused efforts, adjustments are being made to
correct results that are not behaving as expected, and lessons are
being implemented into the business to avoid repeating mistakes in the
future. As shown in Figure 12.10, the vision has been decomposed into

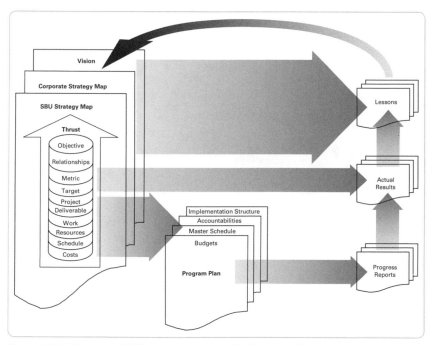

Figure 12.10 Strategic DNA Components in the Strategy Life Cycle

integrated *Strategic DNA* components that support an iterative learning lifecycle for the strategy. If done properly, the organization is now a more adaptable, strategically focused learning culture aligned in pursuit of a clear purpose. Its next strategy lifecycle should be easier to implement.

Most organizations plan their strategies for a multiyear planning horizon and integrate the plan's resource needs into annual operational plans. Multiyear strategies should be revisited at least annually, if only to identify real resource needs for inclusion in the next operational plan. Unfortunately, because plans are rarely adjusted during the year, many of these annual revisits seem to turn into painful replanning exercises. The continuous improvement aspect of the *Strategic DNA* lifecycle should not replace these annual reviews, but it should make them less drastic and less intimidating.

Footnotes

Introduction

1. *Strategy Maps.* Robert Kaplan and David Norton. HBS Press, 2004
2. *The Balanced Scorecard.* Robert Kaplan and David Norton. HBS Press, 1996.
3. *The New Corporate Cultures.* Terrence Deal and Allan Kennedy. Perseus Books, 1999.
4. *The PMBOK Guide®: A Guide to the Project Management Body of Knowledge, Third Edition.* Project Management Institute, 2004.
5. *The Fifth Discipline: The Art and Practice of the Learning Organization.* Peter M. Senge. Currency, 2006.

Chapter 1

6. This method evolved from an approach developed at Sears, Roebuck and Co. that was described by Bob Frisch in the article Vision Engineering: Taking Speculation Out of Strategy. *Gemini Consulting Transformation Magazine*, Autumn 1997.
7. Post-it® Notes are a trademark of the 3M Corporation. Its "super-sticky" type of Post-it is recommended for workshop use.
8. Value Innovation: The Strategic Logic of High Growth. Kim and Mauborgne. *Harvard Business Review*, Jan-Feb 1997, and *Blue Ocean Strategy*, Kim and Mauborgne, HBS Press, 2005.

Chapter 2

9. Strategy map from Ivrnet Inc. used with permission.
10. The Harvard Business School Press has published four books by Robert Kaplan and David Norton about the Balanced Scorecard. They are *The Balanced Scorecard* (1996), *The Strategy Focused Organization* (2001), *Strategy Maps* (2004), *and Alignment* (2006).

Chapter 3

11. *The Balanced Scorecard,* Kaplan and Norton. HBS Press, 1996. Preface.

12. *The Human Problems of an Industrial Civilization, Ch.3.* Elton Mayo. MacMillan, 1933. Cited by Steve Draper in the online document http://www.psy.gla.ac.uk/~steve/hawth. html (28 March 2005).

Chapter 4
13. In *Alignment* (p.190), Kaplan and Norton suggest a similar three-part scheme with common, shared, and unique objectives.

Chapter 5
14. Aha! is a decision facilitation software tool from Chinook Solutions, Inc.

Chapter 6
15. Choosing the Right PMO Setup. William Casey and Wendi Peck. *PM Network Magazine,* February 2001. P. 40.
16. Priority Decisions. Ross Foti. *PM Network Magazine,* April 2002.

Chapter 8
17. *The PMBOK Guide®: A Guide to the Project Management Body of Knowledge, Third Edition.* Project Management Institute, 2004.
18. *PM for Dummies* is a particularly user-friendly guide for beginners. More advanced titles are available from the PMI bookstore at http://www.pmi.org.
19. Sharpie® is a registered trademark of Sanford, a Newell Rubbermaid company.
20. Wikipedia provides a very useful overview of the PERT method first developed by Booz Allen Hamilton, Inc: http://en.wikipedia.org/wiki/PERT.

Chapter 9
21. Broadly discussed and usually credited to Kelley, D., and Conner, D.R. (1979). The Emotional Cycle of Change. In J.E. Jones and J.W. Pfeiffer (Eds.), *The Annual Handbook for Group Facilitators.* LaJolla, CA: University Associates. Pp. 117-122.

Chapter 10
22. *The PMBOK Guide®: A Guide to the Project Management Body of Knowledge, Third Edition.* Project Management Institute, 2004. P. 257.

Chapter 11
23. Microsoft Excel® is a registered trademark of the Microsoft Corporation.

Further Reading

Leadership and Management

- *Managers, Not MBAs*. Henry Mintzberg. Berrett Koehler, 2004.
- *The Naked Corporation*. Don Tapscott and David Ticoll. Free Press, 2003.
- *Execution: The Discipline of Getting Things Done*. Larry Bossidy, Ram Charan, and Charles Burck. Crown Business, 2002.
- *Good to Great: Why Some Companies Make the Leap ... and Others Don't*. Jim Collins. Collins, 2001.
- *The Essential Drucker*. Peter F. Drucker. Collins, 2001.
- What Makes a Leader? Daniel Goleman. *Harvard Business Review*, Nov/Dec 1998.
- *Working with Emotional Intelligence*. Daniel Goleman. Bantam, 1998.
- *Zapp! The Lightning of Empowerment*. William Byham and Jeff Cox. Ballantine Books, 1997.
- *The Change Management Handbook*. Lance Berger, Martin Sikora, and Dorothy Berger. Irwin, 1994.

Decision Making and Prioritization

- Priority Decisions. Ross Foti. *PM Network Magazine*, April 2002.
- Making R and D More Effective at Westinghouse. Ted Foster. *Research Technology Management*, Jan/Feb 1996.

- *First Things First.* Stephen Covey. Fireside, 1994.
- *Decision Traps.* J. Edward Russo and Paul Schoemaker. Fireside, 1990.

Vision and Strategy
- *Blue Ocean Strategy.* Chan Kim and Renée Mauborgne. HBS Press, 2005.
- *Strategy Maps.* Robert Kaplan and David Norton. HBS Press, 2004.
- *The Strategy-Focused Organization.* Robert Kaplan and David Norton. HBS Press, 2001.
- *Strategy Safari.* Henry Mintzberg, Bruce Ahlstrand, and Joseph Lampel. Free Press, 1998.
- Value Innovation: The Strategic Logic of High Growth. Chan Kim and Renée Mauborgne. *Harvard Business Review*, Jan/Feb 1997.
- *Transforming the Organisation.* Francis Gouillart and James Kelly. McGraw-Hill, 1996.
- Structure and Meaning of Organizational Vision. Laurie Larwood and Cecilia Falbe. *Academy of Management Journal*, Jun 1995.
- *Competitive Advantage.* Michael Porter. Free Press, 1980.

Performance
- *Beyond the Balanced Scorecard: Improving Business Intelligence with Analytics.* Mark Graham Brown. Productivity Press, 2007.
- *How to Measure Anything.* Douglas W. Hubbard. John Wiley, 2007.
- *Culture Management through the Balanced Scorecard*: A Case Study (Ph.D Thesis). P. M. Woodley. Cranfield University, 2006.
- *The EVA Challenge: Implementing Value Added Change in an Organization.* Joel M. Stern, John S. Shiely, and Irwin Ross. John Wiley, 2001.
- *The Balanced Scorecard.* Robert Kaplan and David Norton. HBS Press, 1996.

Program and Project Management
- *Project Management Sophistication* and *EPMO.* Parviz Rad and Ginger Levin. AACE International Transactions, 2007.

- *The PMBOK Guide®: A Guide to the Project Management Body of Knowledge,* Third Edition. Project Management Institute, 2004.
- *Creating the Project Office: A Manager's Guide to Leading Organizational Change.* Randall Englund, Robert Graham, and Paul Dinsmore. John Wiley, 2003.
- *Project Management for Dummies.* Stanley Portny. Hungry Minds, 2001.
- Choosing the Right PMO Setup. Casey and Peck. *PM Network Magazine,* February 2001.
- *In Search of Excellence in Project Management.* Harold Kerzner. John Wiley, 1998.
- *Critical Chain.* Eliyahu Goldratt. North River Press, 1997.
- *Principles of Project Management.* Project Management Institute, 1996.
- *Project Planning, Scheduling, and Control.* James P. Lewis. Irwin, 1995.

Learning Organizations
- *Managing from Clarity.* James L. Ritchie-Dunham and Hal T. Rabbino. Wiley, 2001.
- Total Quality Management and the Learning Organization: A Dialogue for Change in Construction. Peter Love, Heng Li, Zahir Irani, and Olusegun Faniran. *Construction Management and Economics,* Apr/May 2000.
- *Adaptive Enterprise.* Stephan Haeckel. HBS Press, 1999.
- Building a Learning Organization. David Garvin. *Harvard Business Review,* Jul/Aug 1993.
- *The Fifth Discipline: The Art and Practice of the Learning Organization.* Peter M. Senge. Currency, 1990 and 2006.

Speaking the Same Language: People, Teams, and Groups

Business Owners

The actual owners of a private business or the group of people charged with the overall governance of the business. The CEO usually reports to this group. Examples of business owners include a nonexecutive board of directors, a board of governors, or the majority shareholder of the business. In smaller private enterprises, it may include all the shareholders; in government businesses, it may be the appropriate minister or a city council.

Business Unit

An organizational subdivision at any hierarchical level. This may include sections, departments, directorates, divisions, operating company's, regions, branches, subsidiaries, and so on.

Change Leaders

Those individuals who direct or influence members of the work force to accept the changes the strategy will bring and who help develop change details during implementation. Change leaders include the leadership team, the broader management team, and the project managers, but they may also include respected thought leaders and an organization's young, assertive, and passionate advocates of change.

Executive Team

The senior operational management of the company. This usually includes the CEO, his or her direct reports, and the executives responsible for each business unit.

Explainers

Those individuals tasked with explaining variances between expected/target performance levels and actual results. They are typically middle managers responsible for the measurement process or subject-matter experts responsible for source performance data. Their early and expert intervention can avoid unnecessary reaction or overreaction to variances by more senior managers.

Leadership Team

The group of people who participate in the decision-making activities involved in the strategic planning process. They are the collective owners of the strategy. This usually includes the executive team, other senior managers, and a few selected specialists. Its configuration depends on the corporate culture and the nature of the strategy. For example, it may include a member of the board and managers from strategic planning, information technology, human resources, or similar functional areas.

The leadership team should not be confused with the stakeholder group, but all leadership team members are also usually members of the larger stakeholder group. External stakeholders may be temporarily included in the group for some elements of the lifecycle.

Management Team

All the organization's managers from first-line supervisors to the executive team.

Program Manager

The individual manager responsible for leading and overseeing the people and work involved in the *Strategic DNA* program and its related strategic projects from initiation to completion.

Program Team

The group of people who lead the strategy implementation on a day-to-day basis. This usually includes individual leaders, the program manager, dedicated program staff, the managers of strategic projects, and any operational managers whose support and influence must be brought to bear. The program team often also conducts performance measurement and reporting functions until the appropriate operational departments can be engaged and assume responsibility.

Larger businesses sometimes expect the strategic planning team to evolve into a program team and implement the strategy it helped design, but they may assign implementation to a separate group.

Project Manager

The individual manager responsible for leading and overseeing the people and work involved in a strategic project from concept to conclusion.

Project Sponsor

The executive accountable for the success of a strategic project. The project manager reports to the project sponsor.

Project Teams (Core, Planning, and Work)

The groups of people who plan and perform each strategic project. As the project progresses, each project team may evolve by expanding from the core team (who develops the business and initial project plans) to the planning team (who designs the detailed project plan) to the work team (who performs all the project activities). At the very least, each team includes a project manager and a project sponsor. The team includes any managers and staff who have responsibility for performing work on the project.

Stakeholder Group

A group of people specifically assembled in support of the *Strategic DNA* lifecycle. The group is configured to ensure that the interests of each principal type of stakeholder are considered. The group usually includes the leadership team and representatives of different stakeholder constituencies (customers, employees, shareholders, and so on).

The leadership team sometimes considers itself to be sufficiently broad that other participants are not required. In this case, the leadership team *is* the stakeholder group.

Strategy Owner

The individual leader who is ultimately accountable for the organization's strategy. This is the CEO, president, or chairman for most corporate-level organizations or the equivalent executive for a strategic business unit. Sometimes ownership is delegated by the CEO to a chief strategy officer or vice president of strategy acting as a strategic quarterback, but the role should only be considered to be delegated if that individual has responsibility for the whole strategy, including its resource priorities.

Strategic Planning Team

The group of people responsible for facilitating and nurturing the *Strategic DNA* lifecycle and performing the legwork for the leadership team. This usually includes a member of the leadership team, the staff of the strategic planning function, and selected individuals who have a broad view of the business. In larger organizations, the strategic planning team might also include external consultants, researchers, and analysts. The strategic planning team effectively runs the Strategic DNA lifecycle until it either passes control of the implementation to the program team or evolves into the program team.

Strategic Quarterback

The executive leader responsible for the overall success of the strategy. The quarterback reports directly to the strategy owner. If the quarterback is not in fact the program manager, the program manager will report to the quarterback.

Speaking the Same Language:
Glossary

This book uses terminology consistent with that established by the Project Management Institute whenever possible.

Brown Paper

Rolls of 4' or 6' wide brown Kraft paper are widely available. Using paper-based materials is invaluable for building large workshop visual aids, because unlike a projected PC image, participants will get out of their seats and take ownership of their thinking. It is used in several chapters of the book for producing visual aids and is often used together with Post-it® Notes.

Decision Gate

A formal control point introduced to provide a consistent standard of project content and definition at specific points in a project's lifecycle without unduly constraining project team independence. The decision gate is sometimes known as a stage gate.

Deliverables

The products, services, outputs, or other outcomes produced by a project. Project deliverables are the intended outcomes the project was created to produce. Work deliverables are outputs that demonstrate completed project work.

Full-Time Equivalents (FTEs)

A workload quantification used for planning and budgeting efforts. FTEs are the equivalent of one employee working full time for the planning period (usually either the duration of a project or a single budget year).

Notes

Original or generic versions of 3M Post-it® Notes of any size or color. They are used in several chapters of the book to facilitate group thinking and discussion in workshop meetings. Generally used with brown-paper wall charts. 3M's "super-sticky" version is highly recommended.

Organization

An entity configured to pursue its own vision, control its own performance, and further an identity that distinguishes it from its environment. An organization may be a business, corporation, government subdivision or agency, nongovernmental organization, trust, foundation, partnership, joint venture, consortium, association, group of people with a common interest, or any other legal entity.

Perspective

Horizontal zones on the strategy map encompassing strategic objectives that share a particular point of view. Several perspectives are arranged on the strategy map in a vertical axis of causality to calibrate the map's cause-effect logic in line with the organization's culture and value chain.

Portfolio

The complete list of all strategic projects selected to be included within the *Strategic DNA* program. The portfolio is usually organized into waves.

Portfolio Wave

A subset of the portfolio of strategic projects organized to group projects of similar schedule priority. Portfolio waves are used to make large numbers of projects more manageable during the portfolio selection discussions of Chapter 5.

Program (also *Strategic DNA* Program)

The group of related strategic projects managed in a coordinated way to achieve a vision.

Project (also Strategic Project)

A temporary undertaking intended to move the value of a performance metric toward its assigned achievement target. Strategic projects are those selected as priority undertakings because they are necessary for the strategy's success. These projects are planned, resourced, and executed in a coordinated manner as part of the *Strategic DNA* program. In some organizations, they may be known as strategic initiatives, actions, priorities, strategies, or even programs.

Risks

Possible events that, if they happen, will have a significant positive or negative impact. The impact may or may not be predictable.

***Strategic DNA* Component**

The many different deliverables produced by each chapter. The basic idea of *Strategic DNA* is to ensure that these components are closely integrated and thoroughly consistent with each other, as they give the strategy its form. The core components include the vision, strategy map, thrusts, strategic objectives, relationships (and their hypotheses), performance metrics, achievement targets, and strategic projects. Subsidiary components such as RACI charts, project resource assignments, budgets, and so on can also be considered components, as they also add features to the strategy and its implementation.

Strategic Objective

A desired outcome described as specific characteristics that represent significant progress toward the actual realization of an organization's vision.

Strategic Thrust

Several related strategic objectives organized into a cause-effect chain that leads to a major strategic outcome. Thrusts are arranged vertically on the strategy map in a horizontal axis of ambition.

Strategy

The direction the organization intends to follow and the business opportunities it will pursue to achieve the vision (how it intends to get there).

Straw Man

A draft model prepared by specialists in advance to facilitate group discussions and frame decisions in a workshop. The straw man gives participants a starting point to disagree with.

Trend (Environmental)

Influences that are sure to happen; they will change the environment in which the organization operates.

Trend (Performance)

A pattern underlying changes in the value of a performance metric measured over several reporting periods.

Vision

The future state an organization wishes to achieve in terms of itself and its business (what it wants to become).

Vision Goal

A desired outcome that represents some of the principal characteristics an organization wishes to achieve.

Vision Concept

An idea that is proposed for consideration as all or part of the vision. Each vision concept represents a configuration of opportunities the executive team might choose to pursue and the investments in assets and capabilities that would be needed to pursue them. An example vision concept might be, "Expand sales into the U.K. through franchising."

Work Breakdown Structure (WBS)

A decomposition to identify and organize the work required to produce project deliverables.

Index